Janner's
Complete Speechmaker
including compendium of draft speeches
and retellable tales

'An invaluable addition to the library
of anyone who must speak in public . . .
I have read it and enjoyed it . . .
It's worth reading and worth having . . .'
The Rt Hon George Thomas MP,
then Speaker of the House of Commons,
now The Rt Hon Lord Tonypandy

'. . . a magic book, indispensable for
everyone in Personnel Management.'
Bernard Dixon, Director, Institute of
Personnel Management

Second Edition

Janner's Complete Speechmaker

including compendium of draft speeches
and retellable tales

Greville Janner

Cartoons by Calman and Tobi

Business Books

London Melbourne Sydney Auckland Johannesburg

Business Books Ltd
An imprint of the Hutchinson Publishing Group
17–21 Conway Street, London W1P 6JD

Hutchinson Publishing Group (Australia) Pty Ltd
16–22 Church Street, Hawthorn, Melbourne–Victoria 3122

Hutchinson Group (NZ) Ltd
32–34 View Road, PO Box 40–086, Glenfield, Auckland 10

Hutchinson Group (SA) (Pty) Ltd
PO Box 337, Bergvlei 2012, South Africa

First published in 1968 under the title
The Businessman's Guide to Speech-making
and to the Laws and Conduct of Meetings
First published under present title 1981
Second Edition 1984
Reprinted 1985

Photoset in Times

Printed and bound in Great Britain by Anchor Brendon Ltd
of Tiptree, Essex

British Library Cataloguing in Publication Data
Janner, Greville
Janner's complete speechmaker.——2nd ed.
1. Public speaking
I. Title
808.5'1   PN4121
ISBN 0 09 158220 2 (cased)
0 09 158221 0 (paperback)

In proud memory of my father
Barnett Janner
Lord Janner of the City of Leicester

Other books by Greville Janner include:

Janner's Complete Letterwriter
Janner on Presentation
Janner's Consolidated Compendium of Employment Law
Janner's Employment Forms
Janner's Handbook of Draft Letters of Employment Law
Janner's Compendium of Health and Safety Law
Janner's Product Liability
Janner's Guide to the Law on Sick Pay and Absenteeism
Janner's Practical Guide to The Employment Act 1980
Know Your Law
and books under the pen name of Ewan Mitchell

Details of Greville Janner's public courses and in-company training
on speechmaking, presentational skills and employment law and practice
are available from Paul Secher, LLB, JS Associates, 2 Abbey Orchard
Street, London SW1P 2JH. Telephone: 01-222 2102.

Contents

Introduction

In business or in social life, competent speechmaking brings success. Disaster on your feet lands you on your back. This book is designed to keep you upright, articulate and successful in speech by showing you how best to think on your feet – to provide the maximum of practical help with the minimum of misery. It is based on a lifetime of experience of hugely varied audiences and of oratorical and presentational occasions in many parts of the world.

The book divides conveniently into three sections. The first describes the basic arts of speechmaking – construction and delivery, audiences and occasions, technical aids – the complete range of basic knowledge and guidance which is the essential equipment of the skilled speechmaker.

Whether you are addressing a meeting of colleagues or of employees at work ... of shareholders in the UK or of stockholders in the USA ... of family or of voters ... whether you are making a presentation to commercial prospects or presenting a guest to an audience or prizes at a school ... the techniques are essentially the same. Their application varies and is vital. Book 1 deals with them all.

You may have to chair a meeting, as major as a mass gathering or as minor as a company committee. In the same book we cover the rules on good chairmanship.

Book 2 contains models – a selection of draft speeches for varying occasions. Some revive great moments from the works of famed orators. They may be read and re-read, analysed and emulated, knowing that they captivated audiences. Others are modern guides. Use both – as precedents. They should help you to make the best of your speechmaking opportunities and to minimise your prospects of tongue-tied collapse.

Finally, in Book 3, I offer a compendium of my own favourite Retellable Tales. Forced to listen to literally thousands of speeches, too many of them with excruciating boredom, I have carefully accumulated an array of over 500 gems. I have used them all – for laughter, effect or emotional impact. Here are my favourites: stories, jokes and epigrams which shine with wit or with vivid language; which delighted audiences; and above all, which made me or others laugh, rejoice or just contemplate.

Watch the moonlight on the Taj Mahal, or the dawn break over the Palace of Westminster, or the light play and change over any other great building and it never appears the same twice. Go back to your bible and re-read your favourite tales and the words will achieve new form and meaning. Put my Retellable Tales before different people or varied audiences – or even the same people or audience in different mood – and they will change their reflection in the mirror or the mood of the moment.

So select and adapt those that suit you and your style as well as your victims and their reactions. With a modicum of that good fortune that every speaker always needs, but which is granted only on unpredictable and joyful occasions, these tales should provide you with a treasure house of spice for the seasoning of your speeches.

This second edition has emerged for a variety of reasons. For the first time *Janner's Complete Speechmaker* is to appear in both hard cover and in paperback. So a comb out became essential.

When it began, I found that the work done and the words written which had pleased me at the time, did so no longer. Styles change. There were chapters and sentences to add, sections and phrases to chase away.

Above all, I submitted the Retellable Tales to the critical eye and ruthless pen of my daughter, Marion. We argued our way through hundreds of stories. Out went those which she believed were irretrievably offensive. In came hundreds of others, selected and approved.

Retitled, revised, reviewed and renewed, resorted and reindexed, my expanded Retellable Tales are a tribute to the united effort of father and daughter – and are offered on the usual basis: responsibility for all errors is accepted by the older generation alone!

My thanks, then, to Marion and to all others who have contributed to the success of this new edition, including those who have (as will appear) given their consent to the republication of quotations. I thank those countless others whose speeches have provided me with examples – good and bad, worthy and laughable, splendid or sad – from which I have culled both advice and retellable tales.

I thank those pupils and delegates to whom I have taught the allied arts of presentation and speechmaking for helping to develop so much of the material in this book – and in its sister Business Books' publications: *Janner on Presentation* and *Janner's Complete Letterwriter*.

Finally: to you, my reader, I wish an overflow of those marvellous occasions when you return home from speechmaking, knowing that the job was well done, the message duly delivered, the audience captivated and content.

London, 1984   *GREVILLE JANNER*

Book One

SPEECHMAKING

First I'll say I'm glad to be here, then I'll tell them the one about the Bishop, then I'll say I'm going to be brief, then I'll talk for half an hour and then sit down to thunderous applause...
. . . .

Part One

The Speech—
its structure and
contents

Introduction:
thinking on your feet

A renowned American trial lawyer called Louis Nizer once wrote a book entitled: *Thinking on Your Feet*. It was the best in its field. Its title encapsulated the essential of every oratorical success – the ability to operate the mind and the tongue in tandem, with body upright.

A famous American President once remarked of his successor that he was so stupid that he was incapable of walking and of chewing gum at the same time. (It has been suggested that the original quotation was even ruder – alleging that the unfortunate man was incapable of walking and of passing wind simultaneously!) If your mind goes blank, you may still be able to read the words on the paper before you, but you will be unable to adapt them to match your audience or its reaction. It will react – you will not. You cannot win.

If you are attempting to plant your own ideas or thoughts in the minds of your audience, you have lost your chance. If your speech has been written for you, then you cannot now hope to make it appear your own.

Any interruption will throw you off your stride. You cannot draw ideas or allusions from your surroundings... refer to speeches that have gone before or to speakers that are to come after... Your speech has lost its spontaneity, its charm and its effect.

Here, then, are the techniques of thinking while speaking – an art essential to the successful speechmaker.

The skeleton of a speech 1

The human spirit can live, flourish and be much admired even when the human body is frail, ugly or misshapen. Some brilliant minds can capture and hold an audience with a rambling, poorly formed oration. Meaning and sincerity shine through and all is forgiven.

But to the businessman who wishes to make a speech in a business-like way ... to the average speaker who wishes to put on an above-average performance ... to the poor or timorous orator, forced into public speechmaking ... the structure of the speech is of supreme importance.

Create the skeleton, clothe it with sensible thought and all that remains is to deliver it. But without a healthy skeleton, the entire speech collapses. So here are the rules on forming a well built talk.

Any speech may conveniently be divided into three parts – the opening, the body and the closing. Take them in turn.

The first and last sentences of a speech are crucial. The importance of a clear, resounding and striking first sentence and a well rounded peroration cannot be over-emphasised. You must catch the interest of your audience from the start and send them away satisfied at the end. So, when building your skeleton, spend time on 'topping and tailing'. Many skilled speakers write out their opening and closing sentences, even if the rest is left entirely unfleshed.

Assume, now, that you have established a relationship with your audience. You have led in with your thanks for the invitation to speak ... your topical references ... your personal remarks, introductory witticisms and greetings to old friends. Now comes the substance of the speech – any speech. It must flow.

Like a first-class book or chapter or article, most fine speeches start their substance with a general introductory paragraph which sums up what is to come, catches the attention of the audience and indicates the run of the speaker's thought. Each idea should then be taken in sequence, and should lead on logically to the next.

Just as each bone of the human body is attached to its fellow, so the ideas in a speech should be jointed. The flow of ideas needs rhythm. Disjointed ideas ... dislocated thoughts ... fractured theories ... these are the hallmark of a poor speech.

So jot down the points you wish to make. Then set them out in logical order, so that one flows from the next. Connect them up, if you like, with a general theme. Start with that theme – and then elaborate, point by point.

Suppose, for instance, that you are explaining the virtues of a new product to your own sales staff. You begin in the usual way by asking for silence, smiling, looking round your audience and saying: 'Ladies and Gentlemen, sales staff of the X Company... It is a pleasure to see you here today, in spite of our reluctance to deprive the company's customers of your services...' Refer to Mr Y and Mr Z by name, congratulating them on their successes. Put your audience at ease. Tell them a joke or a story. Then launch into your theme.

'I have called you together today to introduce our new product.' (There it is, in a sentence.) 'Our research department has produced it. Now you must sell it. If you understand and exploit its full potentialities, you will not only benefit the company, but you should also add considerably to your own earnings.'

Personalise your message. Give your audience true incentive to listen. Whet their appetites for the substance to come.

Now for the speech proper. First, name and describe the product in broad terms. Next, preferably with the assistance of diagrams, transparencies or slides, describe the product in detail. Then take its selling features, one by one: 'The following features are entirely new...' Spell them out and explain them. 'But the following features are retained – they were too valuable to be lost...' (Once again, maintain logical sequence.)

'So there, Ladies and Gentlemen, we have our new product – and you are the first to see it. You will be supplied with full sales literature within the next week. It will be available for your customers by ... The rest is up to you. I wish you the very best of good fortune.'

Precisely the same rules of construction can be applied to any other discourse. Whether you are pronouncing a funeral oration over a deceased colleague or congratulating an employee on completing 25 years' service ... whether you are making an after-dinner speech or haranguing your workers at the factory gates ... whatever the circumstances, wherever the speech is made, if its skeleton is sound and solid, then even if the body is not as strong as it might be, the audience may not notice. But ignore the skeleton and the speech will prove a rambling disaster.

In the beginning... 2

'In the beginning, God created the heavens and the earth.' What a marvellous first sentence, in the world's eternal best-selling book!

Now pick up any national newspaper. Read the first sentence in any news story and it should grab your attention, excite your interest and tell you to read on. It will also encapsulate the theme.

Ask any author or journalist and he will tell you that he may spend as long on preparing the first sentence as he does on the rest of the piece. A good opening is crucial to any presentation, written or oral.

Unlike the writer, the speechmaker has the starting benefit of a formal few words to get used to the acoustics and to settle into his audience. Do not rush them. 'Ladies' ... pause ... 'and' ... pause 'Gentlemen', – not 'Ladies-and-Gentlemen'. Look around and allow your audience to fix its attention on you, its minds on your words.

Next: create rapport. Latch onto some aspect of the introduction you have just received, or to a topicality of particular interest to your listeners.

My late distinguished father (to whose memory this book is dedicated) was an MP for a total of some 30 years and then a life peer. I was (and often still am) introduced as his son – often by that well intentioned cliché: 'The distinguished son of a distinguished father.' I have a standard opening which never fails: 'On behalf of my late father and myself – thank you for your kind introduction. When he was alive and active, we often got invited to meetings in mistake for each other. I treasure a letter, framed in the smallest room in my house, which was actually addressed to: "The Rt Hon. Lord Greville Janner QC MP, House of Commons, London." It begins: "Dear Sir or Madam!" The man was taking no chances!'

Listen to any experienced speaker and you will find that he has opening gambits of his own – you will find a batch of some favourite standbys at the start of my Retellable Tales.

Once you have created contact with your audience and reassured them that they will be interested in your theme and will not be bored by your presentation, then – and only then – you launch into your subject. Your first sentence should be like those in the book or the newspaper – aimed precisely at the issue. Here are some random examples from one front page:

- 'The Prime Minister will return from her overseas visit tonight to find her Government in visible and increasing disarray over its controversial decision to ...'

- 'The American shuttle Challenger returned to orbit yesterday from an eight-day mission ...'

- 'The Coal Board yesterday closed a pit where the Miners' Union had withdrawn essential safety cover ...'

- 'British American Tobacco announced yesterday that it is withdrawing from direct sales distribution in Britain, with the loss of over 1,800 jobs, mostly in Liverpool ...'

You could start any of those sentences with the words: 'Did you know that ...?', or 'We have come together because ...', or 'It is essential for our industry/organisation that we should recognise that ...', or 'As our local/trade newspaper announced on its front page only today ...'

The sprinter who has a bad start can rarely win his race. The speechmaker who fails in the beginning is unlikely to succeed in the end.

3 In conclusion

Nothing so becomes a good speech as a fine ending. And nothing can be more ruinous than a weak termination trailing off into silence or into a lame 'Thank you'. So lavish as much care on the tail of a speech as you do on its top. Consider some common flops:

- Mr Brown rushes his last few sentences, gathers his notes and slides almost surreptitiously back into his seat.

- Mr Black ends his talk in what appears to be the middle of a sentence or the height of an anti-climax.

- Mr Grey, who has been allotted 30 minutes to speak, runs out of material after 20, but is determined 'not to let the audience down', and says: 'In conclusion', 'finally', 'before I conclude', 'lastly', and 'to end up with', at least twice each – each time rekindling hope in the minds of his audience that he really means it.

- Mr Green thinks that he is narrating a serial story and leaves his audience in suspense by over-running his time, panicking and then forgetting to propose the resolution, which was the sole object of his speech.

- Mr Blue realises that he is not going to conclude his prepared talk within the time available if he keeps going at the same speed. So he runs out of script and breath at the same moment, leaving his audience miles behind.

- Mr Dark forgets that a peroration should be brief – and drags it out interminably, embellishing thoughts that were in the body of the speech, introducing new ideas in the guise of a summary of what he had said.

What, then, makes a really good ending or peroration? It should round off the speech and, in most cases, include the following:

- A summary, in a sentence or two, of the main purport of the speech;

- Any proposal or resolution arising out of the body of the speech; and

- A call for support or warm words of thanks.

If you were to attach the peroration to the opening, they should between them contain the core of the entire speech. The opening says what is coming; the closing says what has gone.

Here are some examples of good closing gambits:

- 'So this project does have great possibilities for our company. To succeed we must at once take the steps that I have suggested. I ask you all to support the resolution and to help put it into useful and urgent effect.'

- 'And so, Mr Chairman, my argument is closed. I have tried to suggest the appropriate action which this company could now take. I believe that if my resolution is passed and put into urgent effect, it will transform the company's finances. I trust that no one will vote against it. I submit, Mr Chairman, that it presents the best possible way out of our difficulties.'

- 'So this company stands in grave peril. The only way out is clear. The action I recommend could transform the situation. I am grateful to all of you for having listened so attentively to my arguments. Please do not reject them.'

- 'There is, then, no need for despair. The future presents great opportunities. But we must not only resolve to carry out the procedure proposed in my resolution, but also to ensure that the action which must follow will have the urgent and active support of us all. I therefore move that...'

- 'So those are the possibilities open to us. And only one of them really carries any hope of real success. It is the duty of this Board to protect and to advance the interests of our shareholders. That duty can only be performed if steps are taken in accordance with the resolution which stands in my name. I urge that it be accepted – fully, wholeheartedly and without amendment.'

* * *

There are many roads to Rome and countless ways to construct the end of the same speech. Purge the old clichés: 'My time is running short...' 'I see that my time is nearly up and I must close...'. Still worse: 'I see that you are beginning to get restless...', 'I have no wish to bore you any further...' Make your summary and your appeal – for support, for money, for understanding...

Other recommended endings:

- 'And so, Mr Chairman, I end as I began – with my warm thanks for your kind hospitality.'

- 'Ladies and Gentlemen, it has been a delight to be with you. I hope that my words will have been of some help in promoting the cause for which you work and in which I – like you – believe so firmly. I wish you, Mr Chairman, your honorary officers, executives, members and workers, every possible success in your great venture.'

- 'And so our Conference is over. It has been a delightful experience to meet you all. I trust that we shall see each other on many more such happy and useful occasions. Meanwhile, I know that I am expressing the warm feelings of all of us when I wish you God-speed on your journeys home and every success in all your ventures.'

- 'I know that the views I have put forward are not universally acceptable. But I know, too, that you would not have wished me to do otherwise than to speak my mind. That I have done, most earnestly. I do hope that the suggestions I have made will be adopted, or at least adapted. But whatever decision you take, I would like you to know how much I have appreciated the kind and courteous attention which you have given to me – and how much I care for the future of this organisation.'

Some people end by saying: 'Thank you' or 'Good night'. A climax is better. A last powerful phrase, left hovering in the air – and beckoning on to the applause.

Then do not rush back to your seat, flop quickly down into your chair, whip out your cigarette case and light up. Like any good trouper, wait for the applause. If it comes, smile or bow slightly in acknowledgement. If it does not, then look your audience straight in the eye. Pause. And then sit down. The end of your speech should make as solid an impact as its start.

Wit and humour 4

Every comedian labours hard for his living. If he is renowned for his wit, he may be able to make his audience laugh (if they are in the right mood) where no laughter is really deserved. Part of the art of any speaker is to let his hearers know what is coming . . . to lead them up to the climax . . . to prepare them to react as he intends.

The well known wit has his groundwork laid ready for him. He no sooner comes to the stage, platform, or microphone, shakes his head or performs some other famous gesture – and the audience begins to giggle. Whether his first sentence refers to 'The Diddy people', his mother-in-law, or simply includes some renowned catch-phrase – the audience is off.

But speak to the most famous men of comedy and you will soon discover how carefully their impromptu laughs are prepared . . . how fickle and unpredictable an audience – any audience – can be . . . how even the best woven tales may fall apart at the seams. You will then realise, if you do not already know it, that of all the skills of the public speaker, putting across humour is one of the most difficult. For the most experienced of humorists, the path is tough. How much more difficult must it be for the beginner?

Still: the humourless speaker is weak. There are few occasions when a word of wit is not appreciated. The longer the speech, the more vital the touch of humour. The more sombre the subject, the more appropriate the tactful, tasteful touch of light relief. Humour is a weapon that every speaker should have readily available.

Humour must be tailored to the audience and to the occasion. This applies most obviously to the risqué, the rude or the plain vulgar. There is never any excuse for the obscene. But an element of dirt may sometimes add spice to the meal. When?

Obviously, the stag dinner is the place for the off-colour story. Conversely, those who introduce the risqué tale into solemn or sombre occasions invite contempt. In between come all the rest. You must judge each occasion as best you can. If in doubt – keep it clean.

Similar considerations apply to the dialect story. There is still a place for the saga of the Scotsman, the Irishman and the Jew. But to copy someone else's accent is generally an error. The only speakers who can do it without undue risk are those who belong to the group satirised.

Scotsmen, Jews, Irishmen, Blacks – they may delight in stories *about* themselves, but usually only when told *by* themselves.

If you enjoy the friendship of Jewish people, for instance, you will soon find that they poke merciless fun at their own foibles. Part of their armour, acquired through centuries of persecution, is the ability to make laughter shine through the tears. No one can tell an anti-Semitic story with half the relish of the Jew. But then, masochism is reasonable. *Volenti non fit injuria* – the volunteer cannot complain of injuries brought about of his own free will. We cause no injury to ourselves when we make jokes at our own expense.

Sadism, on the other hand, is always unpleasant, and even a hint may be harmful. Minorities may consider themselves the subject for good humour. But the laughter is thin when the gibes come from tongues other than their own.

So be careful not to obtain cheap laughs at the expense of others. Many of the best jokes – and those most appreciated – are those about yourself.

'We Welsh...,' says the speaker with a smile, 'have, through our very name, given birth to an important word in the English language...'

'As you know,' says the speaker in broad Scots, 'I yield to none of my compatriots in the meanness of my approach...'

'We foreigners find it very difficult to understand you English. I know that m-i-s-l-e-d spells misled. But when I pronounced t-i-t-l-e-d the same way, everyone laughed at me.'

None of this is great humour. All of it has been heard before. But then, as one famous comic put it: 'There are basically only two jokes – the mother-in-law and the banana skin.' Make the joke fit the occasion and the audience.

The best way to suit the occasion is to extract the humour from the surroundings and from the people present. But how do you put it across? Here are some hints.

First, you must give every impression of confidence. It is a mistake to say: 'I was going to tell you the story about...' and then to tell it, half apologetically. Believe in the comedy or you will never induce your audience to do so.

That confidence must be retained, even in the face of defeat. If a joke falls flat, never mind. Pretend it was not intended to be funny and carry straight on. Alternatively, face up to the situation and say: 'Sorry... it wasn't a very good one, was it? Never mind – how about the tale of...?' Or: 'Sorry about that – I'll do better next time. But you must admit that after a meal such as we've just had, it really is the height of sadism to expect anyone to attempt to entertain you!'

Timing is all-important. This means that the joke, witticism or humorous thrust must be well placed in relation to the speech, the content of the talk or lecture, the mood of the audience. But it especially means that the joke must be told at the right pace... with the correct emphasis ... with the appropriate pauses.

Listen to any first-class comedian at work. Half his effect is achieved by timing. He knows when to wait and when to rush forward. So listen to the experts – and copy them.

Some speakers keep a book of stories, notes of humorous tales that have gone down well and which they would like not to forget. Certainly the jotting down of the punch line on the back of a menu card or in the front of your diary can provide useful ammunition. It may also have the opposite effect – it may help to save you from the gross error of telling an audience the same story that it heard the last time it met.

To avoid this fate, take some regular attender into your confidence. 'I'm thinking of telling the story of...' you say to the chairman. 'Do you know it?' If he says no, then the chances are that you will be safe. If he has heard it, then find out whether it was told at the same gathering. If in doubt, leave it out.

Jokes are for others to laugh at. Giggle at your own stories and you detract from their effect on your audience.

The best stories have a sting in their tails. The laughter should build up. The audience should expect the laughs. But if the first climax brings laughter and turns out to be a false one, giving rise to an unexpected twist, then the story has been a success.

The formal tale also has its place. But the bright phrase, the witty aside, the colourful remark – these are more important. If you cannot think of a suitable, funny story for the occasion, never mind. Some humorous thought may come to you as you speak. If it does not, at least make sure that your speech is shorter than if you had been able to lighten its darkness with a few shafts of light-hearted laughter.

Finally, mull over my Retellable Tales (Book Three). Use and adapt to suit yourself, your occasion and your audience.

5 Overstatements

Hyperbole – that is, exaggeration for effect – has its place, and is often used by humorists. There is nothing funny about a thin man – but a matchstick man, a creation of skin and bone, a fat head on a puny frame – that's different.

About the only time that deliberate exaggeration helps the presentation of a serious case is when that case is thin. 'If something is too silly to say, you can always sing it,' says the operatic librettist. 'If logic and argument are surplus,' says the skilled speaker, 'then it is just possible that if you shout loud enough, exaggerate sufficiently, thump with sufficient force, you may numb the minds of your audience.'

This type of behaviour is the last resort of the advocate and should only be used when *in extremis*. Otherwise, your exaggerations are likely to boomerang ... to cause laughter ... to ruin such case as you have. Two horrible examples:

● Reference to the speech immediately preceding: 'That magnificent and moving oration that we have just heard... that tugged at our heart strings and must now open our purses...'

● 'I only saw her passing by, but I shall love her till I die,' said Sir Robert Menzies, then Prime Minister of Australia, enthusing at a dinner in honour of the Queen. However well loved the Queen undoubtedly was and is, Sir Robert's hyperbole brought only ridicule in its wake.

Words, like drugs, may be highly beneficial in the correct quantity and dosage. Over-indulgence may cause death. Moderation pays.

Repetition 6

Repetition should be deliberate. Shakespeare did it best. 'Brutus is an honourable man...'

Or read Martin Luther King's masterpiece (page 175): 'I have a dream...'

Repeating other people's points generally spells disaster: 'Mr Jones has put all the arguments which I had wished to put forward...' Try instead: 'Mr Jones has put forward his case with immense skill, and I commend it to the meeting. However, there are several aspects of his remarks which, I think, require further emphasis.'

'I will not bore you by reploughing the furrows so thoroughly covered by Mr Jones.' Watch out. Boredom is on its way. That sort of introduction, combining mixed metaphor with cliché, is a sure sign of impending audience distress. Leave the meeting if you can.

Then there is the man who repeats his points in the same words. Most well constructed speeches should begin with a summary of what is coming: a full-blooded exposition of those points in the body of the speech and another brief summary at the end. 'To summarise, then: if we are to achieve success, we must take the following steps. First... second... third... and, above all...'

English is a rich language. If you cannot think of similes, consult the invaluable *Roget's Thesaurus* – which should be on the desk or at least in the library of every speaker. If you must repeat yourself, at least try not to do so in the current and boring clichés, which are merely a sign of speeches made without thought, and so reveal the thoughtlessness of the speaker.

7 The cliché

Labour's one-time Foreign Minister, Ernest Bevin, used to say: 'His speech was nothing but clitch after clitch after clitch!'

Clitches are horrible, however pronounced. Still: one way to while away the speeches of others is to compile a list of them, in hideous use. Some examples, culled from a recent company meeting:

- 'In this day and age . . .'
- 'Each and every one of us . . .'
- 'We are escalating towards disaster . . .'
- 'We must give of our best . . .'
- 'No politicians are to be trusted . . .'
- 'We must stem the tide of ill-will . . .'
- 'The ship of State is heading for the rocks . . .'
- 'Blood, toil, sweat and tears – that is the only recipe . . .'
- 'The present system of taxation is destroying us . . .'
- 'Our expansion plans are going full steam ahead . . .'
- 'Let us stand up and be counted . . .'

There is no limit, is there? Each is common, hackneyed, trite and commonplace (see Roget's Thesaurus, paragraph 496). Even though the sentiments expressed may be wise, sage, true, received, admitted, recognized (same paragraph), that flexibility of the language which can cloak even the most uninspiring and unoriginal thought with at least the appearance of charm or originality has not been brought into play.

After a particularly monotonous, cliché-ridden speech made by a dull guest in the Cambridge Union, Percy Cradock (Now Sir Percy Cradock, advisor to the Prime Minister on foreign affairs) brought the house down with the following: 'I know that we have all greeted each sentence expressed by Mr . . . with something of the wretched anticipation felt when one notes the approach of an old but extremely seedy acquaintance.'

Contrast the effect made on the dowdy woman by a new hairstyle, a chic outfit and modern accessories and the moral needs no emphasis. No longer is she seedy. Her familiarity has a new and interesting flavour. She is now worthy of our attention. She is ready for the wooing.

It is no hyperbole to say that the oldest thought in the newest dress can have a rare and surprising appeal. 'There's nothing new to say about this subject,' is a cliché. 'Consider the problem from this new angle,' is a worthy start – and if the angle is sufficiently acute, its familiarity may well be forgotten.

You will not regard yourself as a bore. Your listeners should share your view. A good start to this hopeful process is to learn to recognise clichés in the speeches of others and ruthlessly to eliminate them from your own.

The great I Am   8

The speaker of excellence treats the sound of his own voice as a drug to be taken in moderation. Restrain your use of the first-person singular.

There are two probable reasons why you have been asked to address the particular audience. Either the people *wanted* to hear you or they thought they *ought* to want to do so. These categories subdivide.

If you have been invited to speak in the hope that you will have something interesting to tell, then you are lucky. Do not push your luck too far by retelling what you are, rather than what you know.

Leave it to your introducer to sing your praises. To do so for yourself is to court ridicule. Oscar Wilde once remarked, 'Fall in love with yourself and you are in for a lifetime of romance!' Fine: but do not do your courting in public.

If you are asked to give advice, do you really need to praise your own success? To tell tales of the trade, you must draw on your own experience and a joke against yourself may be highly successful. But you do not need to alert your listeners to your excellence. Do so and they will not believe you. Fail to do so and they may think up the idea for themselves.

Naturally, if you have been the rounds of similar businesses, factories, offices or workshops to your own, at home or abroad, and are asked to give your impressions ... if you wish to express views and to make it clear that they are yours and not those of your organisation or, perhaps, of your board, your partners or colleagues

... if you wish to lighten the darkness of some drab subject with a personal anecdote – then go ahead: 'I once met ... in Birmingham,'; 'I was told the tale of ...'; 'These are my views, I repeat, and if they turn out to be wrong, you will know where to place the responsibility.' All fair.

But 'When I last saw the Prime Minister ...'; or 'Now, I don't like to drop names, but when I was spending a weekend recently with Lord and Lady Blank in their country estate ...' Terrible.

Remember the story of that famous General, Lord Montgomery of Alamein, whose first-person anecdote was accepted because of his undoubted greatness. He was telling an audience about his battle tactics. 'I could not decide what to do next,' he said. 'I thought to myself: "My God, what is to be done now?" "General," came the answer, "you decide. I have every confidence in you." So I did!'

Of course, people like to be given the inside information. Don the cloak of apparent modesty.

All this becomes even more important when you are Guest of Honour – which is not necessarily the same as the honoured guest. Maybe your hosts want your money ... your support ... your services ... your backing. Maybe they are simply hoping to lubricate you sufficiently to obtain some useful information which, in a less cordial or obligated moment, you might never give. Whatever the reason, you are on show. So play up to it. Be grateful that you are to be honoured and not reviled. Help to keep it that way by making your speech extremely modest. Or try my father's favourite: 'After all those kind words, Mr Chairman, I can hardly wait to hear myself speak!'

'It is extremely good of you to honour me in this way,' you might continue. 'I fully appreciate that your intention is, through me, to honour my company ... my organisation ... my entire Board ...' (*or as the case may be*). 'We are deeply grateful to you.'

In the body of the speech, tell them about the work your organisation is doing. Give them as much inside information as you decently can. If you are honoured for long service, then reminisce – and mention as many individuals amongst your audience as you can.

'Now Bill Black over there ... he'll remember when we were both involved in an embarrassing disaster in 1967 ... Sir Michael Brown – whom we are all very pleased to see amongst us – shared many an exploit ... Richard Jones, whose sobriety is a proud tribute to the breathalyser ...' and so on.

Everyone honourably mentioned is flattered. You have achieved the all-important, informal touch. Your audience are your friends. The ice is melted and you are revealed as a man of the people instead of the complete egotist some had thought you to be.

Then continue: 'You are indeed lucky to have in your active ranks tonight and always, Mr Reginald Property ... Mr James Industry ... and that lady, famous for her good deeds, Mrs Jewel.' The guest who gives honour will receive it.

'I now close ...' (one hopes because of the time of the clock and not the time you have taken in your speech) 'but before doing so, I thank you again for the great kindness and generosity you have shown me. I have enjoyed being with you. I hope that we shall meet again often and always on happy occasions. And may this organisation/company/institute (etc.) flourish for many years to come, under your leadership.'

Turn to the chairman, bow to your audience ... You have produced a resounding ending to a good speech. Your hearers will tell you so – and mean it.

Grammar – 9
and the spoken word

The old, pedantic rules for writing have largely been discarded. Freedom of expression and freedom of speech have followed in its wake. Sentences without verbs... split infinitives... They offend the ears of some but are generally forgiven. Still, here are some general rules which may prove helpful.

* * *

The most common grammatical error lies in the use of the first person. 'Between you and I' is wrong. So is 'Dr Brown and me were most impressed with our welcome' and 'You and me must give some careful thought to this problem'. If this sort of problem worries you, discuss it with a friend whose grammar is impeccable. If in doubt, change the sentences around and you will soon find whether your usage is or is not correct.

Thus, if you are inclined to say: 'You and me must go', try instead: 'Me must go' – and the error becomes obvious. Or: 'Thank you on behalf of Mr White and I for your kindness' cannot be correct when you leave out Mr White. 'On my own behalf... on my behalf... on behalf of Dr White' – but obviously, not on behalf of I!

Swear words and obscenities are best excluded, even from the stag-dinner oration. Some listeners will always be offended. But slang and modern idiom are expected. If in doubt, put the words 'in quotes'.

If in doubt about the precise meaning of a word, either avoid it or consult a dictionary. If given the choice between two words, one long and the other short, choose the shorter. Good old Anglo-Saxon monosyllables are usually the most effective.

Sentences, too, should be kept short. Apart from your audience losing the thread, you may yourself do so. 'Now, where was I?' is a sad admission of a speaker's failure.

Avoid statistics where you can; apart from the possibility of being found out, the effect of an understandable approximation is much greater than the spelling out of some lengthy figures.

Clichés should be 'conspicuous by their absence'. You should 'leave no avenue explored' in your attempt to avoid phrases of this sort (see Chapter 7).

You may use material full of sound and fury but signifying nothing. The higher you get in the government of a country or of an organisation, the more frequent those occasions become. But in general, direct speech is better than indirect, the active voice rather than the passive, the straightforward far preferable to the insinuation.

10 Brevity – the soul of success

Mort Mendels, long-time Secretary of the World Bank and top sufferer from the awful speeches from others, boasted a cartoon on his office wall. It showed a man being carried out of the Senate on a stretcher. 'Talked to Death!' was the caption. The corpse might as easily have been emerging from any one of thousands of meetings anywhere in Britain or the USA.

The man who stands in front of the mirror admiring himself for long periods is rightly regarded as a freak. But at least no one else is disturbed. The man who so rejoices in the sound of his own words that he imposes them at great length upon his fellows should be relegated to the same privacy.

Have you ever heard an audience complain that the speaker did not go on long enough? Far more listeners complain at the sluggishness of their watch hands. And on the rare occasions when they do want more from the speaker – well, he can always be invited again.

'If you can't strike oil within 15 minutes, stop boring,' the oil man is alleged to have told his apprentices. He could have been talking to a course on public speaking.

The importance of this chapter should not be judged by its brevity. Indeed, so vital is its theme that we shall return to it in Chapter 20.

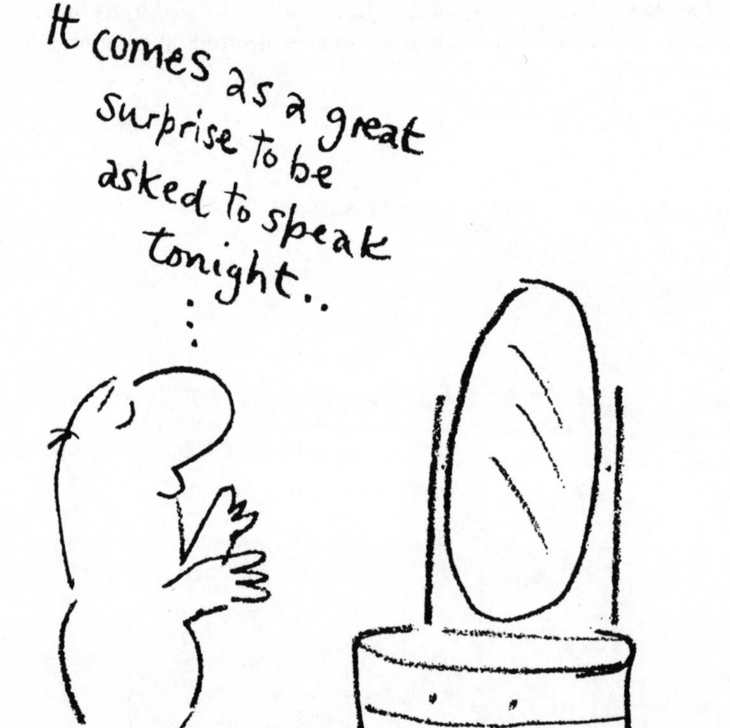
It comes as a great surprise to be asked to speak tonight..

Part Two

The arts of delivery

Controlling your nerves **11**

Human beings – which term includes most speech-makers – habitually have and suffer from nerves. I have seen great athletes coughing and moaning before races ... experienced public speakers shaking and trembling before a major appearance ... world leaders in agony before a crucial press conference ... So join the club.

Nervous tension is a necessity for the performer in any sphere. It releases that amazing and invaluable secretion, adrenalin, which sharpens and tones up the functions of body and mind alike.

So if you do not feel nervous, your performance is unlikely to excel. Greet your anxiety with expectant understanding. It will in due course be your ally.

Accepting, then, that pre-presentation nerves are an inevitable necessity, how can you control them?

First: recognise that once you start moving, they will disappear on their own. The runner may retch as he limbers up but *never* once he is in his starting blocks. The public speaker may shake before he begins but once his first words ring out and he actually hears his voice, he stops worrying whether his vocal cords will freeze.

Second: remember that your feelings are internal and your audience will not know of them unless you are inexperienced enough to tell them. Therefore:

- *Do not* say: 'I am a bag of nerves ...' or any equivalent.

- *Do* look them straight in the eye.

The absence of eye contact is the greatest single give-away of the nervous presenter. An experienced audience may look for a tongue flickering over dry lips, but if the speaker keeps his eyes on floor, ceiling or notes, he is in trouble. So you look your audience in the face. Fix your eyes to theirs and they will concentrate on what you are saying and be far less likely to notice your mistakes.

Third: avoid whatever form of nervous twitch is your personal affliction. Do not:

- Put your hand in front of your mouth – you will muffle your words while leaving your nerve ends visible.

- Keep your hands in your pockets – a slovenly discourtesy made worse if you rattle coins or your keyring.

- Jiggle your handbag or bounce it up and down on the table.

- Twist your hair ... excavate your ear ... pick at your nose, however delicately ... open and close buttons of your jacket .. or engage in any other of those less entrancing pursuits of the nerve-ridden.

Above all: come to your presentation prepared with adequate notes, properly laid out (Chapter 32); knowing your case and (deep down, if not on the surface) confident that you can deal with your subject. Your nerves can then return to their quietude and you can make your presentation at your ease.

That said, here are a few hints to help you either to control your nerves or at least not to show how you are feeling:

- Take whatever position, sitting or standing, that suits you best. Sometimes, you have no choice; often, you can say to the chairman: 'Do you mind if I sit?' Or, alternatively: 'If you have no objection, I shall talk to you standing.'

- Do not be afraid to change your position during the course of your presentation. Maybe you should sit further back, with your rear end tucked into the angle of the chair – or perhaps you should sit and lean forward, until you have taken the measure of your audience. If standing, try putting one foot ahead of the other – this is also better for your voice production.

- If you are superstitious, by all means keep your favourite mascot or charm in your pocket or handbag – but do not rely on it so much that if one day you forget it, your confidence collapses. And please do not allow your nervousness to drive you into clicking your ball point, twiddling or tapping your pen or dashing doodles across a visible pad.

- If a pre-presentation drink will really relax you ... or a tranquilliser stop you from coughing or retching ... then take one. But test your reactions first on some other, unimportant day, just in case you end up befuddled. If in doubt, leave it out.

A man I know was wrongly charged with arson. An honest, decent person, he arrived at his trial stuffed to his eyeballs with tranquillisers. He was not at all nervous. But he never answered the question he was asked; he was convicted and sentenced to three years' imprisonment; and it took the combined efforts of an investigative radio team and another MP and myself to get him released. Tranquillisers cost him an agonising year in jail.

So regard drink and drugs as an absolutely last resort for nerve control. Confidence comes with preparation, practice – and training.

Style 12

For the speechmaker, style and success are synonymous. But the common idea that style will suffice without taught techniques is arrogant and ridiculous. So is the converse – the chip-on-the-shoulder, foot-in-the-mouth inferiority complex approach to public speaking in any form, especially endemic among too many business people at or near the top.

I invited a tycoon to address a private dinner. 'Sorry,' he replied, curtly. 'Nice of you to ask. You and your friends in Parliament do the speaking. I do the work!' What he really meant was: 'I'm afraid of opening my mouth while I'm on my feet in case I make a fool of myself.'

Another told me: 'I came up the hard way. I leave speeches to you fellows with the education.'

An education does no one any harm and many top people who missed it in their youth are unashamed to learn, when their money can buy them time and tuition. And presenting yourself to a public does take courage and is certainly an acquired skill. But if you have that intangible, inexplicable magic – that style of your own – you should not fear its public display. Printers and potters produce identical replicas, good or bad. Your style is unique and rules are made to be broken.

Take the orator's pause, for instance – a crucial weapon in the armoury of timing. (See also Chapter 17.) The space between words or sentences or thoughts should not be blurred by that most awful of sounds – 'er'. To 'err' (or to 'umm') is human – to pause, divine!

The art of successful speaking is to know the case you wish to present; to understand and to use the basic skills which will enable your audience to hear, to comprehend and to accept your words and their intent; and to stamp the process with your own particularity.

It follows that you should use the services of the speechwriters with rare care. Unless you can find the writer who can step into your style as well as your mind, you are probably better off with a researcher. By all means use a ferret to produce your raw material, but knock it into your own shape.

If the speech or presentation is worth your while to make, is it not worth your own time to prepare? Then remember another of Churchill's dicta: 'If I have to make a two hour speech,' he rumbled, 'I spend 10 minutes in preparation. If it is a 10-minute speech, then it takes me two hours...'

The stylist is as brief as his impact and his message permit. There is no reason why the executive who is blunt, direct and lucid in conversation should allow his speech to deteriorate into long-winded and indirect blather, the moment he climbs to his feet.

Just as there is no one successful style in business – or, for that matter, in athletics or in football, in philosophy or in politics – so the executive who seeks success on his feet will project his personal individuality, his individual personality.

Asked the difference between education and training, a professor replied: 'If your daughter came home saying that she had received sex education, you would doubtless be pleased; but if she said she had enjoyed her sex training...'

The executive needs education in the basic skills of speechmaking and presentation, which are universal. They range from voice production to microphone technique, from the skills of the construction of a speech or presentation to the art of the destruction of the arguments of others. But his training in the use of those skills should be devoted to the creation and improvement of his own style.

True education and the best training teach the student – however mighty – to make the best of his own talents.

No presenter of ideas or maker of speeches has ever excelled the wondrous Shakespeare. 'This above all,' he admonished, 'to thine own self be true...'

If truth is the life of style, insincerity is its death.

13 Appearances count

If self-presentation is an essential for self-preservation, then you must make your appearances and hence your appearance count. If your presentation is disembodied, you must take special care with your voice. You have no other way of showing your enthusiasm and your sincerity, your confidence and your command of the subject.

In person or on television, you are notable by your visibility. And while, for instance, dandruff may go unobserved at a meeting, on TV it stands out from a blue suit like chalk on a blackboard. So you *must* take note of detail.

Start, though, with the overall effect. How do you wish to appear? Authoritative, distinguished, sound and sensible? Then no doubt you will wear a dark suit, with modest tie. Relaxed, informal, man of the people? Then wear your light-coloured suit and maybe an open-necked shirt. The choice is yours. The persuaders may try to influence your decision. But ultimately you make up your own mind.

Celebrated caricaturist Ranan Lurie, once said to me: 'Your father got his appearance right. A combination of pointed head, central bulk and above all of red carnation made him instantly recognisable. You, alas, are simply a pleasant and happy looking individual without even a treble chin.'

I convinced him that he should look more closely and he would see that I have at least six arms, most of them working at the same time. But I now usually wear a carnation.

Start at the top and work down. Do you cultivate polished head (David Nixon) or bushed hair (David Ben Gurion)? Do you groom your crowning glory (Margaret Thatcher) or allow it to dominate you (Michael Foot)? Do you permit your hair to turn grey or white (most men) or enjoy retaining or even enhancing its youthful blaze (most women)?

Do you wear your uniform (dark suit or working overalls)?

Safely married and at home or on holiday with your husband or wife, you may decide that appearances are skin deep and matter little. But when you appear in public, you woo the public – so present yourself with pre-studied care, or take any unacceptable consequences.

Body talk 14

The speechmaker may usefully study Dale Carnegie's classic *How to Make Friends and Influence People*. But Desmond Morris's *The Naked Ape* – followed by his *Manwatching* – should give your speeches an extra dimension of excellence. In particular: you will learn how others give themselves away through bodily indications, and how you can avoid doing the same.

For instance: eye contact is crucial to successful speechmaking, whether seated or on your feet. Lowering or swivelling your eyes or failure 'to look people straight' in theirs is a classic symptom of nervousness.

The more your stomach wobbles, the more you should hunt for a friendly face in your audience and talk to it, eyeball to eyeball. (See also Chapter 11.)

Keep your gestures to the minimum. They should emphasise your words, not detract from their meaning. Keep your body still when talking. Be upright to dominate your audience.

You may wish to move around, to involve your audience or for effect. Or, like myself, you may have back trouble and be able to run, jump or climb but not to stand still. Then get a high (or bar or draughtsman's) stool, or perch on the edge of a table.

The effect of a gesture depends not upon its vigour or expanse. The more economic your movements the better. If you make your presentation seated, keep your hands away from your face and your mouth. To command your audience, do not slouch – sit straight. Avoid minor, irritating gestures – from nail biting to finger or pencil tapping to rattling coins in your pocket. Concentrate on the body of your presentation and keep your own steady and still.

Your facial expression should match your topic. President Jimmy Carter used to speak with a fixed grin on his face. Eventually, a professional speech teacher showed him on a video screen how wicked it looked to preserve that smile when talking about, for instance, those who had died in Vietnam. He stopped.

After chairing a memorial meeting, I was admonished for smiling on the platform. My neighbour had told me a wistful and loving story about the deceased. No matter. When on show, your face must reflect the mood of the occasion.

Conversely: if you are asking your audience to laugh, your face should indicate that a joke is on its way.

15 Stance and gesture

Words matter; movements distract.

We all recognise the speaker who strides up and down while

talking, like the American lawyer in those television courtroom scenes. In Britain, lawyers stand still and their speeches are the better for it.

Acrobats doing a tumbling act must gyrate and mime. Those who rely on words stand still and confine their movement to their faces.

The more motionless you stand, the greater the chance of your speech reaching the minds of your audience and making its impact.

What do you do with your hands? Hold the lectern or rostrum before you. Grip the edge of the table. Put your hands behind your back, *à la* Duke of Edinburgh. Or simply hold the cards for your notes, firmly and calmly in front of you?

Keep your gestures sparing. The rarer and the more restrained the movement, the greater its effect. The days of the ranting, tub-thumping, rebel-rousing, arm-waver are gone. The businessman who 'hams' is regarded (not always correctly) as an insincere show-off.

A contemptuous shrug ... an occasional, accusing finger ... a reference to the heavens and hand pointing to the sky ... all have their place in the skilled speaker's repertoire.

You wear spectacles? Then use them as an occasional weapon. To emphasise a point, remove them gently from your nose ... hold them still in your hand ... bend forward and glare at your audience ... brandish your glasses and then return them to your nose and your speech to its theme. Even the odd jab with the closed spectacles can be dramatic and useful.

Speakers with spectacles need not be shy. Many excellent performers who could do without their glasses, even for seeing their notes, deliberately wear them. Do not fear poor eyesight. Like other defects, it can be turned to good effect.

Generally, though, the speaker should use his tongue, his face and his mind, not his feet, his arms or his fingers. Otherwise, his audience may take to their heels.

Voice production 16

The human chest is a sound box. The voice should reverberate and carry. As a stringed instrument gains its volume through the resonance of its sound chamber, so the human voice should resonate through the chest.

Try saying the word 'war'. Through your nose and voice alone, it produces a puny sound. Now take a deep breath; put your hand on your chest and sigh out the word until you can feel the vibration. Deep and resonate sound reverberates an idea to immense effect.

The opposite also applies. To attract and to hold the attention of an audience, you do not need to shout at them. The dramatic effect of a whisper may be intense.

Vary and change the volume and tone of your speech, but always within the hearing of your listeners. Address the woman in the back row. Imagine she is deaf – she may well be!

Take special care not to drop your voice at the end of a sentence. Thoughts should rise to a climax, not fade with the final breaths of a phrase. To avoid monotony, vary tone, speed and volume. When standing, put one foot ahead of the other; throw out your chest; stand well and with pride and your voice will emerge with effect and without effort.

If seated, do not slouch. Lift your body in the chair and stretch your voice out into your audience.

Practise privately. Voice production needs a quiet room and a mirror. Remember: an unheard voice produces wasted words.

17 The pause

The pause is the speechmaker's most useful weapon. Handled with confidence, it hides nerves ... gives time for thought ... and above all, is the basis of all dramatic timing.

Take your cue and your breath from the impresario: 'Ladies and Gentlemen' – pause – 'it is my honour to present' – pause – 'for the first time in this country' – pause – 'none other than' – pause – 'that most famous of all singers/comedians/boxers...' – long pause – 'Mr' – pause – 'John' – pause – 'Smith!'

Refine that into the chairman's introduction: 'Ladies and Gentlemen' – pause – 'Mr John Smith!'

The pause precedes the words and the sense mounts to a crescendo at the end of the sentence.

Churchill used the pause more and better than any other great orator. 'We... er... have no intention of allowing that... er... maniac to demolish our lives...' Each pause and each 'er' whetted the appetite for his next attack on Nazis and their leader.

For those of us who are not Churchills, to 'er' is to err! If you cannot think what to say, keep silent. Your audience will believe that you are searching for the *mot juste*. Even if your mind is blank, look fierce, look around, stand firm. When you are ready with your next pearl, drop it.

At the start of your speech, talk or intervention, you must keep silent until you have the full attention of your audience. Pause.

If you are interrupted – whether by the drop of a window, the shrill of a passing jet or the intervention of a colleague or interrupter – wait again for silence before you proceed. Pause ... not as the sign of indecision or weakness, but using the speaker's great weapon – and the one that the inexperienced speechmaker uses far too little.

The pause before a crucial word is the orator's superb trick. 'If we do not take the steps I have suggested, I foresee only one result' – pause – look around – wait: 'disaster...'

'We all remember the terrible days of...' – pause. You are only using an extension of the suspense motivation, employed at the end of each properly constructed instalment of a radio play... the end of the chapter of a tightly written crime story... you are keeping your grip on your audience.

'After hearing all the views of this committee, I have come to my decision. I think that we have no alternative other than... to...' Wait for it... keep them waiting...

Of course, the pause must not be too long. Just as brevity of a pause may show lack of confidence and cause it to lose its effect, so too great a pause may emerge as 'ham'. To overdramatise is as bad as to underplay. Only experience can teach you how long to pause. Only practice can show the maximum period for the best effect. If in doubt, pause longer.

Under stress, time tends to pass slowly. Prepare an important speech and rehearse it more or less word for word and time yourself on a stop-watch. Then make the same speech on the important occasion and get someone to time you. You will get through it quicker under stress. Only when you must expect and deal with interruptions ... including applause ... will the converse apply.

While gaining that experience, then, consider the most common occasions for pauses:

- *The opening*   Make sure that your audience have settled down and are ready to hear you – whether you are making a major oration at a rally or a minor intervention at a board meeting.

- *In mid-sentence*   To emphasise a vital point.

- *After an interruption* Once again, your audience must be settled in to hear what you have to say.

- *Before your last few words* 'And now, Ladies and Gentlemen, I beg you once more to support your Board...' pause 'so as to ensure...' pause '... that this modest organisation...' pause '... will continue to flourish.' Pause. Look around at those from whom you expect applause. And then sit down.

Which brings us to the final hint. Applause is a most helpful and invigorating leg-up for any speaker. If you did not want it, you would not speak. We all like to be liked. We all wish our words to be accepted. The 'hear hear' or clapping is as gratifying to the speaker as the groan is a misery. It is essential to anticipate and to deal with the cheers – to fish *for* them and to pause *after* them.

It is rare that a pause should be used against the groaner. By all means look round and glare at the man who has the temerity to jeer at you. Then leap back at him with both feet. 'Those who want to see this venture succeed will not assist by that sort of behaviour...' Or: 'I do not think that you, sir, are assisting your cause by behaving in that manner.' Or, if kindness seems to be the best way to deal with the situation: 'I am sorry that you should see fit to jeer, sir. If you would be good enough to wait a little, you will hear the reasons for my last remarks. And you will find that they are correct.'

Then pause. Allow the effect of the jeer to die away. Do not pause so long that the interrupter is encouraged to have another go. The borderline between the effective and the defective pause is a narrow one. Each case must be judged on its own. Far more speakers rush forward in haste, than regret the (apparently) confident wait for silence, attention... effect.

The pause is even more vital – and less of a risk – when fishing for cheers. If you are nervous, follow the sound theatrical first-night tradition of organising your own claque (see Chapter 29). 'We must give the impression of vast enthusiasm for the new project. So when I say how confident I am that it will be a success...' pause '... clap!' (The pause gambit is even useful in ordinary speech.)

An audience generally likes to know when applause is expected. 'We are all pleased to welcome our guest-of-honour from abroad – pause – 'Monseiur' – pause – 'Jaune.' Turn to your guest – pause for the clap.

'Here, Ladies and Gentlemen, is the first sample of our new

product. I present it to you...' pause '... with pride...' pause '... I trust that you will sell it, to your profit and that of the company...' pause. Look round. Someone will probably say 'hear, hear...' if only to please you.

One possible approach if no one applauds is to attack them for their silence. 'Gentlemen, the success of each of you, as well as that of the company, depends upon the way you push this product. I invite you...' pause '... to greet with pleasure' pause 'this new success from our research department.'

If that does not do the trick ... if you cannot drag up the applause you want, then never mind. Move on. Change your tack. Alter your approach. Try again. But do not rush. Wait. Control your audience.

Do not be afraid of the pause. The old saying 'Silence is golden' has no more vital and accurate application than in the world of the spoken word. Silence is a weapon as valuable as speech itself.

Interruptions 18

Interruptions are to the skilled speaker like a raid to the commando – a challenge to draw out his resources and to test his mettle. Handled properly, the heckler can rouse the audience and put them on the speaker's side. The unexpected break may bring variety to a dull occasion.

From the platform or head table, the speaker has a total advantage. Used properly, the interruption should bring or keep the audience in sympathy with the speaker, his case, or both.

To reap the benefit of useful interruption, the speaker must be alert. Tied to a script, written or memorised, he may be thrown off balance. If he cannot think on his feet, he should have remained seated.

Consider some common examples. Take the shareholder who comes to a company meeting to criticise. He shouts interruptions. How do you deal with him?

Maintain your dignity. Quiet but firm appeals for a fair hearing usually earn applause. 'I appreciate that you have a point of view to express and you will be given full opportunity to do so. Meanwhile, please have the courtesy to listen.' Or: 'I ask you to give my viewpoint the same fair hearing that I have given to yours.' Or: 'I listened to you/your case without interrupting. I ask you to accord the same courtesy to me/to mine.'

You could try: 'If you would be good enough to listen to what the Board/the company has achieved and is now proposing in the present difficult circumstances, you will learn something to your benefit'.

If the moment has come to attack, try: 'If you would listen to me, sir, instead of to yourself, you would be doing both of us a favour.'

If you are coping, the chairman should not intervene. If the meeting gets out of hand, then he must do so. At best, he will bring calm; at worst, ask or require the interrupters to leave. Still: a wide-awake speaker can usually keep his audience in reasonably good humour and win a hearing without use of force.

Some interruptions are healthy and helpful – whether or not they were intended to be so. The humorist's outcries can often be turned against himself. The scream of a jet engine overhead may drown you for the moment, but given you the opportunity to draw some moral about the point you are making. Even a friendly remark addressed to a member of your audience arriving late may save you both from embarrassment, as well as give you the opportunity you may in any event need to sort yourself out ... to vary the pace of your talk ... to give your audience the chance to relax for a moment, to shift about in their seats and to prepare for the rest of your speech.

The speaker must show self-confidence and self-command so as to achieve command of the situation and of his audience.

If you are needled by interrupters and are tempted to panic – pause, smile, retain control. The rowdier the meeting ... the more disconcerting the interruption ... the more aggravating the break in your train of thought – the more important it is for you to demonstrate to your audience that you are not to be thrown off your balance.

Go to a first-class political meeting and watch the accomplished politician at work. Listen to him provoking then downing his hecklers. Watch him prompting his audience to turn on the interrupters. A few inefficient hecklers will do his work for him, rouse his supporters, bring the uncommitted to his side and enliven what might otherwise be a dreary occasion.

The more spontaneous the reply, the wittier the retort, the speedier the counter-attack, the more effective the speaker and his speech. A weak riposte now is comparably better than that brilliant barb that you afterwards wish you had thought of at the time.

Do not let the interrupter put you off your stroke. Make use of him.

Passion 19

Passions must be felt, recognised and controlled. Allow your mind to cloud with passion and your performance will collapse.

Studied calm is a powerful weapon. Let your audience share your feelings, but know that your mind guides your heart, or you will not influence their ideas, their votes or their pocket books.

You may wish your audience to feel sorrow *with* you, but they must not feel pity *for* you. You want them to laugh *with* you, but if they laugh *at* you, all will be lost.

So direct your words at your theme and not at your own feelings. Conclude with a thundering peroration or an icy blast, but retain your speech as a well constructed, carefully presented offering.

Passionate eloquence has its place in the pulpit, but rarely works at a company meeting, an organisational gathering or a public conference. Open emotion seldom pays. If you must let off steam, do it at home.

Timing 20

Time is the enemy. Judge and use him well and your speech or presentation should prosper.

An experienced businessman is expert in time management except when he is on his feet. Aloft in his private joy, he ignores both the minutes and the agony of his audience.

'Did I speak too long?' enquired the managing director.

'Not at all,' his host responded. 'You helped to shorten the winter!'

Whether you are making a speech or a presentation, your object is to capture, to captivate and to convince your audience. This means keeping it alive, not boring it to death.

. . . I could listen to him for hours'? How common is its converse: 'I thought he would never stop. . .'

As a post-graduate student at Harvard, I debated at the famous Norfolk Penal Colony. My partner was Anthony Lloyd, now a High Court judge. Our opponents were Bill Flynn, forger, and Buzzy Mulligan, in for manslaughter. American debating is a tough art, with strict rules on timing, and judgment by both content and presentation.

We were briefed by Flynn. 'Remember, please,' he said, 'that in this place time is served, not enjoyed! Minutes, hours and days are notched up on the wall. Your audience is sensitive. Last year, we welcomed two debaters from your Cambridge Union. The opener did not start off very well. "It is a joy," he said, "to address a captive audience!" It is no fun being one!'

The subject of *our* debate was: 'This house welcomes the advance of the Welfare State.' Bill's opening was classic: '*We* live in a welfare state, don't we? Does anyone want to stay?' Loud cries of 'No, no...'

Mulligan matched him. 'The arguments of the gentlemen from England are as dud as my partner's cheques!' Loud cheers.

So respect your audience and its immobility. In Parliament, if you overrun a sensible time, you will empty the chamber, leaving behind only those who have to stay because they are waiting to speak. To antagonise any other audience – especially one that is either standing, or seated in discomfort – all you have to do is to speak too long. So work out your timing in advance; adapt it to your audience; and keep in touch with them while you speak.

A vicar found only one parishioner at his evensong service. With grim determination, he followed the prayer book to the letter and included a splendid half-hour sermon. When all was over, the vicar shook the sole listener's hand most warmly. 'Even if there is only one cow in the field,' he said, 'he must still be fed.'

'Indeed he must,' replied the parishioner. 'But you don't have to give him the whole load of hay!'

In general, the smaller your audience, the shorter you should keep your speech or your presentation. Why not use the time to communicate, to listen, to invite and to answer questions, to establish and to keep rapport? The object of your exercise is to win friends and to influence business? Then do your audience the courtesy of including them into your time calculations.

You recognise the importance of time in your business? You operate that inherently inhuman 'clocking' system for your workforce and perhaps even for your junior management? You regard such measures as part of the necessary discipline of commerce? Then at least apply *self*-discipline to your utterances, otherwise you will be talking to yourself, metaphorically if not literally.

So start by arriving on time. I once heard presidential candidate, Adlai Stevenson, apologising for turning up late at an election rally.

'I am deeply sorry. There is no greater thief than a man who steals the time of another. It is the only commodity that can never be recovered.'

Plan the timing of your speech. Recognise that while time creeps slowly for the prisoner, it races for the speaker. Concentrating on your subject and your audience, you will not notice the passing minutes.

So always overestimate the time you need and you will seldom be wrong. If you are preparing a half-hour presentation, then plan for 20 minutes. You can always use the balance for questions.

Speechmaking? Then ask the chairman – or even a colleague or confederate in the front row of your audience – to give you a signal when you have, say, five minutes left. Do not wait for the gavel to descend or the light to flash.

A well known politician hideously overran his time at a dinner. The next speaker whispered to the chairman: 'Can't you stop him?' The chairman lifted his gavel but it slipped from his hand and hit his neighbour on the head. As the poor man slid under the table he was heard to exclaim: 'Hit me again! Hit me again! I can still hear him!'

Or why not prop up your watch well within view? Most skilled speakers have no compunction in doing so, so why should you?

I use a watch with an alarm. I set it for 5 minutes after my speech is due to end. I am happy that it has yet to sound off.

If you do not have a watch or clock within easy view, you must consult the time with due cunning. Your glance at your wristwatch will be noted by your audience – which is at least less disconcerting than your audience looking at theirs.

A vicar once said to an inattentive parishioner: 'Now, Mr Brown, I don't mind when you look at your watch during my sermon. But when you take it up to your ear and shake it . . . !'

Queen Elizabeth has elevated the art of surreptitious watch-watching to its ultimate. She wears hers on her right wrist, facing inwards. When she holds out her arm – whether to shake hands, to lift her cup or even in a simple gesture – time appears before her eyes.

'The moving finger writes, and having writ moves on', said Omar Khayyam in his famous *Rubaiyat*. Once past, it is beyond recall. But when the moving finger writes, at least the words may later be corrected, the article or presentation cut short, subbed down, compacted.

Thoughts may be unspoken, but not a speech. Take the time of others and it can never be repaid.

My Lords, ladies & gentlemen —
Pray silence
for ...

Part Three

Handling your audience

Handling your audience **21**

An experienced speaker may not talk to his audience. He looks around for a kindly face. Even among the most hostile gathering, there is usually someone from whom he can extract a friendly or tolerant smile. He then talks to that person.

The speaker who looks over the top of his audience, out into space, indulging in soliloquy, is only a mite better than the one who keeps his head lowered and mumbles into his notes.

Audiences are people. They want to be entertained. They have presumably come to the gathering out of interest or curiosity – if not in what you are going to say, then in what the meeting is to undertake. Keep their interest by talking *to* them – and not over their heads, literally or metaphorically. Look at them. Speak to them.

If asked to address a gathering, try to find out the sort and the size of the audience. Your preparation may depend on the number of listeners. Are they skilled or unskilled, simple or learned, well versed in your topic or new to it, likely to be friendly or hostile?

If you are working to put through a business deal in private you would tailor your talk to the nature, personality, interests and sensitivity of your hearer. Only common-sense? Well, if more public speakers would apply that same sense to their audiences, the market for public speaking would not be spoiled as it is. People would go to meetings, instead of preferring their television sets. And speakers would be a great deal more successful than most of them are.

Whatever and whomever your audience may be, watch them while you speak. See whether they are concentrating, or shifting around in their seats. If you have held them still for some time, then stop. Pause. Take a sip from your glass of water. Fiddle through your notes. Give your audience the chance to relax and then to resettle. No one can concentrate for any lengthy period of time without a break.

If your audience is restless when you do not intend it to be so, you must restore your hold on it. If you have been serious, then throw in a joke, a story, an anecdote. If you have been speaking at high volume, then switch to a confidential tone. If nothing works, then wind up – either permanently or for an extended question time.

There is no more important rule for the public speaker than to keep a hawk-like watch on his listeners. It is different, of course, if you are talking to yourself – ignore this rule and you soon will be.

One of the speaker's problems is where to look. Facing your audience and fixing them with your eye is a problem. Why? Know the reason and the problem becomes easier to beat. Consider one paragraph in that most revealing of books, *The Naked Ape*, by Dr Desmond Morris:

> A professional lecturer takes some time to train himself to look directly at the members of his audience, instead of over their heads, down at his rostrum, or out towards the side or back of the hall. Even though he is in such a dominant position, there are so many of them, all staring (from the safety of their seats), that he experiences a basic and initially uncontrollable fear of them. Only after a great deal of practice can he overcome this. The simple, aggressive, physical act of being stared at by a large group of people is also the cause of the fluttering 'butterflies' in the actor's stomach before he makes his entrance onto the stage. He has all his intellectual worries about the qualities of his performance and its reception, of course, but the massed threat-state is an additional and more fundamental hazard for him.

There it is. We fear those who stare at us. But if you want to lift your head above the crowd, you must expect people to stare at it. Learn to stare right back.

22 Audience recognition

The best training sessions on the speechmakers' skills involve people at the same level (see Chapter 37 on training). No one is beholden to, jealous of or dependent for his living upon anyone else. The same principle applies to most presentations themselves.

When lecturing in-company, I try to induce my clients to bring together people at approximately the same level. If they want to include the boss, I warn them that the atmosphere may freeze, the jokes fall flat. The participants may be too apprehensive of their living to venture into asking or answering questions when a foolish moment could lose them promotion or even their jobs.

I once addressed all the executives of a catering company, on Health and Safety. The first part of the morning took off in a gale of laughter and I was able to implant the required knowledge into an audience, relaxed and receptive.

After coffee, everything froze. I only understood what had happened when I learned that the boss had, to everyone's knowledge other than mine, joined us after the break; and that earlier in the week he had sacked 20 executives.

So if you get the chance to choose your audience, aim not at uniformity of personality or approach but at a similar level within the organisation. If you venture into the highly personalised and difficult task of teaching any of the arts of presentation, take extra care.

All these urgings are for the benefit of your victims themselves. They are also for you.

You may on occasion have to talk upwards, either to superiors on their own or to those embedded in a mixed audience. The basic rule is: never show up anyone in the presence of his superior. Tread on a man's dignity, said the sage, and he will hate you for life. Make him look small or stupid in the eyes of superiors or inferiors and you have acquired an enemy.

If the person whom you have managed to lower in the eyes of others happens to be your superior, then he is unlikely to raise you on his list of loyal disciples fit for promotion. If instead you have made an idiot out of a colleague, in the eyes of your shared boss, then you had better protect your back.

Banter and teasing – even harassing and tormenting – are invaluable weapons in the trainer's armoury. But they must be used with sensitivity or they will rebound off their target and strike you down.

If I have a boss in the room with his subordinates, I ask him for his opinion. His subordinates get praise, not ridicule. Dignity must move in both directions, even if the result is boring.

If you are addressing an assembly of your elders, then indeed your mettle will be tried. How do you know and show more knowledge than they possess, without making them dislike or fear you, as present pain or future rival? How do you show respect without crawling; humility without being humble?

Tact, sensitivity, intelligence, common-sense and all those other virtues that you possess in such fine measure – you will now need them all. Plus good luck.

* * *

These rules apply especially to presentations to children, young people, or students. Have you ever been guest of honour at a school prize-giving? Or taken part in a university debate? Or given a talk about your business or your hobby, to a youth club or group?

Those who talk down to the young are blighted. If you treat them as equals, with luck they will not only listen this time but ask you again. You fail to prepare your subject at your own risk. The young are swift to spot a fraud or a phoney. They have an instinct for the insincere.

Naturally, you will adapt your style and your material to your audience and to your intent. You would not talk the same to your sales force as you would to your shop stewards, nor use the same material when explaining why pay has to be held down as you would if launching a new product or scheme.

Sales people, for instance, are an extroverted race apart. Outgoing and thick-skinned by the nature of their craft, and crafty to the core of their nature, they (like all other good professionals) only respect knowledge and expertise that at least equals their own. You must talk their language if you wish them to listen.

A sales force needs to know what you are going to provide for the market and when and how. It needs detail on territories and prospects, on targets, plans and projections.

Shop stewards have a different job. They are elected to look after their members and only if you can satisfy them that your proposals are indeed in their members' interests can you reasonably hope that they will co-operate with you.

Your sales force are as much employees as your workforce and their physical independence and initiative is far greater. But if the workforce is unionised, then it has a different type of independence, fed from the knowledge of its own unified strength.

In times of recession, union power recedes. Who will follow the leader into industrial action if unemployment is a lurking possibility? Sometimes, the car workers – although they have put up with mighty dictation, in the name of survival. Sometimes, the water workers, railmen, coal miners or others with great industrial clout born of monopoly and of the unquenchable demand for their services. But even they may sink into the shaft of recession.

Anyway, if you are talking to union representatives, you should match their knowledge and determination with your own. Give them the maximum of information, accurate and honest. Recognise their loyalty to their union and to its members. If you can harness their members' interests to your own, you are in business.

Or suppose that you must address your managers. They are your colleagues, so treat them as such.

There is a peculiar and almost universal belief that communication between management and unions in British and in American industry is poor. In reality, it generally ranges from good to excellent. Communication collapses within management itself, getting worse the lower down the line you go, or the more varied the companies within the group.

Ask yourself: who has greater access to *you*, the convener or shop steward, or the foreman or line manager? Are you *not* on first-name terms with the union chiefs while keeping your distance from your own middle or (especially) lower management?

UK law encourages this sad trend. You are required to give information to your unions for the purposes of collective bargaining. But do you bother to inform your own colleagues in management, if not beforehand then at least at the same time?

Ask more middle or line managers how they get sensitive information and they will tell you: 'We ask the shop steward. He's got access to the boss.'

When you speak to your managers, remember that they are probably more disgruntled than your workforce. Indeed, some of them are probably paid less than some of those they supervise. This unattractive result of employees receiving overtime, bonus rates and the like while management must work 'for such hours as may be necessary for the proper performance of their duties' and then at fixed rates causes vast ill will.

When you address your colleagues, recognise their problems, personal as well as managerial. Respect their jealousies and meet them head on.

Subordinate managers work *for* you? Fine – but *you* are also working *for* and *with* them. Get your approach into focus and your presentation should succeed.

* * *

Few executives or managers confine their conversations, speeches and ovations to their superiors. Most must at least spare an occasional word – and sometimes, a great string of them, dignified by the name of 'speech', 'lecture', 'talk', 'harangue' or 'presentation' – for their juniors.

So recognising that even a God-like chairman or a managing director must speak to those below him – and that there are very few who will talk only to Him – here is your guide to addressing your staff or employees, workforce or salesforce or others upon whose success your own job and future may well depend.

● Do *not* talk down. The patronising, condescending boss will never get the best from his team. Instead, chat them up . . . build them up . . . create in their minds the belief that they are part of a team which you are both happy and suited to lead.

- Regard these staff or employee talks as important – otherwise why should they? Follow the same procedures for them as you do for any other notable presentation – including careful preparation. There is no one other than your immediate family who is more likely to spot or to be sensitive to your errors than your colleagues.

- Approach the subject matter and your effort to put it across from the viewpoint of colleague or a team leader, and one whose income just as much depends upon their successful effort as their living does on yours. Together, you can make *their* business survive, blossom and flourish. But pull the business apart and it will fail – to the loss of all.

23 Sensitivity and tact

A first-class presenter will react to his audience. He will watch them with care; coax them into concentration; convince them with his themes; enthuse them with his message.

From the moment you enter the room, sensitivity is the key to stylish success. It will, for instance:

- Guide you to the top man – so that you greet him; respect him; take care never to demean him; and, where possible, flatter him – if only by asking; 'Have I covered the points that you would wish?' Or: 'How would you deal with this matter in your organisation?'

- Help you to steer the conversation, discussion or presentation in the direction you wish – especially if it has veered on to an unexpected and unwanted course.

- Enable you to invite audience intervention or participation and make the best use of it. Just as any politician worth his salt will welcome a heckler, so the presenter should be pleased with interventions which enliven his task and enlighten him on his listeners' interests and anxieties.

- Ensure that you avoid jargon, terminology and complications – especially in territory well known to you, but not to any or all of your listeners. You must never presume that others have too much knowledge. After all, Mr X may be new to his department or Mr Y, who should have prepared the ground before your talk, may have omitted to do so.

- Assist in recognising those people who would like to ask questions but are shy to do so for fear of revealing their ignorance to their colleagues. This applies to seniors, who must never be humbled before their subordinates; and to juniors, whose promotion depends upon their listening superiors.

- Keep humour as your ally and do not use it to humiliate those upon whose goodwill you rely.

- Help you to know when your audience is getting restless or inattentive, so that you alter course, style or speed ... introduce a story or a joke ... invite your listeners to ask questions ... or simply say: 'Are there any points that need clarification so far?'

- Sharpen your tact – so that, for instance, if someone asks a question which shows that he was either not listening or stupid, you say: 'I'm sorry. I am sure it was my fault. Let my try and explain again', or: 'It's a very complicated concept and I am so sorry that I did not succeed in explaining it clearly. Let me show you on a chart ...'

If you do go wrong ... make a mistake ... cause unintentional offence ... then apologise. An apology tells its recipient that he was right and you wrong ... it raises him in his own estimation and does you no harm.

Make sure that you write down any names which you may have to quote – the chairman, the managing director, the company, the guest ... and that you spell them correctly. People are very touchy about their names, which are themselves.

Train yourself to think ahead, so that you are not only watching your audience's reaction to what you are saying at the time, but thinking ahead – towards your next sentence, idea, theme ... or change of rhythm or style.

If your listener looks at his watch, watch yours. You will know that time is on his mind. And be prepared to move ahead on your notes ... discard cards on which they are written ... and either advance to your close or involve the timewatcher. 'I am sorry, Mr Brown,' you might say, 'that we are approaching our time limit. But are there any other points which *you* would like me to deal with?'

I once heard a computer salesman explaining to a major company in a depressed area why they should spend money on his equipment. 'We could help you to reduce your staff by 50 per cent if you buy one of our computers,' he announced. I could see each of his listeners saying to himself: 'I wonder whether I would be one of the staff that would go.' The contract was lost. Sensitivity matters.

These sensitivities apply to private as well as to public presentations – from person to person to a platform address. But when you are eyeball to eyeball, eye contact is both easier and more relaxed. The larger your audience, the greater your temptation to treat it as remote, but the greater your need to relate your sensitivities to those of your individual listener. Otherwise do not blame him if he takes as little interest in you and your message as you do in him and his reactions.

If the intent of your presentation is to enthuse, then you must inject enthusiasm into your words and make them as infectious as possible. If the essence of a fine presentation lies in self-control leading into control of your audience, sensitivity is the presenter's top asset, and its absence an insurmountable obstacle to success.

24 Personal attacks

The word 'gentleman' has been defined as meaning 'one who is never unintentionally discourteous'. The mature speaker never unintentionally loses his temper. He also does his utmost to cause offence only by design.

Outside the realm of politics, most wounds are both regrettable and regretted. 'The moving finger writes; and, having writ, moves on: Nor all thy piety nor wit shall lure it back to cancel half a line, nor all thy tears wash out a word of it.' With one, off-guard moment, you may acquire an enemy for life, unnecessarily. The uttered word cannot be erased.

Humour and wit are vital to the speaker. But many a jest, however kindly meant, has been taken amiss. There is all the difference in the body of wit between pulling someone's leg in private and tweaking his sensitive tail in public. The same joke that went down splendidly at the dinner table may be a disaster when told from the platform.

No section of the public is more concerned with its own dignity than people of commerce. Lawyers may be pompous, but they recognise the bitter court battle as part of their trade – it bears no reference to their personal friendship outside court. The private jest is seldom resented; but the businessman whom you attack in public may not wish to speak to you in private.

The seasoned politician revels in the 'cut and thrust' of debate. In most cases, he is able to dissociate the nature of an opponent from his public words. There is no such code in the world of business.

It follows that apart from the laws of defamation, it is as well to keep the discussion on ideas, not personalities. If you do attack your opponent, be sure of your ground. Make certain that his discomfiture is intended and that it has a reasonable chance of leading to the results you seek. The thoughtless, careless, unprepared and vicious outburst in public may wreck a friendship, a partnership, a board, a project. Whether you are speaking at a comparatively small meeting or a mighty gathering, be careful. You are not alone. If your attack is ill-chosen, you soon may be.

If you must attack a personality, then prepare your case with special regard to documentation: letters, quotations and firm facts. The more bitter your resentment, the quieter and the more apparently reasonable your tone should appear. Lose control of yourself and you will probably also lose control of both situation and organisation.

Find out in advance whether your words are likely to be well received. There is no worse time to be shouted or voted down than during a personal attack. If the moment arrives for a personal vendetta, select your time and place with assiduous care. By launching an attack, you invite a counter-attack. By mentioning the name of your opponent, you may give him the publicity that he seeks plus – in the eyes of those who believe in fair play – the moral right to reply. Instead of being in sole occupation of the platform, you may have to surrender it to an opponent whom you would prefer to lurk unseen.

If your opponent descends to personal attack, it is rarely wise to lower yourself to his level. Your object, after all, is to win your case – to convince your audience of your rectitude ... of the usefulness of your activities ... of the excellence of the way in which you are running the business – or, conversely, of your opponent's error. The sharp intellect is a better weapon than the rough tongue. When the theme is laced with incivility, the audience may suspect a lack of factual backing or of self-control – or both.

If you have a half-hour to spare and are near a court of law, watch how lawyer advocates do their job. They must 'handle the judge'. As one distinguished practitioner put it: 'What matters at the Bar is not to know your law but to understand your judges'. So watch the professionals and learn from them.

Try, in particular, to find a judge or a magistrate who is known to be 'difficult'. Happily, the majority of men and women on the Bench are courteous and, in general, kindly. But there are exceptions – most of them well known to the profession. And even the best of human beings suffer from ulcer, backache or matrimonial troubles.

So watch how lawyers politely but firmly stand up to the rigours of the unfriendly judge. Quietly, firmly and respectfully – and sometimes with considerable courage – they refuse either to be brow-beaten into premature silence, or provoked into unseemly loss of temper. They well know that their client's chance of winning his case is never helped if they lose their self-control.

For the average speechmaker – the company director, trying to talk sense into the heads of his board in revolt ... the salaried director or company secretary, dealing with the irascible chairman or managing director who is seeing fit to dress him down at a board meeting, or with an angry shareholder, making loud-mouthed, unwarranted and personal attacks against the company at a company meeting – the 'other cheek' policy is seldom out of place.

- 'I am extremely sorry that Mr Jones has seen fit to deal with this serious matter in such a vituperative fashion ...'

- 'If Mr Jones would be good enough to listen to what the Board has achieved, I think he will regret the manner in which he has referred to it ...'

- 'We are all here for a common purpose – to advance the business. The sort of remarks that have just been made are likely to send it into retreat. They can give comfort only to our competitors ...'

- 'We will answer each criticism, in turn. We will ignore the personal and regrettably offensive manner in which some of these attacks have been made.'

- 'If Mr Black really is, as he says, concerned for the welfare of this organisation, I trust that when he has heard the case for the steps which he has so bitterly criticised, he will not only have the good grace to withdraw those criticisms, but also to apologise to those whom he has inevitably hurt by his unkind remarks. I hope that such was not his intention. He is, as we all know, a kindly man, and we all appreciate what he has done for the company. We know how deeply involved he is, emotionally and otherwise, in its success ... and no one will bear him the least ill-will because he has spoken his mind ... But ...'

● 'We all appreciate, I know, the customary frankness with which Mr White has dealt with this resolution. We do not appreciate, however, the personal insinuations he has made – which can only detract from the genuineness of his case and the real concern with which he and those who support him – and, indeed, many of us on your Board – view the circumstances he discussed ...'

Hostility breeds hostility, and an aggressive approach invites a like response. The converse also applies. Surprise your critics with your moderation, understanding, sensitivity and those views may mellow. It is, in any event, an approach far more likely to succeed than the frontal attack.

Once you have let rip with your hostility, not only has the reasonable possibility of future friendly relations been gravely affected, but you have even discounted the off-chance that the critic was really on your side all the time. Any experienced politician will tell you that some apparently hostile questions are asked at meetings so as to obtain an answer for the benefit of those whom the questioner wishes to convince, and not for the questioner's benefit at all. 'All right, don't listen to me ... We'll ask old White ... He'll tell you a thing or two ...' Blast the questioner for being an idiot and you have obliterated a friend and confirmed a foe in his enmity.

If you must lose your temper, then at least do so with deliberation. Choose your moment and your words with equal care. If you must tear at your opponent – do it properly.

A judge once said to a famous advocate: 'What you are saying to me is going in one ear and out the other.' To which the lawyer replied: 'That, my Lord, does not cause me any surprise, having regard to that which lies in between!'

But most of us think of the best repartee when the occasion is past. While swift retorts often produce acclaim far beyond merit, the rude, unkind, offensive or angry outburst ... the facetious, sarcastic, ironic or spiteful suggestion – these breed contempt, derision, stony silence – and defeat for the speaker, not for the individual towards whom the words are directed.

25 Credits

Few speechmakers object to being thanked or resent receiving credit, even where it is not strictly due. But most get upset if their merit is not recognised or if thanks are withheld – especially if credit due to one goes to another. So the good speaker is as liberal with his praise of others as he is parsimonious with his praise of himself. The listener who feels that you recognise – and are prepared publicly to laud – his worth is more likely to be receptive to the excellence of your arguments.

Here, then, is a sample, generalised opening attack on an audience.

'First, I would like to express my appreciation to various people here. Were it not for Mr Brown, this gathering would never have been organised at all. Were it not for Mr Black, the company would be in grave difficulty. Were it not for Mr White, the scheme we are about to discuss would never have been born. In paying tribute to them, I express my gratitude to all of you for giving them the support and backing without which they could not have put forward this essentially constructive project.

'Now, let us look at the project.' Your audience is softened up. They are ready to listen to some constructive criticism from you.

Or: 'Under the chairmanship of Mr Green, this project has made great headway. With Mr Brown as treasurer and Mr Blue as honorary secretary, it is hardly surprising that it has gathered momentum. And now it is up to us to help them by applying constructive minds to the scheme they have created.'

'I know they welcome criticism designed to forward their work. We all appreciate that their enthusiasm is only increased by suggestions, coming from people like ourselves who only want the scheme to succeed. They know that there is no element of destructive intent in the views that some of us hold. I am sure that you will give careful consideration to our submissions.'

Flattery? Certainly – but legitimate. Praise? Yes, indeed, and with every appearance of sincerity. Credit, thanks, tact – and all designed to prepare the ground for your forthcoming attack. It is not only armies that do best when they advance from the side, and there is no shame in a swift strike from the rear.

To test the importance of these rules, listen to someone who ignores them. Beware the benefactor scorned... the doer of good deeds that go unrecognised... the creator whose idea, invention or brainchild is fathered onto another.

There exists, or course, the occasional *eminence grise* – the spectral backroom boy who takes as much pride in praise going to others whom he has built up as does the father who basks in the reflected glory of his child's exploits. But even he appreciates the oblique reference to the power that made the throne secure, to the modest mind that 'wishes to remain anonymous but must not go without being thanked... Those of us who are fortunate enough to realise just how and by whom the work has been done salute our silent and modest friends – we are grateful to them.'

As the editorial mention and the praise of a product which appears in the general pages of a newspaper are the public relations man's delight – and worth more to him than the advertisement that he has to pay for – so the 'plug' in the course of a speech and as part of it is often more valuable to the maker and more appreciated by the person referred to than the formal and expected vote of thanks. But even that is a weapon not to be despised in the campaign to get your own way – as we shall now see.

Persuading – 26 the art of advocacy

Barristers, said Dean Swift, are men 'bred up in the art of proving that white is black and black is white, according as they are paid'. He left out of account, of course, the ethics of the legal profession, which may often require its members to keep faith with the court by acting (and speaking) against the interests of their clients.

Advocacy is an art; deception an evil. Still, the Swift aphorism is too good to forget. And even the business person may often be forced to propound or to defend in public policies or decisions with which, in private, he disagrees.

It is not only the Cabinet that must stand by majority decisions. The same normally applies to the board of a company, to the partners of a firm, or to the committee of an organisation. Either you accept democracy – allow your views to be overruled when the majority of your colleagues are against them – or resign. If you remain in office, then you must stand by your colleagues. This may mean engaging in their public defence.

So the advocate may not only have to propound views that are unpopular with his audience, but even some that find little favour with himself. Business people customarily attack lawyers and politicians as sophists and word-twisters. But just listen to that executive trying to make the creditors' meeting 'see sense' ... the chairman attempting to extract himself (and possibly the company secretary) from trouble ... the sales director, drilling his sales force about an unpopular (and perhaps not very satisfactory) product.

There is little art in persuading the convinced, preaching to the converted, or keeping your team behind you when they all agree with your views or policies. To argue a difficult case – or even one that seems impossible – is a far greater challenge. Business people may take many a leaf from the brief of the skilful lawyer-advocate.

Start with the quiet, sincere but firm approach. Call it 'the soft sell' if you like, but the studied lack of histrionics lies at the root of the modern persuader's art. Gone are the days of the ranter, the arm-waver, the loud shouter. The theatrical tugger at the strings of the heart may still have his place in revivalist meeting or chapel, but he is a stranger to the court of law – and should be equally so to the company or organisational meeting.

The more your audience starts against you, the greater the importance of moderation – especially in your opening. Here are some well tried gambits for the man in a minority:

- 'I fully appreciate the difficulty of my task in convincing you that ... But I hope and believe that if you will be good enough to give my case a fair and full hearing, you will be as convinced as I am that ...'

- 'Mr Black, who has just addressed you, is an experienced advocate and has presented the case against with skill and eloquence. But there is another side to the picture. Before coming to a decision, I am certain that you would wish to hear both sides of the story, fully explained ...'

- 'Many of us were saddened to hear the vehemence and even the venom with which the case for ... has been put. While many of the attacks have apparent validity, when you go beneath the surface, all is not as some of our friends have suggested. I am sure that this committee/organisation/meeting would not wish to take any decision on such a very important matter without having had both points of view put before it. I shall put mine, as briefly as possible: but I would be grateful for your indulgence, Mr Chairman, if I take a little time to explain my case ...'

- 'This is a small committee of busy people and we should expend no more time and energy in surplus pursuit of Mr X. He has made mistakes and is paying for them. Let us look to the future. Instead, let us look at some of the achievements of Mr X. He let us down? Yes – but he has also laid the foundations for our future success. First ... Second ... Third ... Fourth ... Fifth ... Sixth ...' By the time you are finished, Mr X appears to be quite a splendid character. If you had started with his virtues, you would have lost all hope of winning your case – and his.

Now, for some traps to be avoided:

- 'Does anyone really think Mr Y has cheated the company?' Cries of 'Certainly ...' Rhetorical questions are a menace. Thus:

- 'Could it conceivably be in the long term interest of this organisation to follow the line proposed by Mr Black?' Shouts of 'Yes!'

- 'Does anyone really think that I do not know my job after all these years?' Loud cries of 'Yes' – and laughter.

- 'I am ... a man ...' pause. Shouts of 'No, no ...' The pause is a vital weapon – but watch where you place it.

- 'You may think that the statements you have just heard from Mr Z are about as untrue, misleading, ill-conceived and plain stupid as one could ever envisage.' This sort of attack – especially by someone in a minority – can only lead to vituperation, and defeat. Softly, softly, catchee monkee...

- 'I am furious ...' Then do not show it.

- 'I could weep when I hear such extravagant attacks.' They all know that tears are not in your line – so away with the crocodiles.

It is nearly always a mistake to walk out of a meeting. Still: there are occasions when there is no decent alternative. If decisions are taken that you regard as illegal, dishonest or so contrary to the welfare of the body concerned that you must dissociate yourself publicly from them, then you may have to leave. But otherwise, stay and fight.

Your chances of winning from without are far less than of working your colleagues or audience round to your way of thinking, from within. If you leave, you are not likely to be invited back. The dramatic exit may be required for the diplomat whose country is publicly attacked in his presence. It is seldom an answer for the orator spurned.

The threat of resignation is, of course, a powerful and a valid weapon. It must not be misused or over-employed. If your colleagues or the meeting would be happy to see you go, then you should not offer to provide satisfaction.

'If this decision is to be made, I hope it will not be taken amiss if I say that I shall have no alternative other than to reconsider my membership.' Fairly put.

'I have worked for this organisation for many years and am anxious to continue to do so in the future. I would not wish to sever my ties nor to be forced into such a position that I would have no alternative other than to do so. I do beg you to reconsider. Or at least, please do give me a fair hearing for the other point of view. I would put it like this ...' You should get that fair hearing.

Avoid: 'If you do not change your minds, then I shall resign.' You invite the retort: 'Go ahead.'

27   In a tight corner

If in trouble, choose your words with special care. To borrow from the worlds of fencing or boxing – if you have been hit below the belt, are out for the count, or in a tight corner, you have three alternatives: you can throw in the sponge ... trade blow for blow ... or duck smartly under your opponent's fist and leap nimbly away.

You are proposing a toast to the bride and groom? The bride's father is dead? The groom's parents are divorced? What do you do? You can surrender by making no mention of the parents. This is abject cowardice, and generally regarded as such. You may neatly duck the situation by a few, carefully chosen sentences: 'The bride's father ... we wish he were not here only in spirit ... but he would have been proud and happy today ... How pleased we are that our groom's parents are both so well – and here together for the celebration ...'

Finally, you can take the bull by the horns (to take an analogy from a sport of another kind). You can start with the sort of comment given above – and then extend it into the appropriate elegy. 'Let us face the blunt truth, Ladies and Gentlemen – no occasion is completely perfect, no life without its problems. How sad we are that the bride's father is not here ... but we admire her mother doubly for the fortitude with which she bore her loss and especially for the courageous and splendid way in which she brought up the bride ... The extent of her triumph is revealed by the radiance of our bride. We rejoice too that the bridegroom's parents sit joyfully together with him, united in his happiness and good fortune ...'

There are plenty of equivalent situations in business. The surrender is achieved by an apology. The counter-attack is explained in Chapter 24. The form of ducking away from trouble, to be adopted in any particular circumstances, will depend upon those circumstances themselves. Here are some useful, opening gambits:

- We fully appreciate the circumstances which have led to your anger and disappointment. But there is another side to the story and we do hope that you will give it your earnest consideration ...

- You are in theory, correct, fair and ...

- I do see your point of view – but am sure that you will give consideration to mine ...

- Yes, we made a mistake – but in good faith. The situation nevertheless remains that ...

- We see your viewpoint. Now do please consider ours ...

- You have set out your case admirably. It is only courteous, then, for me to set out as fully as possible the situation as we see it ...

- We believe that your complaint is based on a misunderstanding. We do see that ... but we would urge you to consider ...

● No, we do not agree with you. But nevertheless . . .

Have you noticed that the man who uses words as weapons employs similar tactics to those of the fencer or boxer? You give way a little, so as to attack a lot. You retreat gently, so as to counter-attack with firmness. You at least pretend to see the other man's viewpoint, so that he will be prepared to consider yours. Alternatively, you politely disagree – and then show your magnanimity, good sense or goodwill by offering a compromise or by giving in on some point, however small.

The French put it well: *'Il faut reculer pour mieux sauter'* – you must withdraw, the better to leap forward. As with weapons of war, so with words of forensic skill, written or spoken. You step back so as to throw your opponent off balance (boxing again).

There are occasions, of course, when there is no room for retreat . . . all escape routes are cut off . . . Then remember the advice given to policemen, in similar but physical circumstances. 'Tuck yourself neatly into the corner and use your fists, your knees, your truncheon . . . At least if you are in that corner, they will not be able to get a knife in your back . . .' Unless, of course, they knock you unconscious and drag you out . . .

Try these gambits, when absolutely desperate:

● If you see fit to make these allegations to third parties, we shall have no hesitation in putting the matter in the hands of our solicitors . . .

● In one, last, desperate attempt to remedy a situation which (we repeat) is not of our making, our Mr Jones will contact you and try to arrange some convenient time to visit your office . . .

● Your threats are empty, their premise groundless. Nevertheless, if you wish to take the matter further, we must refer you to our lawyers . . .

● We regard your allegations as both impertinent and groundless. If they are repeated, we shall take such steps as we are advised by our lawyers, to protect both our position and our good name . . .

● If you are so ill-advised as to carry out your threats, then kindly direct all future correspondence to our lawyers . . .

● Our lawyers will be in touch with yours . . .

The debater who contents himself with making his own speech, without referring to those which have gone before, does not do his job. Many discussions – in public and private meetings of companies and organisations of all sorts – are in reality debates. The skilled speaker must study the art of reply.

The proposer of a motion or resolution is normally accorded the 'right of reply'. He opens the debate or discussion and, before the vote is taken, he has the privilege of closing it. His second speech should not be a mere repetition of his first. He should deal – courteously, clearly and firmly – with the intervening debate.

The respondent should thank those who have spoken in favour of the resolution. Directly or by implication he should congratulate them on their perspicacity. 'I was not surprised to have the warm support of that respected businessman, Mr Brown – but I was grateful for it nonetheless... Mr Green is highly experienced in the trade and I do hope that everyone here will give his words due weight...'

'Mr White comes to us from a different side of the trade. So it is all the more significant that he approves of this resolution...'

'Mr Green, is, as you will all know, an extremely skilled and public-spirited lawyer. We must all be grateful to him for the careful analysis he gave to our problems – and for the legal light that he cast upon the dangers of action suggested by those who oppose this resolution.'

The skilled respondent demolishes his enemies. 'I am sorry that Mr Diamond has not appreciated the warnings given by Mr Black...' 'If Mr Stone had really considered the argument that... I feel sure he would have come to a different conclusion...' 'Mr Ruby is wrong. The facts are not as he has suggested. The true position is...'

Then sum up your arguments once again, in a few brisk, crisp sentences. Commend your resolution to the meeting – and hope for the best.

Use notes when replying. No one will expect you to remember all that has been said, without careful jottings. Once again, the card system is best. You may, if you wish, deal with the questioners or opponents in turn, but you would probably be better off to rearrange the comments and criticisms to suit your argument.

Remember: a reply is a speech like any other. It needs a good opening; a sound body; and a proper end. Some suggested openings:

- 'Thank you, Chairman, for permitting me to reply to some of the points raised...'

- 'Mr Chairman, I suggest that nothing that has been said against the resolution has in any way destroyed its essential validity...'

- 'We must all be grateful to those who have taken part in this debate. Even those who oppose the resolution do so in the interests of the company. But as, I think, we have seen from the speeches of Mr Brown, Mrs White and Mr Black, its opponents have not really grasped the advantage of the course of action suggested – and the risks of following any alternative...'

- 'The differences between us, Chairman, have been fully aired. Every possible alternative has been thrashed out. But, at the end of the day, are we not still left with only one real possibility? The resolution must be passed.'

Some of these rules also apply to many responses to toasts. Do *not* ignore the speeches that have gone before. *Do* deal with any points of criticism or suggestion raised by previous speakers. Do *not* fear to use notes to remind you of the words of others. And *do* make certain that your speech is properly constructed.

You have one great advantage over the man replying to a debate. His speech must not only appear extempore, but must actually be so. Yours may be carefully prepared, provided that you cover up that preparation by reference back.

29 Advance organisation

In Italy, opera singers employ claques. They pay the organisers who then ensure that the star receives the appropriate (or even inappropriate) applause, at the right time. If any star sees fit not to pay, then (as one of them recently remarked) 'We are quite capable of whistling and cat-calling instead.'

Those who speak in public may also have a claque – paid or unpaid. If the opportunity arises, no harm is done by ensuring that you get off to a good start, or that your words appear to be treated with such delight that (with luck) your opponents may prefer to stay silent.

People are like proverbial sheep, particularly in public. They want to be on the winning side. Few have the courage to speak their minds openly in the face of a vociferous majority. 'What's the good of it?' they say – not realising that if they only did speak, they might well win. And they might discover that the noise-makers were in reality no more than a loud-mouthed minority.

The most inoffensive type of claque work is easily organised. 'Please show me some support,' you say to your friends. 'If you do not give me some loud "hears, hears", I shall stop trying. I refuse to be shot at on my own.'

Alternatively: 'This is going to be a difficult audience to warm up. If you would be kind enough to start the clapping when I am called upon to speak, I shall remember you in my will!' It only takes one or two people to clap the speaker and the rest join in – but if no one starts, he goes on 'cold'.

Again: 'I am going to tell them the story about the ... so laugh!'

Of course, you may carry your claque along with you because they are under some obligation. Maybe you employ them ... are the kind benefactor on whom they rely ... have patronage in your gift. In that case, no preparation should be needed. Wise lawyers soon learn to laugh at judges' jokes – and whenever possible to produce any of their own ideas in the guise of words of wisdom dropped by the Bench.

If you are on strange ground or among an unfamiliar audience, do not be afraid to ask your friends to give you the appropriate leg-up. One day you may be able to return the compliment.

Of course, advance 'softening up' of an audience may often go far deeper than this. If you have a case to advance, do your best to sound out your audience. If you have a resolution to propose, make sure that someone will second it. The proposer without support is a miserable fellow and, in most cases, would have been better off to keep silent. A good speaker not only prepares his case, but also his audience and his supporters.

Of course, this preparation should not show. One reason why inexperienced speakers often take too little care in the preparation of their material is that they have seen how apparently easy the experienced speaker makes it all seem. Be not deceived. In general, the higher the polish, the greater the elbow grease ... the more relaxed and effortless the style, the more careful the preparation.

Natural speakers may need to take less care than the rest. But follow one of them around and note how his performance varies.

When he stumbles, repeats himself, goes on for too long, breaks the basic rules of good speaking and starts to bore his audience – he has not prepared his speech.

The better the preparation of the material and of its reception, the less obvious that preparation will be. The more it shows, the less its effect. If audience preparation shows it all, the insincerity of the claque may rub off on your speech, and that could mean disaster.

So choose your supporters with as much care as your words, but do not be too proud to prepare both with equal attention.

If you are the chairman, make your preparations with special care. If there is to be a question time, prime someone to ask the first question – otherwise the silence may be unreal and embarrassing and ruin the evening.

If you have to appear neutral but need to espouse a particular viewpoint, make sure you get its best proponent ready with his speech – and someone else available to do a later mopping-up operation. If preparing a team, the basis used by most athletes for relays is helpful. The anchor man – your best – goes last. The next best goes first. The third does the third leg. The worst goes second. Or you may want to put your anchor man first – particularly if he has a right of reply.

If you are not the chairman, but are especially interested in a particular topic or anxious to speak on it (or if you have to leave early or arrive late) do get the arrangements set up in advance. Most chairmen will oblige. They will probably be glad to have advance notice of your intentions, so that they can plan operations accordingly. Planning is the partner of success.

Part Four

Aids, notes and venues

Microphones 30

Once upon a time, you had to speak to be heard. Nowadays, a whisper will do. The microphone has long since arrived. Know how to use it. Well employed, it is a trusty ally. Over-employed or misused it will blast away your audiences for ever.

A voice was a pre-requisite for a singer – no more. With the aid of the 'mike', the men and women of alleged music can make their fortunes without, in many cases, enough power in their lungs to fill a telephone booth or a breathalyser. Alternatively, they may belt out the tune, but the nuances and expressions that the opera singer spends years learning to create are absent. The effects that brighten so many otherwise even more miserable musical moments are created by the microphone – by the tricks of the audio trade.

Not everyone required to speak in public is blessed with the voice of a Churchill. Some of us have voices that refuse to be produced. Never mind. We can learn much from the masters and mistresses of the mike.

First: make sure that your mike is switched on. Tap it with an inquiring finger. Even more professional: flick or click your fingers – the sound of the tap or click should reverberate. At least you will know that the microphone is live. Dead mikes kill unborn speeches.

Next, adjust the microphone to your convenient height. Whether it is a standing or a table model, you will probably find a turning ring near the centre. With luck and some reasonable wrist power, you should be able to fix the mike at just below the level of your mouth. The top of the speaking part of the instrument will then be almost level with your lips.

If presented with a neck mike, rejoice. Test and adjust so that your voice emerges at the correct volume. Then forget about it.

You may prefer, though – as I do – to use a wandering mike on a long lead. You retain your freedom of movement; the mike becomes as much a weapon for you as it is for stage and television performers who hold one by preference, when the wizards of the world of acoustics could well amplify without; but mind your volume. Tuck your elbow into your waist and co-ordinate your forearm movements with those of your head, so that the mike stays at the same distance from your lips.

However long you have to keep your audience waiting, take your time to adjust and position your microphone. With the volume and position adjusted, you are ready to begin. If your voice emerges clear and undistorted, all is well. If there is a scream, a whistle or a shriek, you are too near or the volume is too loud. If your voice emerges as if from outer space, with Martian echo or eerie ululation, then adjust.

'Fellow directors... ' Silence. Lift up your voice: 'Will someone kindly switch on this mechanical marvel?' Laughter. The engineer scurries around and flips the appropriate switch. 'Thank you.' Screams and whistles from the machine. More laughter. 'There's no need to overdo it.' The engineer tries again. 'Fellow directors ...' Silence. 'Are you receiving me?' you say, smilingly tapping the dreaded instrument. 'Do you hear me at the back?' Loud cries of 'No, no' and more laughter. They are laughing *with* you and not *at* you. You have command of the situation. You are waiting until the conditions are as you require before you start speaking.

With luck and perseverance, the microphone will be put into proper order. If it is not – or if reception is intermittent or unpleasant – then you must make up your mind whether or not your voice will carry unaided. Is it better to risk being unheard than to submit your audience to squeals and screeches from the machine? Will you succeed in interesting your audience when the microphone is playing up? Have you, perhaps, a genius in the place who can adjust the amplifier, the loudspeaker, or some other unmentionable or unpronounceable part of this gadget? Think on your feet – fast.

'I shall do without the microphone,' you belt out. 'I hope that you will all hear me.' Applause.

Alternatively: 'I apologise for the inefficiency of this miserable apparatus. I think I had better submit you to the occasional grunt and growl, so that at least I may grant you the pleasure of hearing a part of my presentation!' Hear, hear!

You are off – to a late and unhappy start. But your audience have seen that you have confidence.

More good speeches are ruined because the speaker is not prepared to take his time and make his preparations with the microphone than for any other reason.

Unless blessed with a neck, roving or even radio mike, be careful how you alter your position. Whether you move towards your visual aids or away from your audience, if you break the thread of your speech you will break the thought of your audience. You should keep the attention of your listeners on your word, not on your movements.

Make the mike your ally. Never panic when it goes wrong. Be prepared to fall back on your own voice power, if you must.

Remember that great orators of the past had to manage unamplified – and they did not do too badly – presumably because they knew the rules on voice production (see Chapter 15).

Visual aids 31

There is an art to all excellence – not least in the use of visual aids. So why is this use so seldom taught? Consider:

- Which aids are best for the particular occasion? Slides (35 mm) are splendid – but expensive and generally only worth using for large audiences; when cost is of little importance; when the slides can be re-used; and when darkness does not matter.

- Do not use your visual aids to replace your verbal message. Your charts, etc., should either:

  Provide the skeleton for your presentation, so as to attract the eye and direct the mind, later to revive the memory; and/or:

  Illustrate and explain through graphs, etc., concepts and/or detail which cannot be explained simply and/or adequately and/or swiftly in other ways.

- Overhead projection transparencies are cheaper than slides; easier to make; can be switched or even amended or added to during the presentation. They should be treated with respect, which means: their contents carefully thought out and the transparencies themselves professionally produced. (These sheets of clear plastic, usually mounted in card frames, are known by a variety of names.)

- Keep the wording on all visual aids to a sensible minimum. This does not mean putting one simple sentence onto a separate transparency – but avoiding a mass of hard-to-assimilate material which is properly divisible into two or more projections.

- Transparencies, etc., should be concise, compact and uncluttered. Use abbreviations and symbols to summarise and to emphasise. Use art work sparingly and for results, not effects.

- Remind your graphics department or other aid makers to make the transparencies with backgrounds *clear* and light – not obscure and dark. The darker the background, the poorer the view. Green or blue as well as black come out well on a white background, as black does on yellow. But red on green, or green on red, are even worse than white on red, orange on black, or red on yellow. Clarity of overhead vision should never be sacrificed for artificial and artistic impression.

- Avoid 'funnies'. Humour is much better presented orally, if only because you can quickly move on and away from a failed joke. If you must use cartoons, caricatures or illustrative, graphic humour, them make sure that it is thoroughly professional.

- Choose your overhead projectors or machinery with care. I deeply dislike those projectors with fans that change the atmosphere when they come on; often do not go off along with the light; and disturb speaker and audience. Watch out especially for those that blow air out sideways, depositing papers all over the show. Better – in any event with a smaller audience – to use a mirror-type, fanless projector.

- Ensure that your visual aids are properly set up before your audience arrive, i.e. properly focused and with the first slide, transparency, etc., in position.

- The first transparency should generally provide an overall summary – to which you can (especially with the transparencies) return, filling in the detail by your further projections.

- To point at a slide, you must use (and have ready) a stick or other pointer. For a transparency, you have four possibilities, which can be used in combination, for variety and as required:

   Point with a pencil, pen or even a finger on the slide itself, casting the shadow of the pointer onto the screen;

   Put your pencil down on the transparency. Do not hold it or the slightest jiggle or movement will create a major flicker on the screen;

   Use pointer or finger on the screen itself – but beware of casting the shadow of your body onto the screen at the same time; and/or;

Use a sheet to cover up that part of the transparency that you do not require the audience to see – and then move it. Use the masking technique sparingly; it irritates audiences who find themselves wondering what is hidden, rather than thinking about what is revealed.

- Changes of transparency should be slick. Hold the replacement in your right hand; remove the existing transparency with your left and put the new one into its place, all in one movement; and practise until you can put the replacement into a firm, central position without fiddling. To recognise a transparency, put its title at the top of its frame; then lay out all of them on your table, with the title of each sticking out above the next.

- Ensure that all the audience can see the machine – if anyone cannot do so, then move him or the screen.

- Be deliberate – do not jog, jolt or jiggle an item on the screen.

- Talk to your audience, not to the machine — and even if you are reading out what is on the screen, do not turn your back on your audience or put your face down to the machine. Try not to turn your back on your listeners.

- Minimise your own movement and that of the visual aids; do not distract from the content.

- Use variety in your charts, etc. – different types, colours, underlining, etc.

- If you draw on transparencies, use water-based pens, which can be rubbed out with a damp cloth – not those that require spirit for removal.

- Visual aids should stimulate interest and not simply provide a technical message.

- Check your pens or crayons in advance. Break up the script by using different colours. Make sure the lettering is large enough to be seen. Use as few words as possible, for instance, do not say 'replaced by' – simply cross out whatever it is that has been replaced.

- Watch any good school teacher using his blackboard and transfer the techniques to your transparencies, slides or flip charts. He will ask his audience questions while he writes . . .

never remove his eyes from his class for more than a few seconds ... and turn sideways when writing, never turning his back to his audience, more or longer than absolutely necessary.

- Do not talk while you are changing transparencies or slides.

- If you show slides, try not to keep the room in permanent gloom while you talk – unless you would prefer not to know when your audience slides off into slumber. Maybe you can place yourself to one side or under a spotlight, or at least turn the light on when the slides are off.

- To avoid the blank spaces of darkness and silence between slides, you can now get what are called 'twin pair dissolve slides'. Operated with two machines, as one slide goes off the screen, another comes on it. However: these prepared slides have to remain in the same order and there is no way in which you can shuffle them. Inflexibility is a high price to pay for apparent slickness.

- Beware of overpreparation. An auto-cued, word-perfect script ... the drama of music and lighting ... the overprofessionalism too often produced by specialists for the use of amateurs – avoid them all.

- To make the best of slides, overhead charts, etc., consider providing copies for your audience – as reference to save them writing, so that they can concentrate on your presentation; and for the addition of their own notes. As in the case of all other documentation, consider carefully whether you would wish to supply in advance (not generally recommended, because busy people seldom do their homework, and often forget to bring it with them on the day); and/or at time of presentation for use during its course; and/or at the end of the presentation, to take home.

The old fashioned but worthy flip chart will never go out of fashion. At its simplest, it consists of a stack of newsprint attached to a board. With pens or crayons, you illustrate your words, the sheets then being flipped over or torn off.

Or you may use and re-use prepared charts, again flippable. I use a helpful variant – a white-faced, steel board with magnetic lines, spots and dots and coloured, water-based pens that write and erase with ease.

Whatever type of chart or board you use, check the easel beforehand. Make sure it is firm, the pegs are well in place, that it will not collapse with dramatic impact, creating havoc with your presentation and possibly injuring you in the process.

When pointing at a flip chart – as at a transparency – use your nearest hand or arm, so as not to have to twist your body and turn your back on the audience.

Notes 32

Some speeches are so important that they have to be read. Every word counts and the occasion is so fraught with peril that you cannot risk getting a word wrong. But read speeches tend to be boring. Even Parliament, some of whose debates are an agony to endure, forbids the reading of speeches. Members may not turn exchange debates into a series of written essays, probably the product of the minds of others.

Remove the element of impromptu and the likelihood of the speech proving interesting recedes. As the audience knows the truth, instead of looking forward to hearing the speaker, it prepares for slumber and boredom. As soon as he starts reading from a script, his audience begins to curl up – mentally if not physically.

To the average, non-professional speaker, the difficulty of constructing a speech as he goes along is almost insurmountable. Even for the expert, preparation is a necessity – and the more complex the speech, the more essential it is to be reminded of its main points, so that none are left out.

The compromise, then? Notes. Have the skeleton of your speech (see Chapter 1) committed to paper, leaving you to clothe it with words, embellish it with new ideas and thoughts, and enliven it with wit as you go along.

What should good notes contain? The first sentence plus the last plus the skeleton. The flow of ideas. The thread of the speech. Brief phrases to indicate the contents of even lengthy paragraphs. Reminders of themes. Pegs on which to hang your thoughts.

You need brief headings for the eye, to direct the flow of speech but not to interrupt it. Except where you must quote, the shorter and clearer the note, the better.

By all means divide up the note itself by using block capitals for the main headings and small script for subsidiary items. Underline in red, blue, green. Set the notes themselves into columns and lay them out so as to catch your eye, just as you seek to lay out your speech to catch the minds and imaginations of your listeners.

Notes are best on cards, preferably not larger than normal postcard size. Each theme, each paragraph, each range of ideas can then be put on to a separate card. Use one side only.

If you have a desk, table or stand to operate from, well and good. If not – as when you speak from the floor at a meeting – then you are not burdened by clumsy sheets, paper that slips through your fingers, scraps of notes that you lose at the crucial moment, sending you into that very fluster that the notes were intended to avoid. Return each card to the bottom of the pack as soon as you are through with it. In case you drop your notes, number each card clearly at the top right-hand corner.

Another advantage of the card system is that if you run out of time you can skip two or three of the least essential – or at least summarise them in sentences and turn them over at speed. They provide your guide without restricting you to an itinerary. They leave you room for manoeuvre, combined with the freedom to think on your feet.

33 Quotations

Your audience have come to hear you, but you may still pepper your speech with apt quotations from the thoughts of others. Quoting, though, is an art of its own. Here are some suggestions on how to perfect it.

Keep quotations short. To quote at length from memory is a form of 'showing off' that is seldom appreciated. You are not engaged in stage soliloquy. To read someone else's words at length is seldom an alternative to putting thoughts and ideas into your own words. The reading of speeches – or even lengthy parts of them – is usually an error. That error is compounded when you are not even reading your own original thought.

Quotations are only worth using if they are thoroughly apt. If your audience is flagging, it is sometimes helpful to 'drag in a joke by its ears'. This legitimate gambit may reduce strain, but the story must be apposite. It is a mistake to thrust an inappropriate quotation into your speech, merely because you have a fond feeling for it.

Attribute the quotation to its true author, if you can. If in doubt, you could try: 'Was it George Bernard Shaw who said ...?' Or: 'I think it was Oscar Wilde who once remarked that ...' Or if the attribution is to someone in your lifetime, you can seldom go wrong with: 'I once heard President Ford remark that ...' Or 'Did you read the saying, attributed to Mr Kruschev, that ...' Who is to prove you wrong? Or maybe try: 'Was it not I who said ...?'!

Make sure that your speech really is strengthened by putting the statement concerned in quotation marks – and as coming from the particular author. When trying to convince a British audience to adopt an American practice, it is sometimes better to adopt the transatlantic arguments, without stating their origin. Conversely, for any foreigner to express a preference for a candidate in an American election is to impose the kiss of death upon him. By all means use the foreigner's arguments, but if you must put them into quotation marks, try: 'A famous Russian was said to have remarked ...' Quote Satan to condemn sin.

The best quotations of all, of course, are those from the mouth of your opponents. 'Today, Mr Jones condemns amalgamation. But who was it who said, just two years ago – and I quote: "Our future depends upon achieving amalgamation. We cannot survive as a small independent unit"? None other than my friend, Mr Jones!'

Quotations from yourself should be avoided. 'Did I not say, six months ago, that ...?' Or 'May I repeat what I said at our trade conference last month?' Unless a speaker has previously been accused of inconsistency and must quote from himself to show that he has not changed his mind, this sort of self quotation is generally pompous and egotistical.

If you have something to say today, say it. Let someone else point to your marvellous consistency ... your wisdom before the event ... your status as a man whose advice should be taken. The best you can do is to make that insinuation. Self-quotation, like self-adulation, is only proper alone or among consenting adults in private ...

34 Statistics

Mind how you use statistics. Everyone knows that they are in the same category as lies and damned lies. If your presentation is to succeed, your figures must at least appear to be accurate.

A queue of graduates applied for a job with a firm of city accountants. Each was asked: 'What is twice one?' Each replied: 'Two.' The applicant who eventually got the job replied: 'What number did you have in mind, sir?'

So when you present statistics, at least indicate their origin – assuming only that you are not ashamed of it.

Next: do not presume that others are as conversant with figures or accounts as yourself. I am constantly amazed at the successful business people who cannot even read a balance sheet. So steer your way between the cardinal sins of talking down to your audience on the one hand and conferring undue knowledge on the other. If in doubt, explain.

Recognising that some human beings absorb by ear and others by eye, but most require a combination of both – and accepting also that your audience is far more likely to be innumerate than illiterate – supplement your words with paper – graphs and the rest – and, where appropriate, with visual aids (see Chapter 31).

35 Files and ideas

First-class journalists (especially freelancers with no access to newspaper files) keep their own careful files of clippings, cuttings, photographs and ideas which they can later incorporate into articles, features or books. Speakers should take a leaf out of their book.

Take jokes, for instance.There are books of allegedly humorous tales for every occasion. I sometimes wonder how anyone ever laughed at any of them. But then each of us has his own style... his own sense of humour... his own preference. Do not be afraid to steal the tales of others. They will be flattered. Jot them down and file them. You never know when they may come in handy.

Then there is specialist material, which can be used time and time again. Most popular speakers are invited to talk on their particular specialities. The first time, research must be done ... facts prepared ... statistics unearthed ... notes made. But if those notes are carefully filed, next time will be a walk-over, though naturally they would have to be adapted for different audiences (see Part 5). But the basic groundwork need not be repeated.

Some speakers favour a filing cabinet, others metal boxes with files inside. Still more make do with loose-leaf notebooks for stories and quotations, ideas and suggestions. The most modern store their gems vocally on tape, or automatically on word processors.

The object of it all is to reduce your homework to the minimum. You have no time to repeat your drudgery. So, however boring the keeping of files or notebooks may be, it is worth the effort in the present to reduce your work in the future.

Once again: the Retellable Tales in Book 3 should save you time and trouble and perhaps form the basis for your own collection, as it does mine.

Venues 36

Too often, the speaker cannot choose his venue. The company meeting, organisational gathering or dinner party is held in a place chosen by others. But even there, he may be able to make the best of his surroundings, if he knows what to look for. In other cases, he can influence (if not choose) the venue for his talk.

The first essential is to try and match the size of the room to the number of the audience. If the room is packed, an atmosphere should be easy to create and the speaker's task is made vastly simpler. Take 50 people and squeeze them into a home and you are likely to have a lively, happy meeting. Lose the same 50 in a hall and the evening is a failure before it has begun. So underestimate your audience. If a few get left outside, never mind. Next time they will come earlier. If some have to stand, or perch on radiators, that cannot be helped. You must avoid at all costs the echoing emptiness of a half-filled hall.

If you do find yourself with a sparse audience, do not panic. Suggest to the organisers that they ask all those present to come right up to the front. People hate being at the front, preferring to tuck themselves away in a nook near the door, the better to make their exit if they get too bored. And it is not only speakers who are sometimes shy. But a capable chairman can wheedle most people into 'helping our distinguished speaker'. If your chairman is inexperienced, then (having obtained his permission) you ask your audience to 'gather round'.

Many times, it is better to abandon the platform, draw the curtains and come down to your audience. If the formal gathering has failed to draw in the crowds, then at least ensure that you have an informal chat, so that your audience go home satisfied with their evening. It is most unlikely that they would be if you regaled them from above with an oration more suitable to a packed and cheering hall than to an almost empty room. Someone overestimated the audience in the first place and created your unfortunate situation. It is now for you to make the best of it.

Other suggestions? If the room is too hot, stop and ask for a window or a door to be opened. Your audience will bless you. If it is too cold, speak to the organisers and see whether they can warm the place. The chances are that they cannot. But at least your audience will know that you are thinking of their comfort. If there are aeroplane noises overhead, stop until they pass. To speak on regardless is a sure sign of inexperience. If a carpenter is banging next door, ask the chairman to use his influence to obtain silence for you. Then wait for the results of his efforts.

Of course, it is far preferable to have these distractions dealt with in advance. If you can get to a meeting sufficiently early, you can sometimes induce the organisers to rearrange the seating so as to suit your theme or your plans. You may want to avoid the use of a platform or to have the chairs arranged informally in a horseshoe, or conversely, to speak to your audience from a higher level. It helps everyone to have things arranged beforehand.

Again, it may pay dividends to have the sound equipment tested before the audience arrives or the lighting adjusted to suit your requirements. No theatre audience expects to have these changes arranged in their presence. No audience for a speech or lecture, a discussion or debate, likes to see them done after their arrival. Punctuality pays. If you wish to make a triumphal entry at a later stage, you can always disappear from the scene until the appropriate moment. And if your chairman or hosts know their business, they will have organised some small room at the back for you to use for your coat and hat and for your refreshment.

But so much depends on the occasion. As we shall shortly see.

Training in speechmaking 37

In Britain, speechmaking has always been regarded as an amateur art. Acquired through a combination of heredity and superior education, it finds no place in the curriculum of school, college or university.

Of course, the true Briton learns to read, spell and count. But it is 'not done' to take lessons in speechmaking or in presentation – which explains why both are commonly so inadequately performed.

The fact that you have bought or borrowed this book immediately places you in some peril – or have you put it into a plain, white cover?

As for lessons in speechmaking – they are for Americans and other foreigners, are they not?

There is, of course, neither educational rhyme nor reasonable logic for this curious attitude. Speaking in private may come naturally; orating in public does not. It requires training and experience. Without the appropriate flair, no level of teaching can produce outstanding results. But without training, public speaking is likely to be a burden not only for the speaker, but more especially for his unfortunate audience.

So do not despise the lesson. If public speaking is a burden on you or upon your hearers ... if you need to practise in private, but with an experienced and critical audience ... if you are prepared to learn from other people's mistakes, rather than from your own – then take lessons.

You do not need to advertise to your customers or clients, your friends or even your family that you are indulging in this particular form of masochism. Whether you are an experienced speaker in need of polish ... an inexperienced performer, promoted to a position of prominence where self-expression becomes crucial ... a presenter of your company's products or services, needing guidance in techniques and practice in their use ... or especially, if you suffer from any form of speech defect or accent impediment – then a good teacher is worth his weight in the compliments he will bring upon you and in the miseries that he will help you to avoid.

The same principles apply to courses in speechmaking and presentation for your staff or your executives. Given even moderate material, the skilled teacher can produce marvellous change.

How do you find your teacher or trainer? As usual: recommendation is the best guide. On the basis of horses for courses, another's guru may suit his needs, but not yours. So experiment.

My colleagues and I organise presentational courses for individual executives – tailor-made for the individual; group efforts, generally for a maximum of six; and large-scale, one-day presentations of basic techniques. Our delegates take their choice.

The more the training is angled at the needs of the individual, the greater its potential. Experience coupled with a video camera and monitor screen are our partners in perfection. The combination of seeing and criticising yourself, together with the vision and criticism of others – outsiders and, if you wish, your own colleagues, taking the same medicine – produces dramatic results in (we find) no more than two days.

If you are prepared to lavish resources on presentations ... on estimates, tenders and quotations ... on promotions and on product launches ... on induction and promotional training ... on employing consultants to advise you on everything from organisation and methods to time and man management – why, then, do you underestimate the need to train for prowess in the marvellous art of the skilled speechmaker and the polished presenter?

The speaker in public may be an amateur at the art, but there is no reason in business or in logic for him to be untrained. If more speakers had more training, listeners would have a far more interesting time – and the speakers would reach for the stars.

38 Practice and perfection

The greater your speechmaking practice, the nearer you should get to ease and to perfection. But 'nerves' produce adrenalin which fires the brain and hones the mind's edge. All great speechmakers are nervous on mighty occasions or they would fail. So greet your 'butterflies' with respect and with courage – the speechmaker (like Roosevelt's mankind) has nothing to fear but fear itself.

So if you approach your speechmaking moment with trembling knees, take comfort. Your experienced colleagues may not show their discomfort, but they will feel it.

The skilled speaker will not twist his hat or his hair, chew his fingernails or tear up bits of paper. He has learned to dissemble his feelings. The speechmaker is an actor who must normally write his own scripts. He must learn to cover up his apprehension.

So banish those terrifying fears that your throat will dry up, your voice crack, your mind go blank. Provided that you have prepared your speech ... that your notes are handy and steady and appropriate ... that you know your subject or can at least hide your ignorance ... all should be well. Never panic or all will be lost.

The more you practise, the more your confidence will expand. So:

● If you attend a meeting, steel yourself. Ask questions.

● If you are offered the chance to propose a vote of thanks, accept. If a small group invites you to address it, agree.

● If you have been dealing with some new and interesting project ... if you have gone on an unusual journey ... if you have something out of the ordinary to tell, then let this be known. Your club or organisation, charity, political group or trade organisation which has previously regarded you as a silent member will be delighted to invite you to speak to its members or to an interested section of them.

● Maybe you have a social function of your own: a dinner party, cocktail party, or company lunch. This time, stand up and say those few words of welcome, of thanks, of genuine greeting. If the speech is to be of any length, then (whatever the social occasion) the rules in Chapter 39 (on after-dinner speaking) will provide you with some useful guides.

Remember: the higher you rise or wish to aspire or to ascend in any field, the more vital it is to express yourself on your feet. The only way to gain experience is to get up on those feet. You will no longer fear becoming the centre of public attention. You will get used to the sound of your own voice, raised in public.

So speak. Your nervousness will fall away when your words emerge and your audience listens.

Part Five

Occasions

After dinner

A captive audience, well wined and amply dined, should be an orator's joy. But more often than not the speaker is too apprehensive to enjoy his food – and instead makes a meal of his speech. Which is unnecessary, if he would only follow a few basic rules.

First, wait for silence. When you have it, look around amiably and begin: 'Mr Chairman, Ladies and Gentlemen...' or as the case may be. Those few words are useful. You discover that you have not lost your voice after all. And your audience (at that stage at least) is ready to listen – and to be entertained.

However heavy the dinner or the company, however important the occasion or mighty the listeners, no one wants a dry lecture on top of a wet repast. So however important your message, do your audience the courtesy of exerting patience. Start with a joke ... a witticism ... a story.

The best jokes are usually impromptu. A friendly jibe at the chairman, the restaurant, the food... an oblique reference to the headline in the evening papers (those of the audience who have read it are delighted to be in on the joke). Otherwise, there are many good opening gambits such as:

'A few moments ago, the chairman turned to me and said: "Would you like to speak now – or shall we let them go on enjoying themselves a little longer?".'

Not long ago, an after-dinner speaker was greeted by a woman, at the evening's end, who said to him: 'Mr Jones ... that was a terrible speech!' He composed himself as best he could – and was then greeted by another woman who said: 'I'm awfully sorry about Mrs Brown ... she has such a long tongue ... and she's such an idiot – she hasn't got a mind of her own ... She only repeats what she hears other people saying!'

'Thank you for your hospitality to my wife and to me. In the words of the proverb: Behind every successful man stands an amazed woman!'

However weak the wit, dry the humour or wet the joke, provided that you put it across with verve, courage or at least a friendly smile, you are on your way to establishing *rapport* with your audience. They will settle back into their chairs, relaxed – and either be receptive to a continuation of merriment or, at worst, they will be the better braced for such message as you care to give.

Now you launch into the speech. Keep it short. Have you ever heard anyone complain that a post-prandial offering was too short, too condensed? When addressed by the best after-dinner speakers, they may say: 'I could listen to him forever...' But even if they think that they mean it, practice would prove them wrong.

The lower down you come in the toast list, the greater the premium on brevity. So why is it that many of the most nervous speakers find it necessary to be the most long-winded? Do they think they can make up with length for their lack of wit, their terror or their dearth of wise words? You may argue your bank manager into submission ... stifle the opposition of your competitors by talking them into the ground ... exhibit superb salesmanship by making it clear that you are not going to leave until you get what you want. But all this is in private. Enter into the public arena in general, or the dinner table in particular, and you must be brief.

As for the after-dinner speech itself, it requires the same careful construction as any other. It needs a flow of ideas as well as of words. The more the words are laced with wit, the more likely that their wisdom will strike home.

So watch your audience. If they drop off to sleep, either tell them a joke or sit down. If they jiggle the cutlery, wind up your sermon. If you want to be asked again, do not outlive your welcome.

As you approach your end, remember what it is you have been called upon to do. If you are responding to a toast, you should start by thanking the man who made it and complimenting him on his wit and wisdom. And you should finish where you began – by repeating, once again, your delight at having been asked ... your pleasure at the privilege of responding to the toast ... and your good wishes to the organisation which has asked you.

More important, if you are making the toast – then do so. Nothing is more discomforting than for the chairman to have to say: 'And now, kindly rise and drink with me...'. That is *your* job. So do it.

The standard formula? 'Ladies and Gentlemen, I invite you to rise and drink with me a toast to the continued success and prosperity of... to the health and happiness of...' or as the case may be. By all means vary it. But by no means forget it.

One toast, incidentally, which should never be varied is that to: 'Her Majesty, the Queen'. If you are privileged to propose the loyal toast, then do so – in those words. No one wants a speech from you, extolling the beauty and majesty of the monarch – still less a defence of hereditary peerages, royal privileges and the like. The same applies to a toast at Jewish dinners: 'Mr Chairman, Ladies and Gentlemen – the President of the State of Israel'. This is no time for a

Zionist outburst. The presence of an ambassador calls for a toast to the head of his state – but unless a toast to the state is one of the non-formal variety, reserve your eulogy to some proper occasion.

Of course: no one should smoke until after the loyal toast and others of the formal, national variety. This explains why some kindly chairmen call on the proposer of these toasts when the waiters are collecting the soup. At least the proposers can thereafter relax and enjoy the rest of their meal, in an aroma of cigar.

Feasts and funerals 40

You may be called on to 'say a few words' on festive and funeral occasions, involving family, friends or colleagues. In general, similar rules apply to those outlined for the after-dinner orator – and elsewhere in the book. But here are some special suggestions for particular occasions.

The funeral

No ill must be spoken of the departed. But, as usual, praise should be sincere and, where possible, deserved.

Tact is essential. You are expected to sum up all the pleasant and happy thoughts and memories which your audience would like to recall about the departed ... to encourage and support those who remain behind, with the knowledge of the affection in which they are held ... to indicate the immortality of the deceased – through those of his works that will live after him.

The obituary will range in length from a full-blown oration to (more likely) an introduction to a request for the audience to stand in memory of a departed friend. The following might serve as a model:

- 'Ladies and Gentlemen, Colleagues and Friends. Before we start our meeting, I know that you would want me to express our deep regret at the loss of our well loved fellow director, James Smith. He was a man of enormous enthusiasm, energy and initiative. He was loyal both to his friends and to the company for which he worked so well for so long. The organisation which he created – in particular in our branch factories – will remain as a permanent tribute to his commercial acumen. We – his friends and colleagues – will miss him. So will the company. I ask you all to stand for a moment in memory of ... James Smith.'

Feasts

Happily, whilst every lifetime contains the seeds of its own sorrow, there are far more joyful occasions than sad ones. Births and baptisms, christenings, confirmations and first communions... The Brit Milah and the Bar Mitzvah (Jewish ritual circumcision and confirmation of 13-year-old boys) ... engagements, weddings (including silver and gold) ... each is the occasion for a word of congratulations at the start of a meeting or of a speech – or for a celebration at which a speech is required.

Of the full-blown variety, the after-diner speech may form the model (see Chapter 39). Perhaps the best advice of all is contained in the saying: the secret of talking to the public is the same as that of speaking to your spouse — keep your tongue in time with your thoughts; if either gets ahead, you are done for!

41 Overseas speeches – and foreign customers

The isolationist businessman is, or should be, as extinct as the proverbial dodo. If you can export, then you should, says every government the world over. If you must import, then do so – but at the most competitive prices. You must bargain with the foreigner, eat with him, drink with him, even expense-account with him – and, in the ultimate, you may well be thrust into making speeches to or at him.

Naturally, if you are blessed with equal facility in the foreign language as you have in your own, your problems are minimal. Then you only have to follow the rules laid down in the rest of this book and all should be well. Subject, of course, to cutting your forensic cloth to the style of your overseas audience, there is no essential difference between rousing, holding, interesting, convincing – or boring – an audience of Englishmen, Frenchmen, Russians or Greeks.

Melodrama goes over rather better in the United States than in Britain. The florid oratory that went out in Britain many years ago still thrives in some parts – and with some audiences – abroad. In general, if you play up to the image expected of you – if you give your audience a touch of urbane wit, rather than roistering slapstick – you are likely to come across best.

Stick to your style when in America and you have every chance of a friendly welcome. I once toured the United States, talking about Britain ... the Welfare State ... even what they choose to call 'socialised medicine'. I met a certain surprise that the Englishman was not cold, reserved, humourless, upper crust and frosty. The image of the icy Anglo-Saxon who will only speak when introduced – and, preferably, when well warmed with alcohol – dies hard. So the friendly, humorous opening acquired an extra significance and importance. Establish *rapport* and you are well away.

Once the overseas audience knows that you really do intend to entertain as well as to instruct – to talk across and not down – they are even more ready than your fellow countrymen to give you a warm hearing. The best tip for heating the atmosphere? Use the language of your hosts.

English and American is the same? In general, yes. But the idiom differs and so do the allusions. The American speaker in Britain who takes the trouble to look at his daily newspaper and to joke about the current crime wave, strike outbreak, political disaster or other local misery does well. When you are talking to overseas listeners, return that sort of compliment.

A simple, well tried opening in the USA: 'You will be relieved to know that I am not about to launch into discussion of whether or not that which is good for General Motors is good also for the country as a whole ... as to the merits or otherwise of the political efforts of the Cabots, the Kennedys or' (*here insert names of local politicians currently in the news*). 'If I am asked whether I support the Yankees, the Redskins or' (*here insert the name of the local baseball team*), 'I shall refuse firmly to enter into your local politics. We British have enough trouble trying to run our own affairs, without risking another Boston tea-party. No. I shall confine myself to a discussion of...'

Another invaluable story. 'I have been asked to comment upon your current commercial crisis. I must respectfully decline. You may know the tale of the dying man who was visited by his priest. "My son," said the priest, "do you renounce the Devil, now and for ever more?" "Oh, Father," said the dying man, "this is no time to be making enemies – anywhere!" Ladies and Gentlemen, as the solitary

Englishman in your ranks, I wish to make no enemies anywhere – so I shall tell you about *our* troubles – rather than venturing to discuss yours.'

Once you have established friendly relations with the overseas buyers, suppliers or fellow traders, if you stick to subjects which interest them, all should be well. They are as anxious to pick up profitable tips from you, as you are from them. Provided that you assume a cloak of modesty, they will wish to hear of your achievements. After all, that is why you have been invited to speak. So do not be shy. Talk freely of your doings and the effort may prove more profitable than you had expected.

Now suppose that you are forced to launch into your speech, to people for whom English is not the mother tongue. There are two main possibilities. Either you address them in English and hope that they understand. Or you speak in the foreign language. The second is infinitely preferable, provided that you have a command of the tongue concerned.

If you are really talking business – putting across facts, figures, theories or ideas in respect of which words must be given their precise meanings ... if what you say may create misunderstandings if the words are not used with their correct nuances ... if shades of meaning matter – then you should stick to English and work through an interpreter, if necessary. It is no tribute to your bravery if you venture into foreign seas without wearing a lifebelt.

On the other hand, it may be that this is an occasion when it would be worthwhile preparing your speech beforehand and having it translated – and then reading it. Make a friendly, impromptu opening (or one which is apparently not read) and the audience will just have to put up with what may not be an oratorical masterpiece but which will at least be strictly accurate. That will teach them to invite an overseas expert to speak to them!

In that case, you should do all you can to mitigate the misery by looking up from your speech ... talking to your audience, whenever you can manage it ... pausing from time to time, to throw in a joke in English – or an apology for having to read your script ... and make sure that you do try to put it across in the accent of the native.

We have all heard the Briton who speaks the foreign tongue as if it were his own. French words read in broad Scots, Yorkshire, Welsh or upper-crust Bath or Tunbridge Wells have a distinctly humorous flavour on the music-hall stage. But to the foreign listener, it is just plain silly.

There is an exception. If you are going to make your speech in English, then you should always prepare a few words, right at the start, in your host's language – or, if you are the host, then in that of your guests. It matters not how badly you mispronounce the words – that adds to the fun. Nobody cares if you make a hash of the grammar or even if you manage to make a ghastly boob which gives words their opposite meaning. What matters is that you make the genuine effort to speak to folk in their own tongue. You pay them the compliment of making what is obviously a brave attempt to be friendly – and in the most genuine possible way.

Start with your usual opening, in English. 'Mr Chairman, Ladies and Gentlemen, Fellow Workers in the — industry...' If you then break into the foreign tongue, you will produce just that element of surprise which should give rise to a very friendly reception. 'You did not know that I was learning Greek/Spanish/Hebrew/Chinese... did you?' (This, of course, in the language concerned). 'After I'd met Mr... in... who speaks such marvellous English, I was shamed into trying. I am only sorry that my efforts have been, as you hear, so very unsuccessful. To avoid any future misunderstandings of what I have to say, I hope that you will forgive me if I return – very gratefully – to English!' All that in the foreign language. Memorise it if you can. Otherwise read it. The fact that you will have got the information and the translation from one of the nationals of the country concerned is irrelevant. The compliment you have paid your audience will undoubtedly be appreciated.

There is an alternative. You can launch right into the 'Mr Chairman, Ladies and Gentlemen ... How are you? Welcome to Britain – we are very happy to have you and hope that you will have a very good time.' All that in the foreign language will delight your audience.

End with 'Farewell – and come back soon,' in the language of your hosts or guests. Then add: '*Jai Hind*' or '*Vive la France*' or whatever 'hail' is appropriate in their land. As usual, if you get the start and finish of your speech right, the rest will fall into shape.

Naturally, if your audience happen to be a mixed bag, then the above rules will have to be modified. I have heard a very successful opening: 'Ladies and Gentlemen, Messieurs Mesdames, Señoras y Señores, Meine Damen und Herren ... welcome to you all – and if I have managed to mispronounce even the few words in your language which I have ventured to speak, I know that you will appreciate why I am going to make the rest of my speech in English – I think it will be easier for us all.' Pause while the audience nod, smile, and chatter. 'Misunderstandings that are created by speakers – especially by politicians – who stick to their own tongue are only exceeded by those who have the temerity to create vast international misunderstandings by murdering the languages of others – and murder is a crime in every country in the world!'

42 Appeals and fund-raising

The art of extracting money from the listener requires careful thought and ready adaptation to the circumstances. The Chancellor of the Exchequer may have political problems, but at least he can enforce his financial requirements. The speechmaker seeking to raise funds for his pet charity ... for a trade or industrial benevolent fund ... or even for some less apparently altruistic outlet ... he must win the cash, pound by pound. How? That depends on the audience and the cause. Here are some suggestions:

There are those who give out of pure kindness of heart. Guilt and self-interest are usually more powerful motives.

There are some who work hard for a charity – and others who do not. But the latter may contribute the money they have earned whilst not striving for the good cause. In their own way, they can do as much for the needy as their more apparently energetic colleagues. Tell them so – by implication.

'There are those of us who are in the happy position of being able to spare time to work for this important charity. There are others who find it impossible to do so. May I make a special appeal to them? Give us the means and we will do the job. It is a job that desperately needs every penny that you can afford to spare – and more...'

What, then, of enlightened self-interest? Maybe it is a question of insurance. The charity deals with the aged, infirm, ill or needy? And you are young, middle-aged or at least fit? That is now. What happens when you get dumped on the scrap heap ... sacked ... struck down by (Heaven forbid) some fell disease? You have a pension? Well, maybe the company will not be in a position to pay it or it will not suffice for the needs of your widow. So, now, when you are in a position to assure your future, do so.

This is seldom said. The better approach is this! 'I ask you to give as an expression of gratitude for the fact that you do not need to make use of this great trade charity for yourself. I hope that none of us will need at any time to occupy a bed in this convalescent home...to receive a payment from this fund...to rely upon the benevolence of others in the industry... But who knows?' Pause, significantly. 'And even if, as we all hope, we escape the necessity for help of this sort, we can be proud that those who do require it can look to us. They have given good service...they have earned every penny that comes to them...they have been smitten by the ill-fortune that we have managed to avoid...' And so on. We all spend money on insurance, do we not? Well, this is a healthy and helpful form of outlet for the same, intelligent response to potential misfortune.

Consider always the best way to confer a bargain. This is generally done with the kind aid of the tax man. If a businessman feels that he can give more by paying less, you are far more likely to get your money...to have a bed endowed in the trade home...to acquire your 'Smith House' or 'Jones Hall'. So check on current covenant schemes, charitable trusts, tax-deductible donations...

'Think of it, Ladies and Gentlemen. Any person paying income tax at the current standard rate can confer a benefit on this charity, out of all proportion to the amount which he has to give up from his own spending. Here are some examples...' Then say how much a gift of £X or $Y per year will mean gross, to the charity. Remember, of course, that when a charity receives covenants, these can provide good security for loans, if it needs the money at once. And it is sometimes possible to get people to give a lump sum on the basis that it will be grossed up for tax purposes over the years. The charity's accountants should know the rules.

Then, remember that lawful blackmail is the charitable fund-raiser's most potent weapon. You phone your supplier. 'Jimmy,' you say, 'we've had such a tremendous call on our benevolent fund that we simply have to raise an extra £50,000. Can I count on you for a thousand?'

Jimmy groans inwardly. 'Certainly, Bill,' he smiles. 'Shall I send an advertisement for the Ball Brochure?'

Use the same tactic in public speech. Look at Jimmy when you ask for funds. He may turn away his gaze, but he may not dare to keep his cheque book closed. After all, when he came to the function or the meeting, he realised that the skinning knives would be unsheathed. Or, even better, corner him in advance. Find out how much he is willing to give. Announce it – as a bait for others, or to shame them into raising their donations to an appropriately announceable level. If you have goodwill, then use it for the benefit of the less privileged. No one will ever tell you of the resentment they feel. It's all in a good cause, is it not?

Of course, whether you can use this sort of direct attack or whether you have to be more subtle...whether you can announce donations at the meeting or have to let the word go round from mouth to mouth...whether you conduct a mock auction at inflated prices, a raffle, a tombola...all depends on all factors in the unhappy case. But one rule applies to nearly all: you cannot afford to be bashful, or to worry about rebuffs, if you are looking for money from the pockets of others.

The best time to attack those pockets is when the mind is weak through the stomach being overloaded or the heart touched by your words. If you have people in a happy, receptive and giving mood, then (literally) cash in on the situation. Either ask them for their donation at the time – and pass round the appropriate banker's order or covenant forms – or at least write to them the very next day saying: 'It was very good to see you last night . . . I enclose herewith banker's order...I am sure that I can count on your further support...'

The speech can never be regarded as a separate entity, divorced from the project it encompasses. If you want funds, then you may have to appeal for them. But the appeal must be tied in with the campaign before and after. The very nature of the speech will depend upon that of the appeal, its preparation, its follow-up, its needs. The production of goods depends upon the market...the resources at your disposal...the economic situation...and all the facts of the case. A speech must be matched to the audience and the circumstances – and no speech more so than that which incorporates an appeal for money.

Any professional appeals organiser will tell you that if you can interest the Jewish community in your appeal, you are well away. And while Jewish people are willing givers to their own communal and Israeli causes, they take pride in taking part in the appeals of others. Perhaps even more important, they are excellent fund-raisers for charities of all sorts. So I reproduce with appreciation an interview in which a successful Jewish appeal-maker gave away some of his secrets:

'I know plenty of people who can make an excellent speech,' he said, 'but not an appeal. The technique is quite different. The man who makes a speech can create the right atmosphere for someone to follow in. The appeal-maker must not waste time making speeches. He needs a couple of minutes to say what it is all about. And, of course, an appeal-maker must never be satisfied with his audience. Whatever he says, he must have the people in a frame of mind when they want to give. He should know when to stop.'

An audience, then, should be like a 'juicy orange — you squeeze, but not until the pips fall out. When you stop is a matter of psychology or intuition.'

When you have finished your appeal, can you tell whether the audience is still with you?

'If they applaud you as loudly when you sit down as when you got up, you can be happy with the job done.

'An appeal-maker must never read a speech. What he has to say must be spontaneous. It must come from the heart. He must never embarrass people but make them feel happy about their giving and leave them in a good frame of mind, thanking him for a successful job. People recognise the sincerity of the appeal-maker. An appeal-maker must be somebody who sincerely belives in the cause he puts forward...

Finally, the appeal-maker must set an example in giving.'

Give, and the world gives with you...the mean man is not an appealing figure, in any sense of the word.

In the open 43

The open-air speech is a comparative rarity. But you should be prepared to make one, if necessary. Maybe it will be at the factory gates, at the dockside, or at some open-air trade show or speaking event. Perhaps it is only a vote of thanks at your local sports day...a talk or a lecture on site...or maybe you have to speak at a rally in Hyde Park, Trafalgar Square or at your local war memorial? Whatever the place and whatever the circumstances, there are certain basic rules on open-air oratory that should help you succeed in any such appearance.

Human voices carry poorly in the open air. So the prime essential for the outdoor speaker is to be heard. If you have a microphone, use it. The same sort of rules as set out in Chapter 30 apply, only more so. The chances of outdoor amplifying equipment going wrong are far greater than with their indoor brethren. The variety that hooks on to a motor-car battery is particularly vulnerable. Listen to the men of politics, next election time. Pity their attempts to be heard – especially when a crowd is all around them and the amplifying equipment points only to the front.

If you have a microphone, remember its outdoor limitations. For instance, if ever you have to speak in a moving vehicle – perhaps from the front of a car or the back of a truck – talk very slowly and distinctly and urge the driver to move as slowly as he dares. People do like to hear what is being cried out at them from a moving object and they get aggravated when it darts past without giving them the chance to pick up the words – however banal or trite those words may be. Usually, there is time for a slogan only. 'Today's the day...come to the carnival...12.15 p.m. at the park...' Then you are gone.

Most outdoor speaking is stationary. Mike or no mike – many of the indoor rules go out the window. For instance:

● The outdoor speaker can be far freer with movement and gesture.

● Old-fashioned oratory – rabble-rousing – is more effective and appears less insincere when out of doors.

● Instead of having an audience ready-made, you may have to collect it. Whereas indoors there is no point in speaking to yourself, outdoors you may have no alternative, so the louder and more provocatively you rant, the greater your chances of an eventual audience.

Some rules of indoor speaking require special emphasis out of doors. For instance:

● Do not be afraid to pause...to wait...to give every possible indication of complete calm and confidence.

● Never panic, no matter what may be thrown at you – even if this is more than mere words. Remember always that the man on the platform has a vast advantage over his hearers. If he is firm and refuses to be ruffled, in the long run he should win.

● Make certain that your voice carries. If you use a battery-operated hand megaphone, pull the trigger tight. As one famous Harvard professor used to say: 'Take your voice and throw it against the wall at the back of your audience and make it bounce off.' If you get hoarse as a result, do not worry. You have joined the professionals. Lose your voice and it will come back. Lose your audience, and it is gone forever.

The giver

You may view presentation or award speeches from two angles – that of the giver and that of the receiver. In either event 'a few words' will be expected of you; in either case, the keynote of the speech is sincerity.

Everyone likes to be honoured. The art of the well turned compliment is appreciated more than almost any other. Flattery given freely and wholeheartedly is always welcome – but it must be given in moderation.

'Mr X is the most brilliant businessman, straightforward and sweet-tempered, a paragon of commercial virtue...' Rubbish. No one will believe it – not even Mr X.

Compare this: 'On the one hand, Mr Smith has been the head of a large and successful commercial concern. He has had to see that business became and remained thoroughly competitive. His has been the unpleasant duty of striking the hard bargain, ensuring that the business was tough and competitive, enabling the enterprise to survive and flourish in spite of the economic circumstances, the bitter and fierce rivalries within the trade, the battle for skilled manpower and for shrinking markets.

'On the other hand, Mr Smith has sought to preserve the good name of the company and its good relations both with its suppliers, customers and competitors and with its own staff.

'That he has succeeded in building up the business without destroying the foundations of goodwill...that he has promoted the economic welfare of the business without demoting or undervaluing the honour and integrity of the Board...that he has earned such a warm regard not only for the company but for himself – those are the reasons why we are delighted to honour him this evening – and why we are so sad at his impending retirement.'

Or take the manager, the foreman or the operative, leaving after long service, or receiving an award for distinguished, long-term conduct.

'We were thinking of presenting Mr Jones with a watch. But we do not believe our staff really want to know the time just when it has become least important to them. And so we felt that this electric tea-maker would be more appropriate and much more useful. It comes with the thanks and admiration of the company – and its gratitude.

'It is also given with the affection and goodwill of his fellow members of staff. They have contributed towards it and I know they hope, as much as I do, that it will remind him – and his wife and family – of the affection and esteem in which we all hold him, and of our thanks to him for his loyal service. We wish Mr Jones, together with his charming wife, a long and happy retirement, blessed with the very best of health. And we hope that he will visit us often. He will always have the warmest of welcomes from all of us, his colleagues and friends.'

No flowery insincerities. No 'schmaltz', no overdone compliments, just straightforward, sincere and sensible words, bound to be appreciated by the person concerned.

Sometimes the presentation of an award is really an excuse to encourage people to come to a dinner or other function, knowing that they would not wish to offend the recipient by being absent. With this sort of award or presentation it is expected that the toast to the recipient will be coupled with a eulogy of the organisation he represents – and/or of the virtues represented by the organisation which is conferring the award. This sort of excuse for an oratorical jamboree is becoming increasingly common, and is not always an altogether welcome transatlantic importation. The public relations man has created a new vehicle. If it comes your way, be prepared to steer it.

'In the new and expanding sauna bath industry, we are proud of our pioneers. This dinner is in honour of Mr Finn, whom we are all delighted to welcome to England.' Hear, hear!

'Mr Finn has helped to put our industry on to the British map. Close on the heels of the central heating boom has come the realisation that sauna bath treatments bring health and true family relaxation. Whilst no public authority should be without one, there is an immense, untapped demand for them in the larger private homes throughout the country.' (The press start scribbling.) 'What better occasion could there be than this to launch the great new drive for British-built sauna baths – we shall create a home demand so as to build up an economic, export potential... And we wish to express our admiration and thanks to our honoured guest, Mr Finn, to whom I am delighted to present this gold pin, in the shape of a sauna bath, as a token of our respect and gratitude.' Loud cheers. The audience rises. Flash bulbs pop.

This is only a slight exaggeration of the sort of award occasion that occurs somewhere, every day. If you are the presenter, the more fatuous the occasion...the less deserving the recipient...the bigger the publicity hoped for – the more your sincerity becomes vital, if the occasion is not to deteriorate into sickening slush.

How do you appear sincere, even when you are not? By playing down. By avoiding exaggeration. By excluding melodrama, theatricals, tears in the eyes or choking in the throat. 'I am so moved that I can scarcely speak...' Then don't. 'Mr Jones is fabulous, fantastic, magnificent...' Superlatives are seldom either sincere or accurate. A few, quiet words of praise are worth paeans of exultation.

The receiver

With luck, you may be at the receiving end of an honour, an award, a presentation or a toast. Praise may be heaped on your receptive shoulders. How do you cope with it?

'I am very grateful to Mr Smith for his most generous obituary,' said Adlai Stevenson.

'There is one difference between a speech of this kind heaping praise on the living, and a funeral oration, extolling the dead,' said Israel's first President, Chaim Weizmann. 'In the former case, but not the latter, there is one listener who is ready to believe in the truth of all that was said.'

More common: 'I would first like to thank Mr Jones for his very kind references to my wife and myself. We are very grateful – and only wish that half of it were true.' Or: 'I am deeply grateful to you, Mr Chairman, for the very generous way in which you have referred to my organisation and to myself. We shall do our best to live up to your high regard.'

Just as it is vital for the maker of the speech of praise to be patently sincere, so the recipient must be clothed in decent modesty. It would be ungracious and insincere to say: 'It's all true...you shouldn't have said those things...' You could hardly say: 'Every word is an understatement...' You may be immodest about your wife: 'All that has been said about my wife is true. I am very proud of her – she's a gem!' But then you must go on: 'I only wish that I could believe the same of the words about myself. Nevertheless, I am most obliged to Mr Smith for having spoken them. Maybe he convinced my wife of their truth, even though he left me in doubt.'

The next stage is to return the compliment by speaking well of the individual or organisation that has had the good sense to honour you. 'I have been very lucky to serve this company over so many years...It has been a privilege to work with you all...I shall miss you...I hope that we shall meet again, very often...' Or: 'Whilst this fraternal organisation has been good enough to make an award to me, I should in fact have been making a presentation to the organisation. The honours are flowing in the wrong direction. I shall try to redress the balance a little by saying why it is that I regard the work of this organisation to be of such enormous significance, especially in the present state of...'

Or: 'It was very good of Mr Smith to speak so well of me. As everyone here knows so well, most of the virtues that he was kind enough to attribute to me were in fact his own. This company is fortunate to be led by a man of his calibre...'

Sincerity and the nicely turned compliment should not be the sole prerogative of the giver.

Finally, the conclusion. 'And so, Mr Chairman, my speech – like my time with the company – has drawn to its close. Thank you, Mr Smith, once again for your very kind words. Thank you, my colleagues, for your goodness to me – and for your most generous gift. My wife and I will treasure it always – as we shall the memories of our association with you. Good luck to you all.'

Or: 'And so, in accepting this award, I thank you all for the compliment you have paid to me – and through me to my organisation. My colleagues and I are all happy to have been able to carry out our work – and we undertake to attempt in the future to exceed the achievements in the past which have caused you to honour us in the present. Our gratitude to you all.'

The sentimental anecdotes you have slipped into the body of your speech...the reminiscences, memories, tales with a moral – all of which go down so well in this sort of situation...these are all rounded off with a final word of thanks. To end, where you began, with your gratitude. It has been a fine occasion – and an excellent speech.

The formal vote of thanks to the speaker is a mark of courtesy as necessary as the word of gratitude to the hostess at the end of the evening. You may not have enjoyed your meal. The company may have been excruciatingly dull. Unlike the fabled hostess who was said to have made her guests feel at home even when she fervently wished that they were, Mrs Black may have made you thoroughly ill at ease. You will still thank her as you leave – and no doubt compliment her warmly on the excellence of her cooking and the pleasure you have had in the company of her other, well chosen guests. Because the compliments are apparently unrehearsed, they may be believed. Anyway, they must be given.

So it is with the guest speaker. He must be thanked. In America, it is normal to make handsome payment to those who lecture, even to Rotary Clubs, friendly societies or business or charitable organisations. The guest speakers are given appreciated thanks, in tangible form. In the UK, the audience considers that it is doing the speaker a favour in listening to him!

When your guest says: 'It was very kind of you to invite me to this splendid, peaceful Highland resort', he probably means: 'I wish I could have thought of some way to refuse your invitation to trek up to your God-forsaken, Arctic, barren development area slum!' So at least bathe him in the warmth of your thanks.

Incidentally, have you remembered to offer to pay your guest's expenses? He would probably be too embarrassed to ask for them and he may even refuse your offer. But to beg for and receive the benefit of the time of a busy speaker and then to expect him to pay for his fare or accommodation is a typically British stupidity. All speakers know the wretchedness of being dragged many miles for a few minutes of speech to a minute audience. That is one of the hazards of the trade. But when he does so entirely at his own expense, in money as well as in time, his irritation is understandable.

What, then, of the vote of thanks itself? How do you best put it across?

Sincerity is the keynote. This rests upon a genuine (if possible) and topical (certainly) assessment of the positive and helpful aspects of the visitor's speech. Refer to his wit and wisdom ... to the full and frank way in which he has dealt with the subject ... to the particular interest that you have had in that portion of his talk which dealt with ... Elaborate on a point or two, to show that you have really taken it in – or that *you* have been taken in, as the case may be. Do not use the occasion to launch into a tirade of your own. Your job is to thank. Do it.

A vote of thanks is a mini-speech. The general rules apply, in abbreviated form.

Write out your first sentence and the skeleton of the speech. But to have the whole speech written in advance is a travesty. 'We have all been extremely impressed with the wise words of Mr Stout,' the speaker reads from his typed card. 'He gave us a very clear exposition of the subject. We have much to think about as a result.' Terrible – an impromptu effort not worth the paper it was written on. Of all the speeches which should never be written out in advance, votes of thanks head the list.

'We are very honoured to have had Mr Slim with us this evening. We realise and appreciate how far he has come. We know and understand the effort that it has cost him. And I know that I am expressing the feelings of everyone here when I tell him how deeply grateful we are to him.' Pause for applause. If you rush on, your audience will not know what is expected of them. There will be a few embarrassed hand-claps and the speaker will not be complimented.

'We listened with great interest to Mr Slim's views on ... I was especially impressed with the concept of ... If my own company does not take steps to put this system into effect, it will not be through any lack of enthusiasm on my part, nor any failing on the part of our distinguished speaker. He has paid us the compliment of laying out before us in the clearest terms the essence of the organisational method which he has distilled through years of trial, error and experience.

'The greatest tribute which can be paid to our guest will be through our adoption of his ideas.' Every speaker likes to feel that he has sown good seed on fertile ground. Treat his words as pearls and he will not think of you as the proverbial swine.

'Perhaps our greatest delight, Mr Chairman, has been in the way in which Mr Slim has succeeded in bringing his somewhat recondite subject to life. He has proved that to tell a tale of ... need not be dull. He has enlivened our evening with wit and humour.

'And so, in thanking Mr Slim for his good words this evening, I can only hope that we shall have an early opportunity of hearing him again. We wish him every success. Thank you, Mr Slim, very much indeed.'

And thank you for a terse, appropriate, sincere, friendly and well constructed vote of thanks. Just to think that the audience inwardly groaned when you were called upon to speak, worrying in case you were about to make the late hour even later... to cause them to lose the last bus or train or the services of their aggravated chauffeurs... or, possibly, to embarrass them by saying what they really thought about their guests. So they were pleasantly surprised – and are likely to invite you to perform the same service again. Or maybe they knew all the time that you would perform this under-rated chore with aplomb, which is why they asked you to do it. In that case, their trust was not misplaced. Thank you, indeed.

Brains trusts 46

Curiously, even prominent people are prepared to take part in so-called 'brains trusts'. The audience gets at least two views for the price of one evening. The speaker – who might otherwise resent the competition and the feeling that his audience really should be satisfied with an evening of him – agrees to participate perhaps because he is delighted not to have to prepare any set speech. Each or all of the speakers are often fooled into accepting because they think that the others on the panel have already done so, or they turn up because they have been asked by someone whom they cannot refuse.

Whatever the circumstances, most speakers have to perform at brains trusts some time or another. So here are some suggestions.

The organisers should provide each speaker with a pencil and pad. They often fail to do so. You should never arrive at any meeting without pen and paper, least of all for a brains trust.

When a question is asked, jot it down. Alongside it, put your random ideas. If you have none, indicate to the chairman that one of your colleagues should open the batting. Something will come to your mind whilst your colleague answers. If it does not, then say: 'I agree', or 'I'd rather not comment on this one, thank you.'

There are questions that may provoke all sorts of possible answers, none of which you wish to give. Do not be browbeaten into words you may later regret.

Each answer you do give should be a small, neat speech. It should have a beginning, a body and an end. It must be concise; and precisely because it is extempore, you may find it considerably more difficult than the ordinary, set effort. There is an art to brains trusting.

You may have to cope with interruptions from your colleagues or from the chairman. Take them in your stride. React to the informality of the occasion. Do not be afraid to break your train of thought – or, if you cannot return to it, say: 'Now, where was I, before Mr Brown's witty intervention?' Someone will remind you.

Conversational informality – that is the key to a successful brains trust performance. You are performing at a dinner party, with an audience to play up to. Make use of your powers of showmanship. React to your audience. Fish for applause and laughter. Relax and enjoy yourself and your audience will do the same.

Well chosen brains trust panels include people with different backgrounds, viewpoints and ideas. Speakers engage in gentlemanly teasing. Jokes against yourself will be appreciated. Smart retorts to points made by other speakers seldom go astray. But the tradition is still that of the dinner party and not of the political tub-thump. Aggressive and unfriendly rejoinders ... rude or unkind rebuttals ... personal remarks to or about other speakers, which hurt (whether or not they are calculated to do so) – these are all to be avoided. The object is to demonstrate your brains, not to tear out those of the other panelists.

47 Conferences and seminars

Business and professional people are often dragooned, shamed or enticed into presenting themselves and their wares at conferences or seminars. To this also there is an art.

Your approach to success depends upon the purpose of the occasion. Is yours, for instance, a promotional exercise, designed to introduce new clients or to stiffen the loyalty of old ones? Do delegates come to learn, from those who are trained and qualified to teach? Either way: you are in show business.

There is absolutely no excuse for a dreary conference. However dull the subject, it can be enlivened by visual aids (Chapter 31); relaxed by wit; brought to life by enthusiasm.

Individual speakers should follow the usual rules of good presentation. In particular, they should know and prepare their materials; communicate with and according to their audience; speak with style and demonstrate with skill.

Whether dealing with a small-scale, teaching seminar or a larger assembly or conference, the excellent presenter will respect his audience. If he wishes them to return, he will also entertain them.

The fact that so many conferences are dull and disastrous is a denunciation of those who organise and who address them. They harm not only their own cause, but they also spoil the market. They forget that while schoolchildren are tied to their desks and to their classrooms, conference delegates can opt for the bar and today's seminar attenders will be tomorrow's absentees. Hence the new and musical disease of 'conference syncopation' – staggering from bar to bar!

The presenter's success depends to a vast extent upon the conditions created for him by the conference or seminar organisers. Check these in advance, preferably before you agree to take part. If, for instance, the room is to be vast and the audience small ... the acoustics echoing and the amplification minimal ... the delegates crowded and unhappy and the food inedible – then do not attach your good name to their bad feelings.

Otherwise and in any event, arrive early enough to check your atmosphere and your apparatus, your audience and your audibility. Pay special regard to the following:

- Is the stage, platform and/or table as you like or need it?

- Stuck as *you* are with the amplification arrangements as *they* are, how can you make the best of them? For instance, will you be able to remove, adjust and/or stroll with the microphone or is it fixed – and if so, is it at your height or at that of a pygmy or giraffe?

- Is the overhead projector or other equipment for your visual aids in proper order and position? If you need assistance in, perhaps, the showing of slides, is it available?

- If you need arrangements for your comfort and convenience, will you get them? These may range from water for a dry throat, to (in my case) somewhere quiet for a lunchtime nap and battery recharge. The same applies to the provision of pre-meal drinks or intermission tea or coffee.

- If you are to be paid a fee for your presentation, are the arrangements clear, recorded or confirmed in writing and followed through? If these are to any extent on a commission, bonus or other arrangement that depends upon the success of the event, then how will you find out what you are owed; and will you need to send an account or invoice?

- Should you require smokers to remain at the back or to one side, or do you want to mix the chimneys with the abstainers?

- Always try to fill up seats from the front. If you are not sure whether the room will be filled, can you insist that no one sits in the back rows until front and centre are full?

- Will you avoid interruptions from the clatter of crockery and cutlery, before and after breaks? Separate reception and coffee rooms will help, but thin partitions destroy the best of plans.

- How will you achieve a climax at the end, so that your delegates/audience leave happy? If you cannot manage flowers for the women, then at least ensure applause for your speakers.

- If you are to be introduced by a chairman or other impresario, has he adequate and correct details for the purpose? If either he or you will introduce or sell your products or services, have you made arrangements for details, samples or goods – or order forms, brochures or other documents – to be properly and prominently displayed?

48 Postscript – pastimes whilst others speak

Part of the price of the pleasure of hearing your own voice is the need to endure the speeches of others. You may, of course, be lucky. The sole guest speaker of an evening only has the introduction and vote of thanks to sit through. During the former, he will be thinking of his speech and – if he takes the advice given in this book to heart – trying to find something in the words of his introducer to quote, adapt or answer, and so establish a *rapport* with his audience. During the vote of thanks, he must simply try to believe that the words spoken of him are true. No one need exhibit false modesty to himself.

Inevitably unlucky is the after-dinner speaker, no matter what his place in the toast list. The chairman of a committee may be able to regulate the speeches of others, but the rest must put up with them. If you happen to be a Member of Parliament, you may be able to escape from the function after you have spoken, perhaps blessed with a three-line whip. ('Mr Jones must now return to his Parliamentary duties. We appreciate all the more that he has spared some of his most valuable time to be with us.') But heaven help anyone else who leaves before the other speeches are complete.

So the art of listening is worth careful cultivation.

In private, the good listener is generally credited with fine powers of perception, intelligence and even eloquence. In public, to fall asleep whilst others speak is the height of bad manners. But how to avoid it?

Every practised speaker is a skilled doodler. There is one handwriting expert alleged to make his living largely by interpreting the doodles of the famous. Much more constructive is the writing of those neglected letters.

The dinner is dull? Too bad. You must try to get your neighbour to talk about his speciality and you may find that he is more interesting than you had realised. The after-dinner speeches are a misery? Then use the back of the menu, toast list, guest list or brochure. Take out your pen and write your correspondence. Look up every now and again at the speaker. No one – least of all the speaker himself – will suspect that you are doing anything other than paying him the compliment of noting his words. My relatives in Australia always know when I have been cursed with dull speeches to hear. They receive missives on agendas, minutes, jotting-pads... anything that happens to be handy.

Of course, you could instead be jotting down notes for the current work which you have on hand. In the unlikely event of the speaker sparking off a constructive chain of thought, make a note of the idea before it flees for ever. If he tells a good story, write it down. If all else fails, and you can fight off slumber no longer, then you must do your best to organise your forty winks so as to attract the least possible suspicion.

An acquaintance has, through long years of experience, learned how to sleep whilst sitting bolt upright and with his eyes open. Most of us must be content with the head rested on the hand, the elbow on the table. Alternatively, the head droops forward and the notes, brochure or agenda are in front of you so that it may (with luck) appear that you are reading – or at least engaged in deep thought.

Every speaker should learn to amuse himself during the unamusing speeches of others, without any appearance of flagging attention or lagging concentration. Spare a thought for the diplomats and the royals, who must do it all the time.

49 Radio – the sightless wonder

Ask any experienced radio producer or interviewer which are the best and which are the worst categories of performers. Odds on the answer will be the same: the best – professionals, like most actors or politicians – especially politicians, because they are skilled at making up their own scripts as they go along. The worst? Executives – industrialists and business people. Believing that their success in commerce qualifies them for harnessing sound without sight, they mumble, ramble and prevaricate and make the worst of themselves and their case.

So if *you* must make a radio appearance, how can you avoid joining the ranks of the awful? I offer a concise victim's guide.

Start by arriving on time. If the interviewer arrives late he is usurping the host's privilege. If you are late, you either miss the show or you will never be asked back.

The ultimate in reporter lateness provided me with one of my few and cherished but as yet unrealised chances to enter the *Guinness Book of Records*. Some years ago, I arrived my customary few minutes early for a local radio recording session. The reporter was late.

After half an hour of patient waiting, I made my revolutionary proposal to the man in charge: 'Let me interview myself!' I suggested. I promised to ask myself only the nastiest and most probing questions. 'You can dub in the reporter's voice when he turns up!' To my delight, he agreed.

I carried out the interview with immaculate courtesy, but dug away at my own weak points, being sure of course to supply succinct and appropriate answers. When the interviewer turned up, by the judicious use of the razor blade he duly dubbed his voice into the questions.

Second: approach radio with a touch of paranoia. As Henry Kissinger once remarked: 'The fact that I'm paranoid does not mean that I ain't got enemies!' Whether you are asked questions by telephone ('down the line') or in the studio, unless you are certain that your words will not be broadcast, take care.

President Reagan was to make a crucial 'state of the nation' broadcast. The producer said to him: 'Now, Mr President, please will you say something so that we can have some sound level. Tell us what you think about our United States economy?'

'I must tell the nation,' said the President, 'that our economy is in one hell of a mess!' Unfortunately for him, the studio had already been linked up to loudspeakers in the White House and Press Room. Despite the frantic efforts of the President's advisers, his words were beamed around the world, to the huge delight of all those who take pleasure in someone else's awful mistake. He has just repeated his error — in his notorious 'In five minutes we bomb Russia' joke introduction.

So concentrate. Ignore the interviewer sipping his coffee ... news flashes on a monitor screen ... people seen through the glass in the control room, or busy 'cutting' tapes in the next studio. Allow your mind to move off your subject and you invite disaster.

The best help to concentration: posture. Sit up.

If your piece is recorded, do not worry if you 'fluff'. 'Sorry,' you say. 'I'll repeat that.' Then do – and leave it to the interviewer or editor to slice out your initial and muddled effort. They will not hold that against you. They have too many miseries of their own to correct and they are professionals.

Sincerity is vital. Without sight, only your voice can convey it. Be concise and relevant. Answer the questions you are asked – briefly, accurately and to the questioner's point.

Brighten your broadcast with stories and analogies. Talk to the interviewer as though you were engaging in ordinary chat with no one listening. Concentrate on him – and forget your audience.

Take care what you wear, for the sound it may make. Radio broadcasters are heard and not seen. A young woman deafened listeners with a crackling roar, every time she breathed. A particularly sensitive directional mike picked up and magnified the sound of her new, stiff-fabric 'bra'. It may have done wonders for her figure, but it destroyed her broadcast!

Avoid noisy bangles, beads or leather jackets. Do not click ball-point pens or fiddle with paper clips. Above all, avoid the rattle of paper. If you work from a script on separate sheets, do not turn them over. Lift each gingerly and silently from the pile.

Avoid drinking too much 'hospitality coffee' before committing yourself on air for any length of time. Mother Nature has often destroyed the best of discussions. And keep off alcohol. Many careers have been ruined through that most hazardous wedding of broadcast and booze.

Nothing is more daunting in prospect, more challenging in reality or more lasting in memory than a broadcast confrontation. If your interviewer gets nasty, keep cool. You lose control of yourself and of your audience at the same moment. Lose command of yourself and you cannot command the argument.

If they want to turn you into a human sacrifice, don your armour. If they wish to make a meal of you, ensure that you are thoroughly indigestible.

Remember: an interviewer's job is to produce good radio. So if you suspect trouble, try threatening to 'dry' if your interrogator is unfair.

If you are faced with guest opponents, battle for your fair share of precious time. And always try to commandeer the ending.

After a particularly bloody radio confrontation, a supporter of mine said: 'You did well – but not well enough. How *could* you let that *(expletive)* get the last word?'

So be courteous and firm. Find out in advance how long your piece will last. Is it to be pre-recorded, in which case your 'fluffs' can be removed but also your best arguments edited out? Or will you go out 'live', so that your errors cannot be erased?

Do not be bullied. A good interviewer asks his questions and lets his victim get on with answering them. If you do not get fairness, complain. If you need time to think the answer to a question, ask to have it repeated. If you cannot properly reply, say so.

If offered an invitation to speak ill of some other person, as opposed to criticising his opinions, remember that broadcast defamation is libel. Keep awake and take care.

Finally: make sure you are off the air before you relax and speak your mind. Many a good broadcast and the reputation of its maker have been ruined at the same injudicious moment. As 'Uncle Mac' once said at the end of the (much lamented) Children's House: 'Well, that will hold the little bastards for another day...'! At least your livelihood does not depend on your radio excellence – so relax, follow the rules and pray for good luck. You'll need it!

TV – 50
your head on the box

Television is every other sort of presentation writ large. It is the ultimate challenge for the speechmaker or other presenter, with (in general) a maximum audience for exploitation and error alike. To the radio dimension of sound add sight, and errors pile high.

Every TV second counts and must be cherished. Compare the cost of buying, say, a 10-second 'plug' on commercial radio as opposed to the same moment on TV. The higher cost of television reflects its potential power and impact.

Every peril in radio presentation is concentrated, condensed and made, literally, visible. Politicians and business people alike are made and broken by the oblong screen. So if you are given the chance to project yourself, your company or cause on the box, here is your victim's guide.

● Keep calm. Arrive early; check the venue; and if your stomach heaves, remember that adrenalin sharpens the mind.

● Prop up your nerves with alcohol and you invite disaster with the same certainty as the drinking driver. So eat well but drink little.

● The make-up person will take charge of your face, but you should adjust your own dress. Remember that the box magnifies the most minor blemishes. Tie askew ... white label sticking up from the back of the dark jacket ... dandruff on the shoulders ... dangling shirt tail, drooping socks, laddered tights ... If you must look slovenly, do it at home.

● Dress in clothes suitable to the image you wish to present and in colours and patterns that do not move, shimmer or 'strobe' on the screen. Checks or narrow stripes on jackets or (especially) dresses, suits or ties are major culprits. Avoid 'flashy' jewellery, in either sense of that word. Best colours: pastel; worst, black and white.

Your face may be your fortune, but put it on television and it emerges transformed – probably much for the worse. So: relax and hope for the best – and follow some basic rules.

- Fix your gaze on the interviewer or at your fellow gladiator, thrown into the same ring for the pleasure of the public. Eye expression is crucial for contact, confidence and conveying sincerity.

  The victim who surreptitiously swivels his eyes — perhaps for a glimpse of the audience or the clock, or a peep at the monitor screen — is done for. Immediately, by chance or by malicious design, the camera switches to him and he looks shifty, cunning, wicked...

  If you are to be interviewed in a separate place or studio from your interviewer, ask for an 'eye-line'. Find out where to look so that you appear to be fixing your eyes in line with your interrogator.

- Keep gestures to the minimum. The rarer and the more sparing, the greater the effect. Watch amateurs on the screen — the unconscious scratchers, twitchers, lip-lickers and nose-pickers, the finger waggers, arm-wavers and (even more disastrous) the pounders of fists and the strummers of fingers.

  So sit up. Animation should come from your face, your eyes, your speech, and not from your body.

- Treat your interviewer with kindness and – as he is probably human – he may return the compliment. As a distinguished colleague told me when he was about to face a particularly notorious interviewer: 'The key words for him are – **re**spect and **su**spect!'

- Smoking will probably be forbidden in the studio and is in any event inadvisable on the screen. My wife smokes, I used to. She says that if we ever get divorced, the co-respondent will be a cigarette. She is right.

- At the start of the interview, do not smirk. Instead, stare straight ahead.

- Then keep still. A distinguished cleric who is a most relaxed and brilliant TV performer once reached down into his brief case, nestling against his leg, with such speed that he went totally off screen – to the huge delight of his friendly viewers but to the misery of the studio.

  Wise judges watch witnesses when they have left the witness box. Intelligent cameras flash on and off, red lights blinking – when the light is on, so is the camera and so are you.

- If you read from a prepared script, you will be helped by an auto-cue. Be not afraid. It is controlled by the performer and the operator will go at your speed.

- Do not look at the clock. The studio manager – probably the person who led you to your seat – will stand within view of the interviewer and will relay his time signals.

  The time to dive in with your capture-the-last-word summary is when the 'come to a close' hand windmill signal starts. If it means interrupting someone else — courteously but firmly — go ahead.

To succeed on the screen, you must project your personality... radiate relaxation without relaxing... confidence without appearing smug or superior... sincerity without gush... the same qualities, in fact, that apply to personal presentations, but with far greater tact.

So how do you achieve these evidently desirable aims? Take training. Watch yourself on a video screen. And get as much practice as the media will allow you.

You cannot practise for an interview, but you can follow the crucial rules. Listen to the question; have it repeated if you do not understand – or if you want extra time to think; then reply to that question, not to some other one that you would have preferred to hear.

A Cabinet Minister was lost while driving through the countryside. He stopped at a village and wound down his window. 'Where am I, please?' he asked a passer-by.

'You are in your car, sir' he replied, unhesitatingly.

'That,' replied the Minister 'is a perfect Parliamentary answer. It is brief, accurate – and adds nothing whatever to the sum total of human knowledge!'

So try to add a touch of information, a spice of wit or a modicum of common sense or your TV presentation is hardly likely to sparkle. But do so by way of addition or rider. 'The answer to your question is ... But perhaps we could ask a different question?' Or: 'The answer is yes – but please remember that...' First answer, then add.

Keep calm. Do not underestimate your opponent. And if you do get defeated, then announce that you will fight back. Or flick away the defeat like a fly from your shoulder, hoping that it does not matter.

Do not be bullied. If interrupted say: 'May I finish my sentence, please...'; or 'If you don't mind, I'll just finish this point then give way...' Then wrap up your argument as swiftly as you can.

Above all, concentrate. Forget the hundreds of thousands of viewers. A moment's distraction may spell disaster. Lose concentration and you lose all.

A producer once said to me: 'I have my faults. But being wrong isn't one of them!' Like my wife. Follow both their instructions and if you mess up your performance, then at least it may be someone else's fault!

Two waiters once passed behind a diner's chair. One said to the other: 'Look – he's eaten it!' If anyone had heard him, he would have been in trouble.

The joy of television is that everyone both hears and sees you and trouble can only be a fraction of an error away.

Part Six

The chair

The chairman as compère 51

The chairman of a meeting – any meeting – sets the tone. If he is dull, the meeting will be boring. If he is in gay mood, the meeting will be of good cheer. If he is long-winded, members of the audience not bound to stay will disappear. If he is angry, aggravated, tactless or unkind, this will soon be reflected in the atmosphere. Not for one moment dare he be off his guard. He is the compère. . . the life and soul of the gathering – or its death and decay.

Consider the ordinary variety programme. The compère is the link man. He holds the show together. If he fails, it falls apart. The same applies to any chairman.

To keep a meeting in good humour, here are some suggestions.

- Do not allow yourself to get aggravated. The more difficult the gathering, the more important it is for you to keep your self-control and your pleasant manner.

- Set the tone before the meeting begins. Try to do your colleagues or your audience the compliment of arriving on time. Spare a few minutes beforehand, if you can, to iron out difficulties and to prevent personal affronts.

- If the meeting is a small one, try not to ignore people who come in late. 'Good evening. Thank you for coming.' Worthwhile words to make a guilty latecomer feel at ease – and obliged to you.

- There is no need to take too literally the old, chairman's warning: 'Stand up, speak up and shut up.' But do try to let others do as much of the talking as you can. Time them beforehand, if possible. Introduce them . . . invite them to speak. . . ask what they think. Link the speakers together and provide the channel through which they communicate. But yourself – talk only when you must.

- Let your audience feel that they have had their say. Do your best to allow an adequate question time.

- Cajole your speakers into brevity and into agreeing to answer questions at the end. The audience that has its questions answered is almost always satisfied.

- Where the session is a small one – a committee or board

119

meeting, for instance – the same principle is even more vital. Let the others put their views before the gathering. Try not to choke off discussion before it comes to an end. Wait until you get the feeling of the meeting that time has come for the particular debate or argument to be wound up.

● Let everyone feel that his presence is appreciated. One way is by saying so: 'We are delighted to have you all with us.' When the meeting is small enough, make sure that everyone has said something. 'What are your views about this?' The quiet man may have more valuable advice to give than the garrulous soul who monopolises the discussion. The timid participant may be more expert than the exhibitionist. If talent is available, make sure it gets used.

● Do not be afraid to season the proceedings with laughter. A few moments spent on a friendly joke may be more worthwhile than ten times as long devoted to argument. Try to avoid the unkind cut. Round the meeting off with appropriate words of thanks – and set the atmosphere right for the next time.

Most of these suggestions could be brought under one word: tact. You are running the meeting. But (except in case of disorder) you should try not to let it be too obvious. The horse knows when it is mounted by a skilled rider who does not have to keep tugging at the reins or hurting the animal's mouth. The best leaders give their followers the maximum feeling that they (the followers) are running their own show. The top compères keep the programme going and ensure that everyone stays contented and awake. The finest chairmen are those who rule through good humour, quiet tact and gentle persuasion.

52 Controlling the audience

Whether you are dealing with a committee of three or a crowd of 3,000, as chairman you must be in control. Except in the rare cases of people who have deliberately arrived with the intention of breaking up the proceedings, your audience have given up their time for a constructive purpose. It may be the wish to advance the company's business and hence their own prospects. They may be seeking knowledge or entertainment. They may wish to extend the work of their trade charity. Whatever the reason, they wish the business of the meeting to be done. And then they will want to get back to their offices or, at the end of the day and with even more fervour, to their homes. A chairman who controls his audience and hence the business of the meeting is appreciated.

So do not be afraid to put your foot down (metaphorically) or (literally) to tap with the gavel. You were elected or appointed chairman to keep order. Do so and you will have the meeting behind you.

Do not shout. A firm 'Order please, Ladies and Gentlemen'; 'Will you please give Mr Black a fair hearing'; or 'I must insist on quiet for our speaker, please' – these are courteous and successful gambits. Occasionally, you might need: 'I'm afraid that if those who are attempting to break up the meeting will not desist, I shall have to ask the stewards to have them evicted.' But much more common is the 'Thank you, Gentlemen', addressed to those of your colleagues whom you hope to thank for their future silence.

You must know precisely what you are doing. You must understand the basic rules of procedure. But if you do make a mistake, then you have two alternatives, and one or other must be grasped as firmly as possible. Either you stand by your error or you smile and apologise.

Alternatively: 'It is clear that the meeting would, in fact, like to discuss this matter. So be it.' Or: 'You are quite right, Mr Jones. I should have allowed the discussion to go further. Please do carry on.' A graceful retreat. You are being decisive even about your indecision.

Still, it is 'the sense of the meeting' that usually matters. The chairman needs antennae. He must be able to judge what people want. He must employ his tact so as not to override the wishes of those who have seen fit to put him in charge of their proceedings. Whilst not pandering to the inevitable mischief-maker — that abrasive irritant and aggravating nuisance which nearly every organisation, body or community seems to throw up — he must nevertheless give even such persons (who may be right on occasion and who have a certain acid usefulness) the opportunity to let off steam. When the meeting has had enough of them, you will know. And so will the aggravators. Sense your meeting – and run it. That is your job as chairman.

53 Order – and disorder

To some extent, a speaker can and must control his own audience. He must command attention. He must know how to deal with his own hecklers. And, if necessary, he must be prepared to tongue-lash those who will not heed his words. But if the speaker fails, the chairman must step in. It is part of the chairman's task to ensure that the speaker gets a hearing (literally as well as metaphorically).

In most cases, a smart rap with the gavel and a command of 'Order' should suffice. If you have no gavel, a smart rap on the table with a coin, pen-knife or lighter, will probably do the trick. It is also both more effective and more dignified than a pounding of the fist which may, in any event, prove painful.

If disorder breaks out, the chairman must know precisely how to handle it. The main rule, of course, is to handle himself with restraint, calm and dignity. He must never lose his head, or he will have failed. With luck, he will have the secretary sitting beside him, to guide him on procedure. But to know the rules in advance breeds the confidence he needs. The secretary should know them, too. So here they are.

54 Debates and procedure

The chairman must study the rules of debate. His duty is to enforce them. Speakers must know the rules, either to follow them or attempt to evade them.

* * *

The chairman is in charge. He has been elected or appointed to his position and is expected to guide and control the meeting. He is in charge of proceedings.

When the chairman stands, everyone else is expected to sit and to be silent. If the chairman cannot obtain order by rapping his gavel and demanding silence, he may have to adjourn the meeting. Unless the meeting is closed, the chairman is entitled to speak whenever he wishes – and to prevent anyone else from doing so unless he wishes. He decides the order of speeches. He will have the agenda but may vary it. He is in charge.

A good chairman rules by consent. For instance, if he decides to change the order of business, he should explain his reasons. If the bulk of the meeting objects to the change, then he should revert to the original order. He is not a dictator.

Normally, each item of business should be discussed separately. If there are steps to be taken – or even if it is to be resolved that there be no action on the matter – a resolution or motion will be 'put'. This can be done informally, where there is either no opposition or a general consensus. But if after discussion has taken place there is no agreement, there should be a vote.

Where the formalities are being preserved, a motion will be proposed and seconded. It will then be thrown open to the meeting for discussion – and the chairman will attempt to call upon someone who will oppose the motion. After the matter has been sufficiently ventilated, the proposer will normally exercise his right of reply. Then a vote may have to be taken.

If the motion or resolution is not on the agenda, the proposer should be asked to phrase it as concisely and clearly as possible. The chairman who has to put a resolution which even the proposer has not put into sensible English (and into words that can be put into the minute book) is in a bad way. The motion should be clearly stated either by the proposer or by the chairman before it goes forward for debate.

The length and number of speeches will depend upon the chairman. But anyone may 'move the closure'. A show of hands will indicate whether those present have had enough of the subject or whether they wish to debate the matter further. If a chairman is in doubt as to whether or not the debate should be closed – or if he feels that it would appear partisan for him to terminate it – then he can easily test the feeling of the meeting, if necessary by asking whether anyone wishes 'to move the closure'.

If it is agreed that the question 'be now put' – then that is what happens. The motion is voted upon.

If a motion is carried that the meeting move on to 'next business', then no vote is taken on the motion. It is often better not to reveal the split in the ranks. Or all sides may prefer to avoid a vote that no one is really confident of winning.

Some organisations allow the moving of 'the previous question'. The effect of this being passed is that the discussion on the current topic terminates and all reference to it is expunged from the minutes. No vote is, of course, taken on the matter in question. There are times when people feel that it would have been better for the organisation or meeting had the discussion not taken place at all. 'The previous question' is a useful procedure.

Again, someone may move that the entire meeting be adjourned. It is not only the chairman who can terminate the proceedings. If those present at the meeting wish to put an end to it, they may normally do so. But, of course, there may be a lengthy debate 'on the adjournment'.

While the debate goes on, there may be interruptions. One common device is a 'point of order'. Anyone is entitled to raise any point he wishes concerning the order of the meeting, at any time. In theory, he is only free to query as to whether the procedure in hand... what the speaker is saying... the chairman's ruling... is 'in order'. He should not stray away to deal with side issues or to use the occasion to deal with the substantive issues. But skilled interrupters can often disguise their disruptive attacks in the form of 'points of order', and so insinuate extra speeches where none would otherwise be allowed.

In some meetings, the custom is for speakers to give way on 'points of information' – but generally, it is a matter for them (the speakers themselves) to decide. The chairman cannot force them to give way, or take any step if they decline to do so. But if the chairman himself addresses the speaker, the latter may remain standing but (like anyone else at the meeting) must accord the chairman the right to speak – and while he does so, must remain silent.

The speaker, then, must 'obey the chairman's ruling'. The fact that he 'has the floor' does not mean that he is entitled to occupy it in the teeth of objection from the chair.

If all motions were proposed, seconded, opposed and voted upon as they stood, a chairman's life would be moderately easy. But there are always amendments to be considered. In general, motions to amend a resolution must (if seconded) be allowed. They should be considered individually and voted upon if necessary. If accepted (whether or not after a vote) they become incorporated into the original motion, which must then be put, as amended. If rejected, they die. An amended motion, once put, can then be the subject of further amendment, with the procedure as before.

Often a skilled chairman can induce the mover of a resolution to vary or extend its terms so as to incorporate the amendment. A peaceful meeting is a chairman's delight. But if an amendment is really no more than an effort to kill the resolution, he may rule it out of order and require the proposer of the amendment to put forward his views in opposition to the substantive motion.

A chairman must ensure that everyone is given a reasonable opportunity to express his views. But he is not bound to allow a minority to dominate. He is entitled not only to select the speakers but also to sort out the resolutions and the amendments, so that the feelings of the meeting may be tested in the fairest way.

Once the meeting has had a reasonable opportunity to express its view, the chairman himself may – with the consent of the meeting – close the debate and put the motion to the vote.

Some additional points:

● Unless a company's Articles (or the constitution of the organisation in question) require motions to be seconded and/or submitted in writing, neither will be strictly necessary.

● No one has any right to speak more than once on any motion or amendment – although the proposer of an original motion (but not usually of an amendment) will generally be given the right to reply.

● Once a motion has been defeated, it should not be allowed back into the meeting under some other guise.

● No amendment can be proposed after the original motion has been passed or rejected.

● Amendments cannot be proposed or seconded by those who performed that service for the original motion; but they can, of course, accept (or speak on) the amendments proposed by others.

● If you wish to frame an amendment, usually the best way to do so is by moving that the words you have in mind be added to, omitted from, or inserted into (as the case may be) the motion or resolution.

Meetings are usually governed by consent and common sense. The chairman must keep his head and never panic. Speakers should help the chair in every case except that in which the chairman has shown himself to be unwilling to act impartially. In that case, the battle is on.

55 The company chairman

Some of the duties of a chairman are prescribed by law. In the United Kingdom, company chairmen should be referred to the *Companies Act, 1948* and in particular to Sections 58, 134 and 141. More important: he should read with care the company's own Articles of Association, which lay down most of his powers and duties in the conduct of the meetings of the organisation concerned.

In so far as the law and the Articles are silent, the meeting may itself decide on its own conduct. As Lord Russell pronounced in 1937:

> 'There are many matters relating to the conduct of a meeting which lie entirely in the hands of those people who are present and constitute the meeting... It rests with the meeting to decide whether accounts, resolutions, minutes or notices and such like shall be read to the meeting or be taken as read; and when discussion shall be terminated and a vote taken; whether representatives of the Press, or any other persons not qualified to be summoned to the meeting, shall be permitted to be present, or if present, shall be permitted to remain; and whether the meeting shall be adjourned. In all these matters, and they are only instances, the meeting decides, and if necessary a vote must be taken to ascertain the wishes of the majority. If no objection is taken by any constituent of the meeting, the meeting must be taken to be assenting to the course adopted.'

In practice, if you can keep the meeting with you, you win. If you lose its support, you fail.

So what of the person who comes to break up your meeting? As chairman, you have the right to order his removal; or you may adjourn the meeting until 'the disorderly element' has gone.

At a company meeting, you need an experienced company secretary at your side. At any other, seek a wise and experienced colleague to advise on points of order and procedure. If he knows his job, he will ensure that you do yours.

56 Introducing the guest

However well you know the person you are about to introduce, have his name written clearly down in front of you. The chances of your mind going blank are remote. But it happens. The most famous occasion? During the 1970 UK General Election when a local

Conservative party chairperson was introducing Mr Edward Heath: 'In the short time since our guest of honour has become leader of the party,' she thundered, 'his name has become a household word. I am proud, honoured and delighted to introduce to you our next Prime Minister, Mr... er... er... er...' Calamity!

Or: 'The name of our guest is a household word in the trade. Ladies and Gentlemen, Mr er... er... er...'

Or: 'Our guest needs no introduction... without further ado, I am pleased to introduce to you Sir Robert... er... er... er...'

(My son, Daniel, once introduced an unknown and undistinguished MP to the Cambridge Union, thus: 'Mr Smith's name is a household word – in his own household!')

The harm done by forgetting a name cannot be undone. It may happen if the chairman has done his homework. But it is far more likely with inadequate preparation. Those abysmal words 'our guest needs no introduction' generally mean that the chairman has not bothered to find out anything about the speaker. Let your secretary dip into *Who's Who... The Wine Producers' Year Book... The International Dictionary of Great Millionaires...* or whatever the appropriate reference book happens to be.

Alternatively, get someone to phone up the man's assistant or secretary or manager and get some details of his doings. Even better, hunt around for a personal and friendly anecdote. The less it appears that you had to do research, the better – but the more research you do, the more effective your introduction is likely to be.

If the speaker arrives and you have no information about him, do not despair. Speakers appreciate being asked. Take the man on one side and say to him quietly, with your pencil in one hand: 'I am to have the pleasure of introducing you to our audience. Which of your many offices would you like me to mention? How would you like to be introduced?'

Every speaker has his foibles. He may not want you to say that he is an ex-president of the Undertakers' Society – he may have been defeated in a recent and bitter election contest. He may prefer to forget that he was the author of a book that resulted in a libel action. On the other hand, he may especially wish you to remind his audience that he is an ex-president of the Oxford Union ... former secretary to James Director ... a champion golfer, as well as a prominent industrialist or trade union leader.

Or suppose that you are introducing a man who has really fought his way up the ladder. Maybe he would like you to refer to his humble origins. Or perhaps he would rather repress them. Unless someone has given you the tip off, you cannot know.

At a recent dinner, a famous, generous and charitable businessman was introduced to his audience as the man who 'not only conceived the idea of the ... School, but had personally raised the very large sum needed to establish it.' Unfortunately, the chairman had omitted to check on how the school was going. Had he done so, he would have discovered that there were only eight applicants for the 120 places and that the entire venture was a flop which the guest of honour was not anxious to recall.

The mixture of embarrassed silence and delighted laughter that greeted this *faux pas* reflected in no way upon the affection which the audience had for the gentleman concerned, whom everyone knew to be a first-class man. But it made the audience feel sorry for him – and for the chairman. The fact that the chairman was another voluntary worker in good causes and a popular man of business in no way excused an error that could so easily have been avoided.

If you are too busy to prepare your introduction, then get someone else to do it (either the preparation or, if necessary, the introduction itself) for you. There is no law to prevent a chairman from saying: 'I shall now ask his ex-mentor/disciple/managing director (*or as the case may be*) to introduce our guest to you.' It does not happen very often – which makes it all the more delightful when it does.

So speak of your guest's known achievements. By all means couple this with friendly or flattering references to his firm or his forebears. But the following are to be avoided:

'We are very pleased to have Mr Jackson with us tonight. His father is a very famous figure in the industry and we know that, in listening to his son, we shall have a treat awaiting us...'

Little better is: 'Mr Bloggs is the distinguished son of famous parents...'

Much worse (but often committed in practice):

'Lord Bloggs is unfortunately unable to be with us tonight. But we are pleased that Lady Bloggs has consented to speak to us. Without further ado, I introduce Lady Bloggs.'

Lord and Lady Bloggs could have been complimented on their splendid and happy partnership. But the disappointment at the absence of the original guest must not be made apparent. Anyway, has Lady Bloggs herself nothing to commend her other than her good taste in husbands? The Honourable James Bloggs inherited his courtesy title. But surely he has done something with his life which the chairman ought to explain? The guests will be curious to hear something of the background of their speaker. Heredity is not all.

Try this: 'Ours is an industry which is proud of its family connections. Many of us are old colleagues and friends of William Harness. We have been delighted to see the active part taken by his son, Roger, in our great charity. Naturally, we honour him because he is the son of our old and distinguished friend. But he is invited to speak to us tonight in his own right. His achievements are many. He is... he was... and we are confident that he will be a leader in our industry for many years to come. Ladies and Gentlemen, Mr Roger Harness...'

Or: 'Tonight, we are honoured by Lady Bloggs. It is true that her husband was to have addressed us. I will not repeat the gaffe of the chairman who once introduced the wife in circumstances such as these by saying: "Sir William's misfortune in being ill is our good luck. We are indeed happy to welcome his wife in his place." We are delighted that the reason for Lord Bloggs' absence is that he is busy selling his goods in the USA and hence keeping up his company's magnificent export record. We are fortunate that he has been good enough to leave his wife behind in England – and to trust her in our company this evening. He is...'

If (as so often happens) the speaker is a last-minute substitute, do not apologise for the fact. 'We were to have had Mr Hodge to speak to us, but he has let us down at the last minute. We are grateful to Mr Black, his assistant, for stepping into the breach. Ladies and Gentlemen, Mr Black.' There are two decent alternatives. Either ignore altogether the fact that Mr Hodge has let you down. Everyone will know it. The word will have gone around; and it may be much less embarrassing if nothing is said. Alternatively, make a virtue out of necessity.

Thus: 'Ladies and Gentlemen. I know that you will all have been very sorry to have heard that our proposed guest, Mr Arthur Hodge, has been struck down by the flu. But equally, you will be pleased to learn that he is making a good recovery. He sends his greetings to us all – I have a telegram from him here.' (That was intelligent of Mr Hodge, incidentally). 'It wishes us every good fortune. And I know that you will want me to reply, on behalf of us all, wishing him the most speedy recovery.

'I cannot tell Mr Black how grateful we are to him for having agreed to come to us at such very short notice. His readiness to step into the breach is just one indication of his loyalty to our organisation... of one reason at least why he has earned the affection of all of his colleagues... He is... he was... he will be...'

Or: 'Our good friend and proposed guest, Mr Arthur Hodge, has, alas, been called abroad on urgent business. We know that he would never have let us down had there been any possible alternative. We wish him success in his venture – may he bring home the bacon – or, to be more precise, may he have every success in exporting his prize pigs. And we are very much obliged to him for having on our behalf asked Mr Robert Rook to address us in his place.

'Mr Rook is already well known to us. He is... he was... he will be ... We know the pressure of work upon Mr Rook and we are extremely grateful to him for honouring us by joining us this evening. Ladies and Gentlemen, Mr Rook...'

There are, of course, occasions when the speaker should not be introduced. For instance: 'I shall ask our chairman, Edward Smith, to propose the loyal toast.'

Or: 'Thank you, Mr Hodge. I am pleased to ask our treasurer, Richard Bright, to propose the vote of thanks.'

The chairman, then, sets the tone and calls the tune. He has many important duties, one of the most vital of which is the introduction of the speakers. He should treat his job seriously. He should apply the same rules to the brief speeches of introduction as he would to longer efforts. An introduction needs a beginning, a body, and an end. The opening and closing sentences matter. Careful preparation (which, as usual, must be as unobtrusive as possible when the speech is actually made) is important. A bad introduction can ruin a good speech – and a potentially fine meeting.

57 Handling the speaker

No area of a chairman's duties is so potentially hazardous as handling the guest speaker. Here are a few hints:

- If you are not sure how your guest pronounces his name, ask him. If his name is to be put in a programme, toast list, brochure or other document, check that the spelling is correct. People are very sensitive about their names.

- Ascertain in advance as much as you can about the speaker. Members of the Royal Family are renowned for their splendid memories. They come into a room and promptly recognise people and even remember where they last met. This is partly because they are blessed with good memories, but mainly because they do their homework. The best way to flatter your speaker is to remember all about him. The surest way to antagonise him is to be indifferent to him and his past achievements.

- If he has incurred expenses, remember to invite him to let you know.

- Remember to say thank you – and to write and repeat your thanks afterwards. You can never express gratitude too often.

- While trying to ensure that the speaker gets a fair hearing, be careful not to interrupt him too often. Competent speakers can handle their own audiences and prefer, where possible, to do so. The chairman should exercise his authority with moderation.

- Prime the speaker in advance as to the length of time you want him to speak, and ask him whether he would like to be reminded when he is a few minutes away from the appointed end. Most speakers will gladly agree, and will not then resent a reminder. If necessary, push a note in front of the speaker, with '5 minutes to go' in large letters. But to do this without pre-arrangement may upset both the speaker and your friendship with him.

Much of the chairman's job is done before the meeting actually begins. If he reads this book beforehand, he should do better at the time. Otherwise, he can bring it with him... in a plain, white cover if he prefers...

So all that remains is to wish you – in the role of speaker or the chairman – the very best of luck. However experienced and able you may be... however carefully you follow the rules I have given... whatever the occasion... there is no substitute for good fortune. Whether you are on your feet or in the chair, may you be blessed with success.

And I mean this sincerely..
However, let me say this...
Possibly you may feel - as I do..
Furthermore, I would add - as a postscript
FINALLY - let me
In conclusion
ZZZZZZ
ZZZZ

Book Two

DRAFT SPEECHES

Part Seven

Model speeches
for varying occasions

Prominent people are frequently invited to declare functions or occasions duly open – from trade exhibitions or fairs to sales conferences, from new premises to the same old annual garden fete run by the local church or by the trade benevolent society.

The opening pronouncement may be one of two varieties, which must be carefully distinguished from each other – the formal opening and the keynote speech. Either way, you may be asked to speak because of your eminence; because of past usefulness or benevolence; in hope of future service or cash – or a mixture of all of them. If you want to be asked again, though, you must do a good job this time.

The following are examples of brief openers, plus skeletons of keynote speeches which, by their nature, are expected to be longer, fuller and likely to provoke thought or action, rather than an atomosphere of generalised goodwill.

Opening a trade fair

Mr Chairman, Ladies and Gentlemen.

Some ancient peoples had disgusting habits – like examining the entrails of animals to see whether the auguries were satisfactory for some proposed enterprise. I have taken a much shorter and pleasanter route – to the greater oracle of this organisation – Mr... He tells me that the preparations for today's gathering have been carried out swiftly, in harmony and without a whiff of industrial ill-will; that advance orders already total half as much again as those received at this stage last year; that we are expecting one of the biggest gatherings in the history of the trade.

What a delight it is, then, for me to sound the tocsin and to proclaim in advance the value, the importance and the success of this year's vital exhibition.

On your behalf as well as my own, I thank our organisers – Mr... and Mrs ... and Miss ..., as well as ... and their staff. If the arrangements look smooth and simple, it is because the organisers have worked so hard.

And now – in anticipation of good companionship, top sales and a continuation and ending to the fair which will be as successful as its inception – I have the greatest pleasure in declaring the fair – open.

Opening an industrial exhibition

Mr Chairman, Ladies and Gentlemen,

We are not as wasteful in this industry as our colleagues who build ships. We will not smash and spill good champagne on the side of our machines (*or: furniture or equipment – or as the case may be*). Instead, we will use the wine to drink a series of toasts.

First, we drink to the prosperity of our trade/industry/company. Today's effort is of vast importance to it and so to us all.

Second, we toast the health of those whose efforts have created this exhibition – from our chairman/chief executive/organiser (*etc.*) at the top of our trees, to the carpenter, the electricians and the cleaners who have firmed down its roots. Our warmest thanks to them all.

Third, we drink to the future of our great new product, the...(*here give details*).

This is an exhibition of machinery/equipment/furniture (*or as the case may be*). It is designed to exhibit products – and to help design exhibits. Its success depends on order and cheques, not on words – however warm or well meant.

Symbolically only, then, I am proud to launch this exhibition. By its end, I hope that we shall drink a toast to the beginning of a new era of prosperity for our trade/industry/company.

Mr Chairman, Ladies and Gentlemen – I declare the exhibition open.

Opening a new building

Mr Chairman, Ladies and Gentlemen,

Like most of us here, I have survived many happy, successful but hideously cramped, cribbed, cabined and confined years in our old premises. It is therefore with delight that I can declare this new building open.

Think what we can now do. Each of us can swing as many cats as we wish; turn around in our chairs without being accused of indecent assault; drink a cup of coffee without worrying whether we have swallowed our neighbour's sustenance.

Seriously, we can now expand our business and, inevitably I hope, our profits – so bringing delight to our bank manager, to our share-holders and to all of us who are a proud part of our enterprise. We hope that we will pack our custom-built building with more and more satisfied customers. Certainly we shall be able to do our work and not only with greater economy and speed but also in greater comfort – and that is important because the environment of our workforce has taken top priority in the plans for our new structure.

Mr Chairman, Ladies and Gentlemen – this is a time for building. The bricks, the mortar, the cement, the steel – all is in place. We must now build the business – and have done with the words – mine or anyone else's. I thank the architects, Messrs...; I thank all of you for putting up with the inevitable discomfort involved in the move; I thank those who have organised this reception and, in particular, our own Miss ... I most happily declare this new building – open.

Opening an old people's home

Mr Chairman, Ladies and Gentlemen,

A sage once divided charity into categories of merit. At the bottom came gifts where the donor was known to the recipient and the recipient to the donor. At the top were those where neither knew the other. This old people's home has been created by the generosity of the trade/industry – individuals, firms and companies – each giving so that others may enjoy their old age.

There is far too much clap-trap talked about old age, isn't there? Autumn years ... senior citizens ... well earned years of pleasurable rest ... Well, that's how they should be. But too often, they are years of loneliness and poverty.

But not for the residents of this home. Here they will have privacy in their own rooms ... companionship in the communal rooms... relaxation in the gardens ... peace when they want it but kindly supervision and help when they need it.

Your committee has had more trouble in selecting residents than it has even had in the raising of the money for the building. With hundreds in need, how do we select the tens who get help? Who are we to select to live here in happiness and who to die alone? All have served the trade/industry; all deserve service from us.

So my functions are twofold. First, I join you in looking back with pride and thankfulness to what has been achieved – and in thanking those responsible. Our special gratitude to... and... and...

Second, we must now service and expand the home.

I once went to a very rich man and asked him for the money to create a building for a certain charity. He replied: 'How are you going to run it ... to staff it ... to pay for it once it is opened? I am tired of giving buildings and then having the same people come back to me and saying: "What's the good of giving the building without the running costs?"'

Well, we have the building – given not by one man but by

many – our thanks to them all. And we have enough to keep the place going for ... months. Did you know that it costs about ... to pay for each resident for each year?

So in thanking you all for your kindness and generosity ... for your presence here today and for your presents to this home in the past – I ask for your support in the future. We close one era when we open another.

Mr Chairman, Ladies and Gentlemen – it is with the greatest of pride – and in the hope and confidence that this home will provide a great comfort and joy to its residents – that I declare the building open.

Keynote – sales conference

Mr Chairman, Colleagues and Friends,

This company lives through sales – and we all live through the company. It is by building the sales that we can not only ensure a prosperous future for the organisation but also for each one of us here. We are part of the same enterprise. This conference has been carefully designed to help us all in our work.

I am happy to introduce to you not only the conference but also our new season's range/tremendously successful line/ to introduce our.../new equipment, specially designed for our market by... *(or as the case may be).*

(Description and explanation of product/service, etc, follows)

The key to this conference, then, lies in expanding our territory and our sales – but with the help of our new lines/products/equipment *(etc.).*

My introduction marks the beginning of two/three days/weeks of intensive discussion/instruction/conference – which I am confident will herald with a fanfare of trumpets the start of a year of distinction and prosperity.

The conference will also enable us to get to know each other socially and to enjoy that good companionship that is so much part of the atmosphere of this organisation. On behalf of your board/directors/chairman, I wish you good days and fruitful discussions – followed by brisk and burgeoning sales and continuing success for the company and for all of you. I am happy to declare this conference duly opened. Good luck to you all.

Opening an exhibition

Mr Chairman, Ladies and Gentlemen,

We are honoured to be holding in our shop/factory an exhibition of paintings by Martha Smith and of sculpture by Roger Jones, drawing their inspiration from our trade/industry.

You will all have seen the brochure/catalogue, designed by our own Walter Brown. One half, read from the top, sets out the work of Martha Smith; the other half, reading from the bottom of the page, lists the sculpture of Roger Jones.

I know that our two guest artists will not be offended if I say that the hanging committee felt a little like the brochure – not quite sure which way up to hang some of the pictures or to stand some of the sculptures. No matter. The shapes are glorious and the colours superb.

You will, I am sure, be as delighted as I was to learn that each of the artists has offered to donate one work to our trade charity. This is immensely kind of them and we are very grateful.

I am told that it took Martha Smith about a week to create each painting and Roger Jones took nearly as long with his larger sculptures. But it is not the time and motion that matters but the spirit.

Many years ago, when a pound was twenty shillings and worth a sovereign of gold, the painter Rex Whistler claimed £500 for a portrait in oils, commissioned by a client. No price had been agreed and he sued on a *quantum meruit*, claiming that £500 was reasonable and right.

Counsel cross-examined him on behalf of the client. 'Mr Whistler,' he said, 'how long did it take you to paint this portrait?'

'Three days,' the artist replied.

'Then are you asking my client to pay £500 for three days' work?'

'No,' retorted the painter. 'I am claiming £500 for a lifetime of work which enabled me to paint this portrait in three days'.

It was not the time that was taken by our generous artists which is the dominant matter – it is their lifetime of skill which has made each of them predominant in his or her own sphere. They are giving us of their own best work. I offer them on behalf of all of us our warmest thanks.

Industry and commerce take pride in design. Individually, we may not be able to be patrons of the arts. But an exhibition of this sort enables us to harmonise artistic forms with our working environments. It is an experiment that deserves success. It is a contribution that we can make to the artist's fame and which the artists make to our pleasure and understanding.

The time has now come, then, for each of us to browse, to look and to learn. There may be some of you who are capable artists – I have trouble in drawing a circle with the help of a compass. A cynic remarked: 'He who can, does; he who can't, teaches.' We might say: 'He who can't visits exhibitions and admires those who can.'

We have an exhibition now and here. I thank the artists for bringing that collection together and enabling us to enjoy it at our leisure. I have much pleasure in declaring the exhibition – open.

59 Guests of honour

To the disabled

Mr Chairman, Ladies and Gentlemen,

Some people are obviously disabled because they are missing a limb..., because parts of their body do not work properly. But I know plenty of people whose bodies are in excellent shape, but who never use their heads. I congratulate this organisation on its work because it helps disabled people to make the best possible use of their assets – and encourages people here, who have absolutely excellent heads, to use them, and to compensate for their physical disabilities.

We must each make use of the assets we have. This organisation helps its members to recognise and to exploit those assets to the full.

Far too many disabled folk are left vegetating at home. You help to get them out into society, so that they are part of the world, making their contribution and enjoying doing so.

Your committee are themselves disabled – but by their work they have not only brought new and vigorous life to others, but have – I know and they know – enriched their own lives in the process.

I congratulate the committee for their efforts; I welcome so many members here today; I am delighted to be your guest of honour – and to give any impetus I can to your efforts, today and every day – and I thank you very much for inviting me.

Now, my friends – on with the party...

Note: This approach is, of course, designed for the physically handicapped. A variation for the mentally ill-equipped follows.

For the mentally handicapped

Mr Chairman, Ladies and Gentlemen,

Our object must be to enable each member of our society to make the best of his assets.

When I went into the Army, many long years ago, my closest friend was a postman's son. We had sat our aptitude tests together.

I found the verbal reasoning and intelligence test extremely easy. The first question sticks in my mind: 'The sun is blue, yellow, green – cross out the answers which do not apply.'

Dick managed the first couple of dozen questions without too much difficulty, but he then came to a dead halt. His vocabulary was tiny.

Next came technical aptitudes. I spent the first half hour trying to assemble a lock and the second a bicycle pump. I failed totally on both. Dick performed all 10 puzzles without the least difficulty.

We all have different talents and the handiwork done by members of this club and on exhibition here today shows how much pleasure they can give to others – and at the same time, to themselves. They have a right to develop their talents to the full – and I congratulate the committee and organisers of this club for the work they have done to enable the members to enjoy their lives.

This place is full of happiness, isn't it? People have the odd idea that where human beings are not blessed with the same degree of mental aptitude as themselves, they are necessarily less happy. Some of the most miserable people I have ever met were of genius level – and some of them were immensely wealthy into the bargain. I congratulate you all on the measure of happiness which this organisation brings not only to its members but also to those who love and care for them.

Thank you, then, for inviting me to be your guest of honour, you, the organisers and committee and your members – and I am at your service and proud to be here among you. The very best of luck to you all.

Note: This speech is essentially aimed at the organisers – with the probability that the members will not understand. You must always decide to whom you are going to speak. If you are addressing a school audience – then never mind the parents, talk to the youngsters. Thus:

School celebration

Headmaster, Parents, Boys and Girls,

I am here as a Governor of the school – which is a grand word isn't it? The Governor of a *prison* is top boss. The Governor of this school is only one of a group – all of whom work together with the Head and his staff to help you, the pupils, to make the most of your time here.

Why, then, is this school different from others? Why should I and my fellow Governors be proud to be associated with it?

First...

Second...

Third...

Well, I expect you know the story of Henry VIII – and what a happy time he had, didn't he? I say to you – as he said to each of his wives in turn: 'I shall not keep you long!'

Didn't he say that? Unfortunately many of the best historical tales are not necessarily accurate. Like the one about Oliver Cromwell. Charles II definitely did dig him up, lift off the lid of his coffin, chop off his head and put it on a pike on the roof of Westminster Hall for six years – that is the ancient Hall of the Palace of Westminster – the only part of Parliament which is still standing almost as it was when it was first built.

What cannot be proved is the old story, that when the head was on the pike on the roof of the Hall, it dripped blood down onto the flagstones for six years. Then one night there was a terrible storm and the head blew down with a horrible thud. A huge cat ran out of the crypt, grabbed the head in its teeth and was rushing off towards the door when the Sergeant at Arms – our sort of Head Prefect – drew his sword, speared the cat and grasped old Cromwell's head.

The next part is true. The head was then taken up to Sidney Sussex College in Cambridge and duly buried. It is there to this day.

I do not recommend that you use that story in your history essays – but I do hope that someone will take you to Westminster Hall one day. If you look carefully enough, you might even find Oliver Cromwell's blood still on the flag stones.

Anyway before my blood is spilled for taking up too much of your time, I will simply wish you well ... congratulate you all on a tremendous year of success ... wish you happiness for the holidays ... (*or as the case may be*).

Good luck to you all.

Note: Personal reminiscence is essential – and can be achieved without being egocentric or immodest. Otherwise, an imaginative tale enlivens any speech. Draw from your own experience or from anyone else's – but do not talk down to your audience – whatever its age.

At prize-givings, avoid telling children how badly you did when you were young – even if it was true, they will not believe it. But do by all means remember the children who get no prizes. Skip the tale of how dreadfully Winston Churchill did as a boy – and try something like this:

Prize-giving

Headteacher, Parents, Boys and Girls,

It's marvellous being top of the class, head of the school, a prefect or a monitor, isn't it? Even being in the top form gives you status. You are a senior character, looked up to by the new pupils.

Unfortunately, no sooner do we reach one pinnacle – no sooner do we get to the top of one mountain – than we slide right down again and, once more, become new boys and new girls – 'freshers' as they call them in college.

All you leavers will be feeling a bit nostalgic today. When you start your new school, university or college – at your work – you will be back down at the bottom again.

Naturally, those of you who have won prizes today – and I congratulate you all – will treasure them as a memento of a happy and successful occasion. But you will be no higher on the ladder than those of your friends, who will be joining you at your work, without prizes. And next time, it may be their turn.

In many ways it is a pity that we have to have prizes at all isn't it? Many people here, I know, will have worked very hard and done extremely well but will not be getting rewarded. Never mind. Your turn will come.

Just think of all the successful politicians and scientists – and teachers – whom everybody congratulated and who won all the rich prizes in civilisation. Ten years later, where are they? Where is the businessman ... the captain of industry ... the big boss ...? They retire and are forgotten about and that is the end of them.

Well, you are not retiring, any of you, are you?

Apart from presenting your prizes, which I shall look forward to doing, my task is simply to wish you all well – wherever you are going, whatever you do. I hope that your ambitions will be fulfilled.

As for those of you who remain – I hope that you will have very happy times ahead. Next year, some of you will reach the top. Enjoy it. Jimmy Durante the famous American comedian, once remarked:

'Be nice to people you pass on your way up because you will pass them again on your way down!'

145

To all of you who are going up or down – and even to a few who are staying still – the very best of luck to you – and thank you for inviting me to be with you today.

Note: Never mind the parents. They will enjoy your talking to the children. But adapt your words according to the age of the youngsters. Chat to them as if they were your own. A child can see through pomposity or insincerity far better than an adult. You may be elevated onto a platform – but pretend that you are in and amongst them. Indeed, it is sometimes possible to climb off the stage. On great state occasions, the dignities and proprieties have to be maintained. But when talking to children, I try to perch on the edge of a table, to walk down among them – or even to remove my jacket and to hang it on the back of a chair – that almost always breaks the ice.

A beginning that I was taught by a member of the Magic Circle – and which requires a certain sleight of hand that I have enjoyed acquiring – goes like this.

Magic opening

Good Morning,

I am sorry that you are all looking so sad. I promise you that I am not going to bore you. So you can relax. There's a chap sleeping at the back – I can see you.

What's this ... (*holding up a coin in left hand*).

It's an ordinary coin, isn't it? (*vanish coin*).

Now where is it? (*inevitable gasps and cries of 'It's in your pocket ... It's up your sleeve ... '*)

No, it's just gone, but you are not going until I have finished talking to you, so you might just as well relax...

Note: At one famous school, there was a long pause before proceedings began. It was a small room, with about 50 restless youngsters in it. I said: 'I am sorry to keep you. We shall be starting soon.' 'I shall say when we begin,' the Headmaster reproved me, publicly and rudely. This sort of treatment of a guest is unusual – but one reproof of that sort is too many. Always consult the organisers, chief citizens or bosses of the place or occasion before opening your honoured mouth.

Equally you must choose your opening – and, for that matter, tailor your speech according to the nature and dignity of the occasion. If in doubt, relax. But there are those that regard too informal an approach as a slur – as not recognising the importance either of the occasion or (worse) those present. Tread warily on the dignity of others.

For the homeless and unhoused

Ladies and Gentlemen,

Some regard homes as chattels to be bought and sold. Others – including everybody here – consider a home to be part of a person's entitlement. So is it not scandalous that so many people are so shockingly housed?

I am delighted to be with you today because you are working to provide roofs for the homeless – and more, to help those in homes to put down their roots and to cope.

Those are the twin challenges. First, there is the physcial worry of providing a place for people to live in decent happiness and contentment. Second, there are many in our civilisation who cannot cope with life, even when they have a home to live in.

It is this last category that provides so many of our most underprivileged and deprived. They are inarticulate; they have no Members of Parliament, because they are on no register; they drift rootless through a world that prefers to disregard them.

Just as those who know no medicine tell the chronically depressed to 'snap out of it', making matters infinitely worse – so those who are able to cope with life tend not to understand the troubles of those who are inadequate.

This organisation... (*set out its objects*).

This organisation... (*set out its successes*).

This organisation... (*set out its remaining problems and how the person can help to solve them*).

To this organisation and all who struggle for it – and to those whom it seeks to help – my warm and affectionate greetings. If my colleagues and I can be of help to you, we shall be pleased – meanwhile, we are delighted to be associated your work.

Note: This sort of speech can easily be adapted for every industrial or benevolent association.

The magic of speech

Speechmakers are (or certainly should be) entertainers. And occasionally we politicans get invited into the entertainment world.The following speech was the first of the evening at a grand banquet held by the International Brotherhood of Magicians in

London. Guests included not only some of the world's outstanding men of magic but a star-studded array of show-business personalities.

Note the break towards the end where (with a borrowed touch of showman's flourish) I introduced a special presentation.

Mr President, Ladies and Gentlemen,

The toastmaster has just whispered in my ear: 'Would you like to speak now, Mr Janner – or shall we let them go on enjoying themselves a little longer?' I think he had forgotten that politicians, like magicians, are part of the entertainment business. The main difference between us is that politicians do infinitely more harm.

I think that there are only two people that can make coins and notes disappear swifter than David Berglas – the Chancellor of the Exchequer – and my wife, Myra. Myra and I are both delighted to be with you this evening.

The first time that I saw David Berglas working – perfectly, as always – was about 25 years ago. At that time, I was running a folk music group in the Brady Boys' Club, in a particularly tough part of London's East End. We were desperately short of funds so we decided to organise a public concert. I asked friends in the entertainment world – who among the great and the famous were the most likely to help us if they could? They gave me three names – all of whom consented.

The first was that spirited and warm-hearted singer, Alma Cogan. The second was that prince of character actors, David Kossoff. And the third was our President, radio and TV's man of magic, David Berglas.

David not only took part in the concert but I remember how he took under his wing a young and very underprivileged magician who specialised in the floating ball illusion, accompanied by music of my group. He encouraged and coaxed and baffled the lad – who adored him.

Since then, I have seen how David has with quiet and dignified reticence used the magic of magic to bring entertainment and happiness to people who have needed it badly.

Several years ago, David gave up his Christmas holiday. He came with me to Leicester and he put on shows for old people, for children and for youngsters in a local reform school.

Tonight I have a surprise for him. I wish to make him a small presentation. I have searched for a 'Berglas' – which I have always presumed was a sort of Holy Grail which casts no shadow. But instead I have found a Wedgwood Parliamentary inscribed goblet – which I will now ask him to accept as a token of appreciation not merely from me but especially from those thousands of people whom he has so freely entertained and helped without any possibility of reward – and who do not enjoy my honour of paying tribute to him tonight.

* * *

Those who believe that politicians and magicians lead wholly glamorous and undemanding lives suffer from a very common and pernicious delusion. But few recognise the strains which these lives place upon our wives. Tonight we pay tribute not only to David but to that splendid lady who has held tightly to him on his roller coaster of fortune for the past 30 years — to Ruth Berglas — and also to their children.

Just as our affection for David is a link between all of us, so the British Ring of the International Brotherhood of Magicians provides a link between men of magic of many lands – a link that holds far tighter than the classic Chinese rings – and the British Ring with over 1,500 members is the largest in the entire chain.

I ask you to rise and to drink a toast – to the British Ring of the International Brotherhood of Magicians – to its President, David Berglas – and to Ruth, his wife. May they enjoy the magic of good health and happy fulfilment together, for very many years to come.

Benevolent or other trade association

Dear Friends,

We are all part of the same trade/industry aren't we? Some of us are more fortunate than others – and those of us who are here today are certainly very lucky.

It has not all been smooth sailing, has it? We can all remember difficult days when we might have been toppled into trouble.

I know some people here who have fought their way back to the top, after slithering into great difficulty, usually by no fault of their own.

However, this benevolent association of ours is designed to help those who have not been fortunate enough to make success a permanence – who need a broad shoulder, to lean on.

The association has many achievements ... (*outline them*). The association has great plans ... (*outline them*).

This gathering today is designed to ... (*set out objects of meeting*).

My colleagues and myself are honoured to be part of your work. I am delighted to be your guest/chairman – and I can assure you that I will do everything in my power to help. 'There but for the Grace of God' go any of us, in our great industry.

60 Introductions, greetings and thanks

To the Minister

Mr Chairman, Secretary of State, Ladies and Gentlemen,

We are all very grateful to the Minister for joining our family *(or: the family of our trade, industry or as the case may be)* when he could so easily and comfortably have been with his own. We appreciate not only what he has said, but the fact that he has snatched the time to be with us today.

I once asked a friend who is a safety officer how he defined his job. 'Oh,' he replied, 'I'm in charge of accidents!' By that token, the Minister is in charge of illness, deprivation and disease *(or unemployment or as the case may be)*. He deals with our problems and his own with admirable calm – and for the sake of us all, we wish him success.

For our part, we recognise the acute dangers created for our society by any condition of unrest. When people regard all politicians with equal distaste, democracy is in danger. A statesman was once defined as a dead politician. We are glad that there are live statesmen like our guest, concerned with the affairs of our land.

(Then refer to one or two points made by the guest.)

So once again I thank the Minister for giving this event the accolade of his lively presence – and I ask you to join me in expressing to him our warmest appreciation.

Apologies for a small audience

There is nothing in the speaker's world more embarrassing than bringing a prominent guest to speak to your organisation, membership or club and then to find that – for whatever reason – the audience is pathetically small. How do you handle the situation?

● Make your apologies as best you can – relying on the foul weather, apparent trade disputes – or any other excuse that seems reasonable.

- If possible, transfer to a smaller room – a few people in a small room make a fine audience – a small crowd is lost in a huge hall.

- Adapt your introduction to the occasion. Thus:

Distinguished Guest, Ladies and Gentlemen,

I know that we will all be sorry that the weather *(the strike or as the case may be)* has kept so many people away. We are to have the treat. We are the fortunate few. I am reminded of a story: Mr Brezhnev and Mr Kosygin were discussing the problems of the Jewish minority wanting to emigrate. Mr Brezhnev said: 'Why don't we let them go?'

Mr Kosygin replied: 'Once you let them out, you will have to release the Ukranians, the Armenians, the Baptists, the Uzbeks. . . and after that, I will go . . . You will be the only person left. . . '

Mr Brezhnev replied: 'No. I shall not be alone. The Soviet Union will be empty!'

We are far from empty this evening, we have here among the most distinguished members/some of our top industrialists/some of the most famous men in our trade.

We have gathered here because we know of the work of our guest – and on behalf of us all, I welcome him to. . .

(Then give details of the guest's work.)

Ladies and Gentlemen, I present Mr. . .

Thanks – surprise tale

Mr Chairman, Ladies and Gentlemen,

I am delighted to propose the vote of thanks to our guest speaker, Mr. . . He is a man of enormous distinction and we are very grateful to him for visiting us tonight.

Perhaps one reason why Mr. . . has become so famous is, curiously, his unassuming and almost deceptive approach. He reminds me of the true story of a Member of Parliament driving home at 3 o'clock in the morning, after a particularly late sitting. He drew up outside the Members' entrance to see whether anyone wanted a lift home and a colleague asked him whether he would take a friend to North London. 'With pleasure' said the MP, and ushered the middle-aged balding gentleman into the passenger seat.

It soon became clear that the guest had been taking advantage of the evening to enjoy the delights of the Strangers' Bar. After giving his instructions as to where he wanted to go, he started dozing off.

'Are you one of the new Members?' asked the politician.

'No, I am a Union Official,' the guest replied.

'Do you live in London?'

'No, in Scotland.'

The MP turned on the radio and the news reader was describing some important union events. 'You had better listen to this,' he said to his guest.

'Oh, I have heard it all before,' said the guest.

About 15 minutes later, the MP asked the guest what his name was. The answer shook the politician rigid – his guest was one of the most famous trade union leaders in the land.

'I am very pleased to meet you,' said the MP. 'I am Member of Parliament for...', and he named his seat.

'You are what?' retorted the guest, obviously startled. 'You are an MP? What the bloody hell are you doing driving a taxi around London at this time of night?'

Once the embarrassment of the misunderstanding had been cleared away, the two men became friends – and have remained friends ever since.

Ladies and Gentlemen, I was the MP – and our guest of honour tonight was that union leader.

We salute him ... we thank him ... and we wish him great success and good fortune in the future.

Thanks to celebrity

Ladies and Gentlemen,

I regret that I have only got to know our guest speaker tonight – personally, that is. Like most of you, I have long admired him from afar – in the press, on the radio, on television – for his devotion to the fate of others. The chance that has brought us together this evening is undramatic – but very welcome.

Mr ... *(naming the speaker)* – we are very grateful to you – and hope that you will join us again often. We wish you well in your work and we thank you for telling us about it.

Retirement

Mr Chairman, Colleagues and Friends,

It will seem strange to attend a meeting of the ... without Arthur Jones presiding over it. In the past ... months/years, he has established himself as the epitome of all that is best in our trade/industry/organisation. There is much to thank him for.

First, I thank him for the kindly way in which he has referred to me. He has been warm, generous and extremely accurate ...

I can therefore say with equal accuracy that his qualities of ... and

... have enlightened his period of office and helped him to create a vibrant organisation.

Most of us here are forthright individualists – or we would not be doing this job. We may disagree as to the best way to serve our customers/clients/firm's business interest. We argue, we debate and we dispute. But we are united in our admiration for Mr...

Let me list some of his achievements during the past ... *(expand on his achievements)*.

And now that his period of office is over, we know that we will receive the same unassuming, kindly and affectionate welcome – and the same help – from him as a fellow member of our ... as we did when he held the highest office and honour that we could give him.

The Poet wrote:

Sound, sound the clarion, fill the fife
Let all the sensual world proclaim
One crowded hour of glorious life
Is worth an age without a name.

Our friend, and mentor, Arthur Jones, has enjoyed his very crowded hour – and he has put glorious life into our proceedings/ company/organisation. We thank him – and we wish him well.

Distinguished guests

Ladies and Gentlemen,

In the unavoidable absence of our President, I have been asked on behalf of the guest to thank our hosts for the spendid, austerity lunch *(smoked salmon sandwiches)*. I would wish this sort of austerity on all businessmen, everywhere.

In particular, I thank our two guests for joining us – and for their enthusiastic words. How they adjust – physically and mentally – to their eternal round of the world is a mystery. Maybe it is due to the sustenance provided by the international smoked salmon sandwich.

One of our guests is a lawyer – the other is a financier. When justice and money come together on the same platform, then indeed we have found common cause.

We have listened with immense care to their speeches – and I can assure them that we are happy to associate ourselves with their work. *(Then a few sentences about that work.)*

We are involved – and we are all grateful to our guests for increasing that involvement. We look forward to seeing our guests back with us again very soon – and next time for a much longer stay.

61 Business speeches

Meetings – of companies and corporations

The lengthier the meeting, the greater its potential for conflict and harm. The Chairman's Report should set the tone; set out essential facts that shareholders need to know; and indicate future prospects.

Remembering that this report will often be published, it should be prepared with care and read with precision. It may be preceded or concluded with embellishments, naturally or apparently impromptu.

I am grateful to Lord Sieff of Brimpton for his permission to reproduce the following typically brisk and model example of a report that he gave to shareholders in Marks & Spencer.

Statement by the Chairman of Marks & Spencer, Lord Sieff of Brimpton

During the last six months, economic recession has deepened, unemployment increased and inflation remained high. In these circumstances our sales are encouraging, particularly as there has been an improvement in August and September.

The recent improvement is largely due to better values in clothing and foodstuffs where, as a result of co-operation with our suppliers, we have substantially reduced the price of a number of major items. Our clothing prices are now only 2 per cent and our food prices 8 per cent higher than a year ago. These improved values have been achieved while maintaining St Michael high-quality standards.

If the present trend continues we expect the full year's profits to be satisfactory.

We have continued our long-term policy of 'Buying British'. In recent years a number of major suppliers have invested substantially in the most modern equipment. By working closely with them we have been able, in nearly all cases, successfully to meet the challenge of imported clothing.

On April 1st we awarded salary increases to our staff three months earlier than last year. As a result, compared with last year, the first six months' costs include an additional quarter's salary increase amounting to approximately £3¾ million. This now completes the rephasing of our salary reviews which we intend to take place at the beginning of April in future years.

Our Canadian operation is making progress. In Europe we face similar economic problems to the UK. A substantial proportion of the merchandise sold is manufactured in the UK and margins have suffered from the strength of sterling.

The Directors have declared an interim dividend of 1.5p per share, the same as last year, which will be paid on 16th January 1981 to shareholders

whose names are on the Register of Members at the close of business on
14th November 1980.

State of the industry

I am happy to have this opportunity to review the state of our
industry – and to appeal on behalf of all of us for government
understanding and help. We have honourably adhered to
governmental guidelines and advice. We have – as Ministers have
sometimes unhappily put it – cut away the fat. But we are becoming
extremely and dangerously lean. First, the dangers. They are many.

We face increased competition from countries where employees
are paid miserably low wages. We contend with the dumping of
goods by suppliers who – directly or indirectly – lawfully or
otherwise – are heavily subsidised by their governments. And no
government appears ready to help us to meet this unfair competition.

We are neither against competition nor imports. We recognise the
needs of others to sell. And we must export to live. We know that if
we place undue restriction on our imports, then we must expect the
same treatment by others to whom we must export. We are against
unfair competition ... *unfair* imports ... *improper* dumping ...
wilful subsidy by others, unmatched by governmental aid to our
ailing industry.

Add to these overseas miseries over which we have no control
whatever the results of our own recession ... the state of the
currency ... the weakness of our economy ... the problems of
overseas demand matched by the collapse of our market – and the
reasons for my anxiety are clear.

So let us plan and plot ... organise and lobby ... work together
for the preservation of our industry. Let us learn from the unions that
individually we are weak, but if we fight and use our unity, then these
times of trouble have brought great lessons for us all.

Remedies

The diagnosis for our trade is clear – cure the recessional
misery.That cure requires capital and investment – but above all,
hope and confidence.

The time for cutting each other's industrial throats has passed. We
must now work together for the survival of..., recognising that
collapse for one is a signal of tempest for all.

So my colleagues and I are proposing the following specific steps,
to draw our plight to the government's attention and to take

constructive help with our problems – not least in preserving employment in this key area of our industry.

First...

Second...

Third...

I commend these proposals to you. I ask you to accept them unanimously. We need more confidence and you need leadership, which we have now united together to provide.

62 Unions and colleagues

Never talk down to anyone – least of all to trade unions. I have watched speeches collapse into ruin at school prize-givings, company occcasions, debates at universities and conferences of trade unions – nearly always because the speaker made it plain that he regarded his listeners as inferior, whether by reason of their youth, their education, their status, or otherwise. Conversely, nearly all the most successful speeches shine because the listener is treated as a colleague, a partner, an equal.

Trade unions are especially sensitive to apparent condescension, even when it is in fact a mask for shyness or apprehension.

The younger and the less educated the audience, the greater its nose for the scent of insincerity. And you only fool your unions once. They will not trust you again. Nor will they accept your invitation to share with them the miseries of recession if you do not also let them benefit in times of profit. Provided that their accounts will not reach the eyes of their creditors, employers are always glad to show the miseries to their workforce. But in days of gloom, the accounts only emerge after due provision has been made for the pension reserve fund and other receptacles for profits that are better unseen.

So the key to a successful speech to employees – and especially to those with the combined strength provided by a well run union – is: the sharing of information, anxieties and hopes, with sincerity and frankness. Or to use a useful American phrase: 'Level with them...'

Disclosure

Mr Chairman, Ladies and Gentlemen,

Thank you for agreeing to meet me today. I would like to explain to you very briefly the position of the company and our plans and hopes for the future. Then I shall be glad to answer your questions.

Our company secretary, Roger White – who is, of course, here with me – has just provided your board with our latest figures. I have provided a summary for each of you – and when I have concluded this introduction, Roger will be glad to join me in answering your questions on these accounts. They provide management with a guide to liability and prospects. And they will give you an indication of the state of business which, of course, provides a livelihood for us all.

Remembering that the period covered is the year/six months/three months from ... to ..., let me summarise for you:

First: the turnover during this period increased/decreased from ... to ...

Second: our workforce grew/diminished from ... to ...

Third: working days lost through absenteeism due to illness rose/fell from ... to ...; and from industrial action rose/fell from ... to ...

Fourth: and do please treat this information as entirely confidential – in broad terms, at the start of this period we had enough orders on our books to keep us busy/on full-time working for a period of ... weeks/months. We can now see confidently ahead only until ...

Our plans for the future are as follows.

We shall make every effort to retain our present workforce. If unfortunately we do have to reduce numbers, we shall try to do so through natural wastage – that is, not replacing employees who leave us. But if redundancies do become inevitable – and I repeat that we hope and believe that this will not occur – we shall consult with all unions concerned; and we shall try to arrange redundancies with the minimum of hardship.

Anyway, I repeat that I hope that this situation will not arise. It is certainly the determination of your board and of all the management team to scour the countryside/the world for orders and to take any steps within our power to keep our organisation – with all its skills, experience and comradeship – together. We know that you know the problems – and how much we appreciate your partnership and help. We believe that together – all of us together – we can survive this miserable recession. Thank you – and now please do ask your questions. We shall try to answer them all – frankly and in the confidence that you recognise that we are all working — together — for the future of this, our works/business/undertaking.

Note: The redundancy section of this speech sets the tone for misery and, of course, should not be used unless that misery is at least in prospect. If you have any alternative joy to offer, then by all means do so. Alternatively, you could use the redundancy section to form a major part of an even more unhappy speech, if redundancies really do become inevitable.

Similar principles apply to speeches to management, thus:

To management colleagues

I appreciate greatly your coming together today. I know how far some of you have had to travel and the difficulty that some of you have had in leaving your work/departments. But it is essential that we confer together so as to decide how to meet the current emergency/how to make the best of the present opportunity/how to avoid *(or as the case may be)*.

First let me refer to the background paper which has been provided to you all. I must emphasise the following points:

1 ...
2 ...
3 ...

The board consider that the following steps should now be taken – but before making any decision irrevocable, we are seeking your views. Our proposals are:

1 ...
2 ...
3 ...

I look forward to hearing your comments and any counter-proposals. We shall value your constructive criticism and your ideas – as we do your comradeship, your partnership and your assistance – without which this business could not be surviving in such excellent shape.

Note: Accounts (as in the previous precedent); a background paper (as in this) – or some other document – prepared carefully in advance, will avoid waste of time; provide the basis for discussion; and reduce the length of your speech.

Sales team talk

I have asked you – our sales team – to join me today so that we can together plan for the future of the entire business. In the past, customers have come to us. In these troubled times, we must go to them – and arrive well ahead of our competitors.

I shall now ask our colleague, Bill Black, to present to you our new product – which will lie at the centre of our effort for the coming year. Bill...

(Mr Black then introduces and explains the product – with appropriate diagrams, charts and/or visual aids)

Now you have seen the product and you know the plans. So how do we beat the competition ... sell well – and justify the skill, the brilliance and the enterprise of our colleagues in research and development? How do we make the most of this great new opportunity? If we succeed, then the company will flourish. Failure is unthinkable – for the company – and for us all.

Note: Visual aids are vital – as a supplement to speech (see also Chapter 31). They are indispensable to (a) explain complicated ideas or machinery; (b) punctuate a lengthy speech or brighten a shorter one; and (c) feed other people's talents into your talk. (See also Janner on Presentation.)

Part Eight

Classic speeches

Extract from Lloyd George's address to over 4,000 people at Limehouse in 1909.

... Now unless I am wearying you, I have got just one other land tax, and that is a tax on royalties. The landlords are receiving eight million a year by way of royalties. What for? They never deposited the coal there. It was not they who planted these great granite rocks in Wales, who laid the foundations of the mountains. Was it the landlord? And yet he, by some divine right, demands – for merely the right for men to risk their lives in hewing these rocks – eight millions a year!

Take any coalfield. I went down to a coalfield the other day, and they pointed out to me many collieries there. They said: 'You see that colliery there. The first man who went there spent a quarter of a million in sinking shafts, in driving mains and levels. He never got coal. The second man who came spent £100,000 – and he failed. The third man came along, and he got the coal. But what was the landlord doing in the meantime? The first man failed; but the landlord got his royalties, the landlord got his dead-rents. The second man failed, but the landlord got his royalties. These capitalists put their money in. When the scheme failed, what did the landlord put in? He simply put in the bailiffs. The capitalist risks at any rate the whole of his money; the engineer puts his brains in, the miner risks his life.

Have you been down a coal-mine? Then you know, I was telling you I went down the other day. We sank down into a pit half a mile deep. We then walked underneath the mountain, and we did about three-quarters of a mile with rock and shale above us. The earth seemed to be straining – around us and above us – to crush us in. You could see the pit-props bent and twisted and sundered until you saw their fibres split. Sometimes they give way, and then there is mutilation and death. Often a spark ignites, the whole pit is deluged in fire, and the breath of life is scorched out of hundreds of breasts by the consuming fire.

In the very next colliery to the one I descended, just three years ago, three hundred people lost their lives in that way; and yet when the Prime Minister and I knock at the door of these great landlords and say to them, 'Here, you know these poor fellows who have been digging up royalties at the risk of their lives, some of them are old, they have survived the perils of their trade, they are broken, they can earn no more. Won't you give something towards keeping them out of the workhouse?' they scowl at you. And we say: 'Only a ha'penny, just a copper?' They say: 'You thieves!' And they turn their dogs on to us, and every day you can hear their bark. If this is an indication of the view taken by these great landlords of their responsibility to the people who, at the risk of life, create their wealth, then I say their day of reckoning is at hand.

The other day, at the great Tory meeting held at the Cannon Street Hotel, they had blazoned on the walls: 'We protest against the Budget in the name of democracy, liberty, and justice.' Where does the democracy come in in this landed system? Where is the justice in all these transactions? We claim that the tax we impose on land is fair, just, and moderate. They go on threatening that if we proceed they will cut down their benefactions and discharge labour. What kind of labour? What is the labour they are going to choose for dismissal? Are they going to threaten to devastate rural England while feeding themselves and dressing themselves? Are they going to reduce their gamekeepers? That would be sad! The agricultural labourer and the farmer might then have some part of the game which they fatten with their labour. But what would happen to you in the season? No weekend shooting with the Duke of Norfolk for any of us! But that is not the kind of labour that they are going to cut down. They are going to cut down productive labour – builders and gardeners – and they are going to ruin their property so that it shall not be taxed.

All I can say is this – the ownership of land is not merely an enjoyment, it is a stewardship. It has been reckoned as such in the past, and if they cease to discharge their functions, the security and defence of the country, looking after the broken in their villages and neighbourhoods – then those functions which are part of the traditional duties attached to the ownership of land and which have given to it its title – if they cease to discharge those functions, the time will come to reconsider the conditions under which land is held in this country.

No country, however rich, can permanently afford to have quartered upon its revenue a class which declines to do the duty which it was called upon to perform. And, therefore, it is one of the prime duties of statesmanship to investigate those conditions. But I do not believe it. They have threatened and menaced like that before.

They have seen it is not to their interest to carry out these futile menaces. They are now protesting against paying their fair share of the taxes on the land, and they are doing so by saying: 'You are burdening the community; you are putting burdens upon the people which they cannot bear.' Ah! they are not thinking of themselves. Noble souls! It is not the great dukes they are feeling for, it is the market-gardener, it is the builder, and it was, until recently, the smallholder.

In every debate in the House of Commons they said: 'We are not worrying for ourselves. We can afford it, with our broad acres; but just think of the little man who has only got a few acres'; and we were so very impressed with this tearful appeal that at last we said: 'We will leave him out.' And I almost expected to see Mr Prettyman jump over the table and say – 'Fall on my neck and embrace me.' Instead of that, he stiffened up, his face wreathed with anger, and he said: 'The Budget is more unjust than ever.' Oh! no. We are placing the burdens on the broad shoulders. Why should I put burdens on the people? I am one of the children of the people. I was brought up amongst them. I know their trials; and God forbid that I should add one grain of trouble to the anxiety which they bear with such patience and fortitude. When the Prime Minister did me the honour of inviting me to take charge of the National Exchequer at a time of great difficulty, I made up my mind, in framing the Budget which was in front of me, that at any rate no cupboards should be barer, no lot should be harder. By that test, I challenge them to judge the Budget.

(Reprinted, by kind permission of Caxton Publishing Co. Ltd, from The Book of Public Speaking, *Volume 3, edited by C. Fox-Davies.)*

George Bernard Shaw: 64
'The Labour Party'

Shaw's speech on his seventieth birthday, at a dinner in his honour given by the Parliamentary Labour Party in 1926.

Of late years the public have been trying to tackle me in every way they possibly can, and failing to make anything of it they have turned to treating me as a great man. This is a dreadful fate to overtake anybody. There has been a distinct attempt to do it again now, and for that reason I absolutely decline to say anything about the celebration of my seventieth birthday. But when the Labour Party, my old friends the Labour Party, invited me here I knew that I should be all right. We have discovered the secret that there are no great men, and we have discovered the secret that there are no great nations or great States.

We leave that kind of thing to the nineteenth century, where they properly belong. Here you all know that I am an extraordinarily clever fellow at my job. But I have not got the 'great-man feeling'. You have not got it either. My predecessor in my professional business, Shakespeare, lived in a middle-class set, but there was one person in that set who was not a middle-class man. He was a bricklayer, and when, after Shakespeare's death, the middle class generally started to celebrate Shakespeare by issuing a folio edition of his works (I haven't come to that yet, but I have no doubt some one will do it), all the middle class generally wrote magnificent songs about the greatness of Shakespeare. Curiously enough, the only tribute ever quoted or remembered today is the tribute of the bricklayer who said: 'I liked the man as well as anybody did this side of idolatry.'

When I began as a young man, Labour was attached to Liberalism and to Radicalism. Now Liberalism had its traditions, the traditions of 1649, of 1798, of 1848, and those traditions are still rampant in what is called the Communist Party. What were those traditions? Those traditions were barricades, civil war and regicide. Those are the genuine Liberal traditions, and the only reason that we can't say they exist today is that the Liberal Party itself has ceased to exist.

The Radical Party was publican and atheist, and its great principle was in the great historical phrase, that the world would never be at peace until the last king was strangled in the entrails of the last priest. When asked to put it a little more explicitly, and to put it into practical politics, they said that the world was full of tribulation and injustice because the Archbishop of Canterbury got fifteen thousand a year and because perpetual pensions were enjoyed by the descendants of Charles II's mistresses.

Now, however, we have built up a Constitutional Party. We have built it up on a socialist basis. My friend, Mr Sidney Webb, Mr MacDonald and myself said definitely at the beginning that what we had got to do was to make the Socialist Party a constitutional party to which any respectable God-fearing man could belong without the slightest compromise of his respectabilty. We got rid of all those traditions; that is why Governments in the present day are more afraid of us than they were of any of the Radical people.

Our position is a perfectly simple one and we have the great advantage of understanding our position. We oppose socialism to capitalism, and our great difficulty is that capitalists have not the slightest notion of what capitalism means. Yet it is a very simple thing. It is a theory of the Socialist Party that if you will take care of private property and if you will make all the sources of production as private property and maintain them as private property, in so far as that is a contract made between persons on that basis, then production will take care of itself and distribution will take care of itself.

According to the capitalists, there will be a guarantee to the world that every man in the country would get a job. They didn't contend it would be a well-paid job, because if it was well paid a man would save up enough one week to stop working the next week, and they were determined to keep a man working the whole time on a bare subsistence wage – and, on the other hand, divide an accumulation of capital.

They said capitalism not only secured this for the working man, but, by ensuring fabulous wealth in the hands of a small class of people, they would save money whether they liked it or not and would have to invest it. That is capitalism, and this Government is always interfering with capitalism. Instead of giving a man a job or letting him starve they are giving him doles – after making sure he has paid for them first. They are giving capitalists subsidies and making all sorts of regulations that are breaking up their own system. All the time they are doing it, and we are telling them it is breaking up, they don't understand.

We say in criticism of capitalism: Your system has never kept its promises for one single day since it was promulgated. Our production is ridiculous. We are producing eighty horsepower motor cars when many more houses should be built. We are producing most extravagant luxuries while children starve. You have stood production on its head. Instead of beginning with the things the nation needs most, you are beginning at just the opposite end. We say distribution has become so glaringly ridiculous that there are only two people out of the 47,000,000 people in this country who approve of the present system of distribution – one is the Duke of Northumberland and the other is Lord Banbury.

We are opposed to that theory. Socialism, which is perfectly clear and unmistakable, says the thing you have got to take care of is your distribution. We have to begin with that, and private property, if it stands in the way of good distribution, has got to go.

A man who holds public property must hold it on the public condition on which, for instance, I carry my walking stick. I am not allowed to do what I like with it. I must not knock you on the head with it. We say that if distribution goes wrong, everything else goes wrong – religion, morals, government. And we say, therefore (this is the whole meaning of our socialism), we must begin with distribution and take all the necessary steps.

I think we are keeping it in our minds because our business is to take care of the distribution of wealth in the world; and I tell you, as I have told you before, that I don't think there are two men, or perhaps one man, in our 47,000,000 who approves of the existing distribution of wealth. I will go even further and say that you will not find a single person in the whole of the civilized world who agrees with the existing system of the distribution of wealth. It has been reduced to a blank absurdity. You can prove that by asking any intelligent middle-class man if he thinks it right that he should go begging for a civil list pension while a baby in its cradle is being fought over in the law courts because it has only got six millions to be brought up on.

The first problem of distribution is distribution to the baby. It must have a good income and a better income than anybody else's income if the new generation is to be a first-class generation. Yet a baby has no morals, no character, no industry, and it hasn't even common decency. And it is to that abandoned person that the first duty of the Government is due. That is a telling example of this question of distribution. It reaches our question, which really is a question which is going to carry us to triumph.

I think the day will come when we will be able to make the distinction between us and the capitalists. We must get certain leading ideas before the people. We should announce that we are not going in for what was the old-fashioned idea of redistribution, but the redistribution of income. Let it always be a question of income.

I have been very happy here tonight. I entirely understand the distinction made by your chairman tonight when he said you hold me in social esteem and a certain amount of personal affection. I am not a sentimental man, but I am not insensible to all that. I know the value of all that, and it gives me, now that I have come to the age of seventy (it will not occur again and I am saying it for the last time), a great feeling of pleasure that I can say what a good many people can't say.

I know now that when I was a young man and took the turning that led me into the Labour Party, I took the right turning in every sense.

(Reprinted, by kind permission of Dover Publications, New York, from The World's Greatest Speeches [*second revised edition*], *edited by L. Copeland and L. Larner.)*

King Edward VIII: 65
'Abdication Address'

Edward VIII's abdication address, which he broadcast to Britain and the world on 11 December 1936.

At long last I am able to say a few words of my own. I have never wanted to withhold anything, but until now it has not been constitutionally possible for me to speak.

A few hours ago I discharged my last duty as King and Emperor, and now that I have been succeeded by my brother, the Duke of York, my first words must be to declare my allegiance to him. This I do with all my heart.

You all know the reasons which have impelled me to renounce the throne. But I want you to understand that in making up my mind I did not forget the country or the empire, which, as Prince of Wales and lately as King, I have for twenty-five years tried to serve.

But you must believe me when I tell you that I have found it impossible to carry the heavy burden of responsibility and to discharge my duties as King as I would wish to do without the help and support of the woman I love.

And I want you to know that the decision I have made has been mine and mine alone. This was a thing I had to judge entirely for myself. The other person most nearly concerned has tried up to the last to persuade me to take a different course.

I have made this, the most serious decision of my life, only upon the single thought of what would, in the end, be best for all.

This decision has been made less difficult to me by the sure knowledge that my brother, with his long training in the public affairs of this country and with his fine qualities, will be able to take my place forthwith without interruption or injury to the life and progress of the empire. And he has one matchless blessing, enjoyed by so many of you, and not bestowed on me – a happy home with his wife and children.

During these hard days I have been comforted by her majesty my mother and by my family. The ministers of the Crown, and in particular, Mr Baldwin, the Prime Minister, have always treated me with full consideration. There has never been any constitutional difference between me and them, and between me and Parliament. Bred in the constitutional tradition by my father, I should never have allowed any such issue to arise.

Ever since I was Prince of Wales, and later on when I occupied the throne, I have been treated with the greatest kindness by all classes of the people wherever I have lived or journeyed throughout the empire. For that I am very grateful.

I now quit altogether public affairs and I lay down my burden. It may be some time before I return to my native land, but I shall always follow the fortunes of the British race and empire with profound interest, and if at any time in the future I can be found of service to his majesty in a private station, I shall not fail.

And now, we all have a new King. I wish him and you, his people, happiness and prosperity with all my heart. God bless you all! God save the King!

66 Winston Churchill: 'Blood, Toil, Sweat and Tears' – 1940

I beg to move,

> That this House welcomes the formation of a Government representing the united and inflexible resolve of the nation to prosecute the war with Germany to a victorious conclusion.

On Friday evening last I received His Majesty's Commission to form a new Administration. It was the evident wish and will of Parliament and the nation that this should be conceived on the broadest possible basis and that it should include all parties, both those who supported the late Government and also the parties of the Opposition. I have completed the most important part of this task. A War Cabinet has been formed of five Members, respresenting, with the Opposition Liberals, the unity of the nation. The three party Leaders have agreed to serve, either in the War Cabinet or in high executive office. The three Fighting Services have been filled. It was necessary that this should be done in one single day, on account of the extreme urgency and rigour of events. A number of other positions, key positions, were filled yesterday, and I am submitting a further list to His Majesty tonight. I hope to complete the appointment of the principal Ministers during tomorrow. The appointment of the other Ministers usually takes a little longer, but I trust that, when Parliament meets again, this part of my task will be completed, and that the administration will be complete in all respects.

I considered it in the public interest to suggest that the House should be summoned to meet today. Mr Speaker agreed, and took the necessary steps, in accordance with the powers conferred upon him by the Resolution of the House. At the end of the proceedings today, the Adjournment of the House will be proposed until Tuesday, 21st May, with, of course, provision for earlier meeting, if need be. The business to be considered during that week will be notified to Members at the earliest opportunity. I now invite the House, by the Motion which stands in my name, to record its approval of the steps taken and to declare its confidence in the new Government.

To form an Administration of this scale and complexity is a serious undertaking in itself, but it must be remembered that we are in the preliminary stage of one of the greatest battles in history, that we are in action at many other points in Norway and in Holland, that we have to be prepared in the Mediterranean, that the air battle is continuous and that many preparations, such as have been indicated by my Hon. Friend below the Gangway, have to be made here at home. In this crisis I hope I may be pardoned if I do not address the House at any length today. I hope that any of my friends and colleagues, or former colleagues, who are affected by the political reconstruction, will make allowances, all allowance, for any lack of ceremony with which it has been necessary to act. I would say to the House, as I said to those who have joined this Government: 'I have nothing to offer but blood, toil, tears and sweat.'

We have before us an ordeal of the most grievous kind. We have before us many, many long months of struggle and of suffering. You ask, what is our policy? I will say: It is to wage war, by sea, land and air, with all our might and with all the strength that God can give us; to wage war against a monstrous tyranny never surpassed in the dark, lamentable catalogue of human crime. That is our policy. You ask, what is our aim? I can answer in one word: It is victory, victory at all cost, victory in spite of all terror, victory, however long and hard the road may be; for without victory, there is no survival. Let that be realised; no survival for the British Empire, no survival for all that the British Empire has stood for, no survival for the urge and impulse of the ages, that mankind will move forward towards its goal. But I take up my task with buoyancy and hope. I feel sure that our cause will not be suffered to fail among men. At this time I feel entitled to claim the aid of all, and I say, 'Come then, let us go forward together with our united strength.'

(Reprinted, with kind permission of HMSO, from Hansard, *Fifth Series, issue No. 1096, volume 360, 13 May 1940, col. 1501 to col. 1502.)*

67 Jawaharlal Nehru: 'A Glory has Departed'

Nehru, first Prime Minister of independent India, addressing the Constituent Assembly at New Delhi on 2 February 1948, three days after the assassination of Mahatma Gandhi.

What then can we say about him except to feel humble on this occasion? To praise him we are not worthy – to praise him whom we could not follow adequately and sufficiently. It is almost doing him an injustice just to pass him by with words when he demanded work and labour and sacrifice from us; in a large measure he made this country, during the last thirty years or more, attain to heights of sacrifice which in that particular domain have never been equalled elsewhere. He succeeded in that. Yet ultimately things happened which no doubt made him suffer tremendously though his tender face never lost its smile and he never spoke a harsh word to anyone.

Yet, he must have suffered – suffered for the failing of this generation whom he had trained, suffered because we went away from the path that he had shown us. And ultimately the hand of a child of his – for he after all is as much a child of his as any other Indian – a hand of the child of his struck him down.

Long ages afterwards history will judge of this period that we have passed through. It will judge of the successes and the failures – we are too near it to be proper judges and to understand what has happened and what has not happened. All we know is that there was a glory and that it is no more; all we know is that for the moment there is darkness, not so dark certainly because when we look into our hearts we still find the living flame which he lighted there. And if those living flames exist, there will not be darkness in this land and we shall be able, with our effort, remembering him and following his path, to illumine this land again, small as we are, but still with the fire that he instilled into us.

He was perhaps the greatest symbol of the India of the past, and may I say, of the India of the future, that we could have had. We stand on this perilous edge of the present between that past and the future to be and we face all manner of perils and the greatest peril is sometimes the lack of faith which comes to us, the sense of frustration that comes to us, the sinking of the heart and of the spirit that comes to us when we see ideals go overboard, when we see the great things that we talked about somehow pass into empty words and life taking a different course. Yet, I do believe that perhaps this period will pass soon enough.

He has gone, and all over India there is a feeling of having been left desolate and forlorn. All of us sense that feeling, and I do not know when we shall be able to get rid of it, and yet together with that feeling there is also a feeling of proud thankfulness that it has been given to us of this generation to be associated with this mighty person. In ages to come, centuries and maybe millenia after us, people will think of this generation when this man of God trod on earth and will think of us who, however small, could also follow his path and tread the holy ground where his feet had been. Let us be worthy of him.

A glory has departed and the sun that warmed and brightened our lives has set and we shiver in the cold and dark. Yet, he would not have us feel this way. After all, that glory that we saw for all these years, that man with the divine fire, changed us also – and such as we are, we have been moulded by him during these years; and out of that divine fire many of us also took a small spark which strengthened and made us work to some extent on the lines that he fashioned. And so if we praise him, our words seem rather small and if we praise him, to some extent we also praise ourselves. Great men and eminent men have monuments in bronze and marble set up for them, but this man of divine fire managed in his life-time to become enshrined in millions and millions of hearts so that all of us became somewhat of the stuff that he was made of, though to an infinitely lesser degree. He spread out in this way all over India not in palaces only, or in select places or in assemblies but in every hamlet and hut of the lowly and those who suffer. He lives in the hearts of millions and he will live for immemorial ages.

(Reprinted, by kind permission of Dover Publications, New York, from The World's Greatest Speeches *[second revised edition], edited by L. Copeland and L. Larner.)*

68 Harold Macmillan: 'The Winds of Change'

Addressing the South African Parliament in 1960 on the theme of emerging third-world nationalism, Macmillan opened his speech as follows.

Sir, as I have travelled round the Union I have found everywhere, as I expected, a deep preoccupation with what is happening in the rest of the African continent. I understand and sympathise with your interest in these events, and your anxiety about them. Ever since the break-up of the Roman Empire one of the constant facts of political life in Europe has been the emergence of independent nations. They have come into existence over the centuries in different forms, with different kinds of Government, but all have been inspired by a deep, keen feeling of nationalism, which has grown as the nations have grown.

In the twentieth century, and especially since the end of the war, the processes which gave birth to the nation states of Europe have been repeated all over the world. We have seen the awakening of national consciousness in peoples who have for centuries lived in dependence upon some other power. Fifteen years ago this movement spread through Asia. Many countries there of different races and civilisations pressed their claim to an independent national life. Today the same thing is happening in Africa, and the most striking of all the impressions I have formed since I left London a month ago is of the strength of this African national consciousness. In different places it takes different forms, but it is happening everywhere. The wind of change is blowing through this continent, and, whether we like it or not, this growth of national consciousness is a political fact. We must all accept it as a fact, and our national policies must take account of it...

(Reprinted, by kind permission of Macmillan London Ltd, from Pointing the Way 1959–61, *Volume 5 of Macmillan's biography.)*

Martin Luther King: 69 'I Have a Dream'

Martin Luther King's evocative black masterpiece of hope – 1963.

I have a dream that my four little children will one day live in a nation where they will not be judged by the colour of their skin but by the content of their character.

I have a dream today.

I have a dream that one day the state of Alabama, whose governor's lips are presently dripping with the words of interposition and nullification, will be transformed into a situation where little black boys and black girls will be able to join hands with little white boys and white girls and walk together as sisters and brothers.

I have a dream today.

I have a dream that one day every valley shall be exalted, every hill and mountain shall be made low, the rough places will be made plain, and the crooked places will be made straight, and the glory of the Lord shall be revealed, and all flesh shall see it together.

This is our hope. This is the faith with which I return to the South. With this faith we will be able to hew out of the mountain of despair a stone of hope. With this faith we will be able to transform the jangling discords of our nation into a beautiful symphony of brotherhood. With this faith we will be able to work together, to pray together, to struggle together, to go to jail together, to stand up for freedom together, knowing that we will be free one day.

This will be the day when all of God's children will be able to sing with new meaning 'My country 'tis of thee, sweet land of liberty, of thee I sing. Land where my fathers died, land of the pilgrim's pride, from every mountainside, let freedom ring.'

And if America is to be a great nation this must become true. So let freedom ring from the prodigious hilltops of New Hampshire! Let freedom ring from the mighty mountains of New York! Let freedom ring from the heightening Alleghenies of Pennsylvania!

Let freedom ring from the snowcapped Rockies of Colorado!

Let freedom ring from the curvaceous peaks of California!

But not only that; let freedom ring from the Stone Mountain of Georgia!

Let freedom ring from every hill and mole hill of Mississippi. From every mountainside, let freedom ring.

When we let freedom ring, when we let it ring from very village and every hamlet, from every state and every city, we will be able to speed up that day when all of God's children, black men and white men, Jews and Gentiles, Protestants and Catholics, will be able to join hands and sing in the words of that old Negro spiritual, 'Free at last! Free at last! Thank God almighty, we are free at last!'

(Reprinted, by kind permission of George Allen & Unwin Ltd, from What Manner of Man: a Biography of Martin Luther King *by L. Bennet.)*

70 Enoch Powell: 'Rivers of blood'

An extract from the speech of Enoch Powell, MP, to the West Midlands Area Conservative Political Centre in 1968 on the Race Relations Bill.

... The other dangerous delusion from which those who are wilfully or otherwise blind to realities suffer, is summed up in the word 'integration'. To be integrated into a population means to become for all practical purposes indistinguishable from its other members.

Now, at all times, where there are marked physical differences, especially of colour, integration is difficult though, over a period, not impossible. There are among the Commonwealth immigrants who have come to live here in the last fifteen years or so, many thousands whose wish and purpose is to be integrated and whose every thought and endeavour is bent in that direction. But to imagine that such a thing enters the heads of a great and growing majority of immigrants and their descendents is a ludicrous misconception and a dangerous one to boot.

We are on the verge here of a change. Hitherto it has been force of circumstances and of background which has rendered the very idea of integration inaccessible to the greater part of the immigrant population – that they never conceived or intended such a thing, and that their numbers and physical concentration meant the pressures towards integration which normally bear upon any small minority did not operate. Now we are seeing the growth of positive forces acting against integration, of vested interests in the preservation and sharpening of racial and religious differences, with a view to the exercise of actual domination, first over fellow-immigrants and then over the rest of the population. The cloud no bigger than a man's hand, that can so rapidly overcast the sky, has been visible recently in Wolverhampton and has shown signs of spreading quickly. The words I am about to use, verbatim as they appeared in the local press on 17 February, are not mine, but those of a Labour Member of Parliament who is a Minister in the present Government. 'The Sikh community's campaign to maintain customs inappropriate in Britain is much to be regretted. Working in Britain, particularly in the public services, they should be prepared to accept the terms and conditions of their employment. To claim special communal rights (or should one say rites?) leads to a dangerous fragmentation within society. This communalism is a canker; whether practised by one colour or another it is to be strongly condemned.' All credit to John Stonehouse* for having had the insight to perceive that, and the courage to say it.

For these dangerous and divisive elements the legislation proposed in the Race Relations Bill is the very pabulum they need to flourish. Here is the means of showing that the immigrant communities can organise to consolidate their members, to agitate and campaign against their follow citizens, and to overawe and dominate the rest with the legal weapons which the ignorant and the

* *Mr Stonehouse was later imprisoned for fraud.*

ill-informed have provided. As I look ahead, I am filled with foreboding. Like the Roman, I seem to see 'The River Tiber foaming with much blood'. That tragic and intractable phenomenon which we watch with horror on the other side of the Atlantic but which there is interwoven with the history and existence of the States itself, is coming upon us here by our own volition and our own neglect. Indeed, it has all but come. In numerical terms, it will be of American proportions long before the end of the century. Only resolute and urgent action will avert it even now. Whether there will be the public will to demand and obtain that action, I do not know. All I know is that to see, and not to speak, would be the great betrayal.

Commenting on this notorious speech, Bernard Levin (in The Times*) compared him to the man who set light to seats in a cinema and rushed out, yelling: 'Fire!'. But a set of current examples of oratorical power would be incomplete without this influential and incendiary effort. Most parliamentarians agree that when on form, the most eloquent Parliamentarians of recent years (filling the chamber when they are on their feet – as opposed to the 'chamber emptiers') were or are: Winston Churchill, Aneurin Bevan, Michael Foot and Enoch Powell – three of whom are represented in this collection.*

71 Axel Springer: 'Nip it in the Bud'

German publisher, Axel Springer, on the resurgence of right-wing terrorism – October 1980.

There is no doubt: the signs of right-wing extremism are growing bloodier in Europe. The seed of violence is sprouting. Since the mid-sixties extreme-left terrorism has bombed itself irresistably into the underdeveloped consciousness of some of the marginal right-wing extremist groups in our society. A fatal reciprocal effect with exchangeable slogans but with the same blind and damnable brutality is taking shape. The track of insanity leads from the blood bath in Bologna railway station over the massacre at the Oktoberfest in Munich to the attack on the synagogue in Paris. Where will it end?

It would be premature to attribute to right-wing extremism a deadly peril to political morality in Europe. But it is imperative to nip the beginnings in the bud, with all our watchfulness and rigour. It is food for thought when in a country which was responsible for the holocaust, right-wing extremist elements ride the wave of hostility to foreigners, when the treacherous murder of two Vietnamese in a foreign workers' hostel in Hamburg releases no storm of public protest.

The writing is on the wall of more than one house in Germany. Heinz Galinski, the untiring chairman of the largest Jewish community in Germany, a man who survived Auschwitz, has therefore taken the right initiative at the right time. He addressed the passionate appeal to the President of the European Parliament, Simone Veil, to throw in the whole weight of her office to put the co-ordinated fight against right-wing extremism on the agenda of the European Parliament. Galinski is right when he points out that right-wing extremism is not a problem for this or that country but a European phenomenon.

Certainly there is not yet cause to dramatise and attribute to the extremists of the right a set of muscles which, thank God, they do not possess. The trammels of our free communal body still hold. Our political party landscape is still unstained by the entry of the incorrigibles as a political force. The German voter – up to and including the last elections to the Bundestag – still proves his maturity as a democrat. The crime of Auschwitz is not yet waste paper of history.

But the young German democracy has not yet been called upon to stand the ultimate test. If we were in misery, in a grave economic crisis, with millions of unemployed, crumbling internal security and under stress in our foreign politics – would we be proof against the slogans of yesteryear?

We are witnesses to the determination with which right-wing extremism tries to get on to the political stage via hostility to foreigners. Our sensitivity, sharpened by the tragedies and the guilt of our history, shows us that extremism of the right again feeds on anti-semitism.

Here we are immediately up against the unholy relation between anti-semitism and anti-zionism. It is not a polemic contrivance but provable that in every place where indifference to the fate of Israel guides the pen, or where even Israel's right to existence is questioned, anti-semitism raises its hideous head. A recent example:

With 20 adherents the 'Führer' of a right-wing extremist group is reported to have been trained early this year for two weeks in a Lebanese training camp of the terrorist organization 'El Fatah'.

We have, of course, enough to sweep at our own doorstep, but it is presumably no stupid coincidence that in France of all countries anti-semitism is stretching its muscles again – in a country which in the European Community in recent years has assumed a pro-Arab pilot function striking at Israel.

Just as left-wing extremism needed a mental field of trivialisation and sympathy which allowed the terrorists to move in it like fish in water, so must we take care that extremism of the right is deprived of its humus at the very beginning of thought on the subject. Nobody who utters reservations against Israeli policies or who gives equal weight to the interests of the Jewish state and to the Arab camp (if there is such a thing) must be assumed to be deliberately embracing the cause of right-wing extremism. But every responsible German politician should face the question of conscience as to whether, if he takes a critical attitude against Israel, he is not unwittingly encouraging those who say Israel but mean anti-semitism.

There is something wrong in a political landscape in which the Federal Chancellor's words calling Prime Minister Begin 'a danger to world peace' can circulate, at first without dementi, then only after protest by Israel followed by a dementi.

Government circles in Bonn were outraged when the Israeli press carried worried commentaries on the outcome of the Bundestag elections, which again brought in the social-democratic-liberal coalition. Was that really surprising? After all the West German Government is a partner in the EEC Venice resolution, which shamelessly favours Israel's enemies. After all Bonn unblushingly shares in raising Arafat's stock and that of his PLO, which is still proud of being a murder organisation. After all, the West German Government favours the establishment of an independent Palestinian state in which exactly those Arabs would rule who till this day have written on their flag the intention to annihilate the Jewish state.

Must not the insanity of people who hark back to Hitler feel strengthened when the West German Foreign Minister, Herr Genscher, as good as files away the 'special relations' between the Federal Republic and Israel, writing in large letters his sympathies for the Arab camp and favouring beleaguered Israel merely with statesmanlike coolness?

How shall a brain untrained in politics digest the Federal Chancellor's neutral declaration, given a few days before the Bundestag elections, that 'We are friends of Israel, but we are also friends of Saudi-Arabia, Jordan and Egypt'? How must one interpret the sad fact that during the entire election campaign no single responsible German politician uttered a word demonstratively for all to hear on the special German obligation towards Israel, especially in the present dangerous situation in the Middle East?

This indifference is a product of a false political and moral approach. The words slip with frightening ease from German lips, that a peace settlement in the Middle East can only be reached by stabilizing the Arab camp. Arab unity – this we know – has only existed, if at all, in the common fight against the Jewish state.

As things lie, anyone who calls for the amalgamation of Arabia forces the campaign against the Jewish state and against the Egyptian-Israeli peace settlement. We must be on the watch. We must not assume the disguise of statesmanship in order to steal away – in the dead of night – from Auschwitz.

(Reprinted, by kind permission of Axel Springer Publishing Group, from Die Welt, *October 1980.)*

Hugh Gaitskell: 72
'Fight and Fight and
Fight Again'

Speech delivered at the 57th Annual Conference of the Labour Party, Scarborough, 1960.

... There is one other possibility to which I must make reference because I have read so much about it – that the issue here is not really defence at all but the leadership of this Party. Let me repeat what Manny Shinwell said. The place to decide the leadership of this Party is not here but in the Parliamentary Party. I would not wish for one day to remain a Leader who had lost the confidence of his colleagues in Parliament. It is perfectly reasonable to try to get rid of somebody, to try to get rid of a man you do not agree with, who you think perhaps is not a good Leader. But there are ways of doing this. What would be wrong, in my opinion, and would not be forgiven, is if, in order to get rid of a man, you supported a policy in which you did not wholeheartedly believe, a policy which, as far as the resolution is concerned, is not clear.

Before you take the vote on this momentous occasion, allow me a last word. Frank Cousins has said this is not the end of the problem. I agree with him. It is not the end of the problem because Labour Members of Parliament will have to consider what they do in the House of Commons. What do you expect of them? You know how they voted in June overwhelmingly for the policy statement. It is not in dispute that the vast majority of Labour Members of Parliament are utterly opposed to unilateralism and neutralism. So what do you expect them to do? Change their minds overnight? To go back on the pledges they gave to the people who elected them from their constituencies? And supposing they did do that. Supposing all of us, like well-behaved sheep, were to follow the policies of unilateralism and neutralism, what kind of an impression would that make upon the British people? You do not seem to be clear in your minds about it, but I will tell you this. I do not believe that the Labour Members of Parliament are prepared to act as time servers. I do not believe they will do this, and I will tell you why – because they are men of conscience and honour. People of the so-called Right and so-called Centre have every justification for having a conscience, as well as people of the so-called Left. I do not think they will do this because they are honest men, loyal men, steadfast men, experienced men, with a lifetime of service to the Labour Movement.

There are other people too, not in Parliament, in the Party who share our convictions. What sort of people do you think they are? What sort of people do you think we are? Do you think we can simply accept a decision of this kind? Do you think that we can become overnight the pacifists, unilateralists and fellow travellers that other people are? How wrong can you be? As wrong as you are about the attitude of the British people.

In a few minutes the Conference will make its decision. Most of the votes, I know, are predetermined and we have been told what is likely to happen. We know how it comes about. I sometimes think, frankly, that the system we have, by which great unions decide their policy before even their conferences can consider the Executive recommendation, is not really a very wise one or a good one. Perhaps in a calmer moment this situation could be looked at.

I say this to you: we may lose the vote today and the result may deal this Party a grave blow. It may not be possible to prevent it, but I think there are many of us who will not accept that this blow need be mortal, who will not believe that such an end is inevitable. There are some of us, Mr Chairman, who will fight and fight and fight again to save the Party we love. We will fight and fight and fight again to bring back sanity and honesty and dignity, so that our Party with its great past may retain its glory and its greatness.

It is in that spirit that I ask delegates who are still free to decide how they vote, to support what I believe to be a realistic policy on defence, which yet could so easily have united the great Party of ours, and to reject what I regard as the suicidal path of unilateral disarmament which will leave our country defenceless and alone.

(Reprinted by kind permission, from the Labour Party Report of the 57th Annual Conference.)

Aneurin Bevan: 73 'Socialism Unbeaten'

Extract from Bevan's speech to the Labour Party Conference following Macmillan's General Election victory of 1959.

What are we going to say, comrades? Are we going to accept the defeat? Are we going to say to India, where Socialism has been adopted as the official policy despite all the difficulties facing the Indian community, that the British Labour movement has dropped Socialism here? What are we going to say to the rest of the world? Are we going to send a message from this great Labour movement, which is the father and mother of modern democracy and modern Socialism, that we in Blackpool in 1959 have turned our backs on our principles because of a temporary unpopularity in a temporarily affluent society?

Let me give you a personal confession of faith. I have found in my life that the burdens of public life are too great to be borne for trivial ends. The sacrifices are too much, unless we have something really serious in mind; and therefore, I hope we are going to send from this Conference a message of hope, a message of encouragement, to the youth and to the rest of the world that is listening very carefully to what we are saying.

I was rather depressed by what Denis Healey said. I have a lot of respect for him; but you know, Denis, you are not going to be able to help the Africans if the levers of power are left in the hands of their enemies in Britain. You cannot do it! Nor can you inject the principles of ethical Socialism into an economy based upon private greed. You cannot do it! You cannot mix them, and therefore I beg and pray that we should wind this Conference up this time on a message of hope, and we should say to India and we should say to Africa and Indonesia, and not only to them, but we should say to China and we should say to Russia, that the principles of democratic Socialism have not been extinguished by a temporary defeat at the hands of the Tories a few weeks ago!

You know, comrades, parliamentary institutions have not been destroyed because the Left wing was too vigorous; they have been destroyed because the Left was too inert. You cannot give me a single illustration in the Western world where Fascism conquered because Socialism was too violent. You cannot give me a single illustration where representative government has been undermined because the representatives of the people asked for too much.

But I can give you instance after instance we are faced with today where representative government has been rendered helpless because the representatives of the people did not ask enough. We have never suffered from too much vitality; we have suffered from too little. That is why I say that we are going to go from this Conference a united Party. We are going to go back to the House of Commons, and we are going to fight the Tories. But we are not only going to fight them there; we are going to fight them in the constituencies and inside the trade unions. And we are going to get the youth! Let them start. Do not let them wait for the Executive, for God's sake! Start getting your youth clubs, go in and start now! Go back home and start them, and we will give all the help and encouragement that we can.

Book Three

COMPENDIUM OF RETELLABLE TALES

Introduction

A lively story is to a good speech as spice to a fine meal. A touch of wit ... a flash of humour ... a shaft of laughter ... each is appreciated by every audience. Again: everyone likes a good story – whatever his, her or its age. The best tales are like wine, they mature with the years.

As I have sat through millennial miseries of meetings and dinners, many of them extremely boring, I have jotted down on menus, notepads and scraps of assorted paper the best of the story-teller's crop. To create this section of the book, I have now raided piles of files ... deciphered scrawl and shorthand ... rejected some tales, too blue or too terrible to retell – and brought together the mixture that now follows.

Each tale – be it a joke, an aphorism, an illustration, a wisecrack or an unwise gaffe – has been well used and much appreciated. I have sorted the accumulated into rough sections – although many stories could fit just as well into several of my groupings. Anyway, if you wish to pick out a story for a special purpose, the index should help. Or maybe you will just enjoy browsing your way through a quarter-century of tales which – told or retold – have brought me much pleasure. Use them in good health, in good voice – and with that good fortune that is the essential prerequisite and precursor of every standing ovation.

A tale is only as good as its teller. Bad workmen blame their tools, poor comedians their scriptwriters. Still: tools and scripts must be selected with care, to suit both user and occasion.

Some of these Retellable Tales will suit you, others will not. Most can be adapted.

Sometimes, I have suggested possible changes, in brackets or footnotes. But do not hesitate to change the material to suit yourself or your audience.

Naturally, it is unhelpful to misattribute a quotation. We may all be prepared to accept the paternity of wise words, fathered off on us by affectionate quoters. But misquoted ideas provide the source of many a first-class libel suit.

So use and enjoy these tales with pleasurable care and they should serve you well.

Presentations, speeches and stories **74**

Opening gambits

As Henry VIII said to each of his wives in turn: 'I shall not keep you long...'. *(Lord Janner)*

Like the time the toastmaster said: 'Ladies and Gentlemen... pray for the silence of Mr Greville Janner...'.

The last time the chairman introduced me and was told to be brief, he began: 'The less said about Mr Greville Janner, the better...'.

Your chairman has just said to me: 'Would you like to speak now – or shall we let them go on enjoying themselves a little longer?'

A woman said to the speaker at the end of his talk: 'You weren't on form tonight, were you, Mr Brown?'
    Another woman who had been listening nearby sidled up to him. 'I am sorry about that,' she said. 'Please take no notice of Mrs Green. She is a stupid woman. She hasn't a mind of her own... She only repeats what she hears other people saying...'.

Why me first?

I have been asked to speak before Mr... because I have several dates in *(naming two months hence)* which I wish to keep. *(Bob Monkhouse)*

Bars?

I have to make a great number of speeches and I am afraid that I have to use the same material on a number of occasions. The speech I am about to make to you is largely a repetition of a speech that I made last week in Sing Sing/Dartmoor/Wormwood Scrubs *(or the nearest prison to you)*. I apologize to any of you who have heard it before. *(Careful — any ex-cons in your audience? GJ)*

Civic slip	I have to address a lot of conferences. Indeed, last week, somebody said: 'Would you please address a meeting of 150 co-operative women'. *(Mayor of Harrogate addressing conference opening session.)*
Royal introductions	While presenting various notables to the Queen at a reception, I remarked that it must be a strain meeting so many strangers all at one time. 'It is not as difficult as it might seem,' came Her Majesty's deadpan reply. 'You see, I so seldom have to introduce myself — they all seem to know who I am!'
Compliments	Mark Twain once said: 'I can live for two months on a good compliment.' You have given me enough compliments for several years... *(Response to flattering introduction. GJ)*
AGM	Chairman: 'We now come to another annual meeting – after an interval of a year...'
Audience	I asked your chairman for details of the people I would be speaking to today – numbers, broken down by age and sex – and he replied: 'Yes, they are...'. *(Clement Freud)*
Conference spirit	Sir Zelman Cowan, former Governor General of Australia and now Provost of Oriel College, Oxford, and Chairman of the Press Council told a luncheon: 'When I was Governor General I had to go to a lot of conferences. Sometimes I got so muddled that I did not know whether the delegates were discussing law or education – you could not tell from the sound of the words – and when I did find out, I discovered usually that it didn't matter! It's not what you discuss at a conference but the spirit that counts!'
Sleep	A new pastor arrived in a country parish. He noticed with dismay that each week during his sermon, the senior churchwarden dropped off to sleep. He put up with this until one week the man

snored. After the service he went up to him and said very gently: 'I am sorry to mention this, but it does set a very bad example when my senior churchwarden sleeps during the sermon.'

'Not at all,' replied the Elder. 'It just shows that I trust you!'

Off the record?

'How did your speech go?'

'Marvellous. Even the journalists put down their pencils and listened . . .'.

A load of old hay

There was only one person at the service at the local church. The vicar said to him: 'Shall I carry on?'

Congregant: 'I am only an old cowhand. If there is only one cow in the field I still feed him.'

So the vicar carried out the whole service. On his way out he said to the congregant: 'How did you like it?'

Congregant: 'I am only an old cowhand. Even if there is only one cow in the field I still feed him. But I do not feed him the whole load of hay!'

Quote

'War has devastating results', as Lenin said. And it would be true even had *he* not said it . . . [*Translatable to, from, or for anyone else. GJ*]

Jokes by numbers

At a jokesters' conference, everyone knew each other's stories so well that they simply used numbers. A man got on the stage and said: '75'. Silence – except for two men who were rolling about in the aisles. When asked why they were laughing, one said: 'I like the way he tells it'; the other said: 'I haven't heard it before.'

Golden silence

A business person must first learn when to make speeches. Then he gets wise and learns when not to make them.

Pronunciation

An American tourist was crossing Westminster Bridge. He stopped a passer-by and said: 'Sir, could you please tell me. Is this river pronounced "Thems" or "Tems"?'

'Thems,' the man replied.

"Gee, I'm surprised,' said the American. 'I always thought it was pronounced "Tems". Are you quite sure?'

'Yeth,' answered the man. 'I'm thertain!'

Preferred position

Addressing a large meeting, a politician was worried in case his microphone was not working.

'Can you hear me at the back?' he called out.

'I can't hear you,' cried a voice from the rear.

'I *can* hear you,' shouted a man from the front row. 'Would the man at the back like to change places with me?'

To inattentive listener

'Can you hear me? That's good... I can hear you too!' *(David Berglas)*

If...

There is no end to the oratorical use of the word 'if' – nor to the stories which may embellish it. If (there we go) you decide to use Kipling's poem, please ladle on your vocal melodrama. As Kipling long ago claimed: 'If you can keep your head when all about you...' The best 'if' story is a reversed chestnut:

'How was the dinner?'

'If the chicken had been as fresh as the waitress... if the waitress had been as young as the wine... if the wine had been as mature as the jokes... it would have been a lovely evening!'

Or there is the French saying: 'If my aunt had wheels, she would be a bicycle!' (*Si ma tante avait des roues, ce serait une bicyclette* – in case you use it to an audience which Canadians call 'Francophone' – which is not always the same as Anglophile!). [*If any reader would care to submit an original 'if' story that I can use in the next edition of this book, I shall be glad to provide a reward. Meanwhile, please do not think that because a joke or a story happens to be known to your audience, they will reject it. A comedian suggested that there are only two basic themes for humour – the banana skin and the mother-in-law. All the rest are variations. GJ*]

Vote of thanks   At least Macbeth knew that when the dreadful banquet was over, he would not be the person required to return thanks.

The end   A guest for dinner who could no longer stand the eternal droning of the speaker passed a note to the chairman: 'Why not put an end to it by smashing him on the head with your gavel?'

The chairman picked up the gavel – but it slipped out of his hand and coshed the guest of honour, by his other side. As the poor man began slowly to sink out of sight under the table, he cried out: 'Hit me again. I can still hear him!'

Churchillian brevity   Churchill often proclaimed that it only took him 10 minutes to prepare a two-hour speech, but two hours to prepare a 10-minute one.

'Our next speaker needs no introduction from me. . . .'

Epigrams and definitions, 75 proverbs and laws

Anger
A sage who is angry ceases to be a sage. (*Talmud-Pesahim*)

Argument
My father told me never to argue with an angry man... (*Nahum Goldmann*)

Average man
A defendant in a negligence action pleaded that 'anyone with average intelligence' would not have suffered damage. With shattering accuracy, the judge replied: 'You should perhaps bear in mind that something like one half of the people in this country are below average intelligence!' (*See also* Public opinion.)

Balance
Churchill once remarked that there is nothing more difficult that holding up a wall leaning towards you except kissing a girl leaning away from you.

People in our industry are well balanced – we have a chip on each shoulder! One chip is provided by Revenue, the tax man... the other by (*the Government, Customs and Excise – or what-have-you*).

Boring
It is the sort of document that is so dull that when you put it down it is difficult to pick up again. (*Malcolm Rifkind*)

Change
The UK Government was considering switching its vehicles to driving on the right-hand side of the road. Anxious about a transitional changeover period, the Department of Transport suggested effecting the alteration 'by stages ... starting with heavy goods vehicles.'

Company
A man is known by the company which he thinks no one knows he is keeping.

Corroboration
Never lie alone. (*Janner's Law*)

195

Cranks	Crank – A man with a new idea until it succeeds. (*Mark Twain*)
Danger from fools	Any fool can throw a stone into a lake; but a hundred wise men cannot get it out. (*Greek proverb*.)
Democracy	Democracy – national or corporate – requires the enlightened balance of satisfied self-interest. (*Janner's Law*)
Deterrence	Deterrence requires existence of powers; willingness to use it; and knowledge by the adversary that it will, if necessary, be used. (*Abba Eban*)
Discretion	If I know something you do not know, then you know that I cannot tell you; and if I do not know anything that you do not know, you will not want to hear me anyway!
Education – and training	The difference between education and training? If your daughter comes home and says that she has been having sex education at school, you will doubtless rejoice. But if she says that she has been having sex training, you would have due cause for alarm.
Enemies	Choose your enemies with care. Make sure that they are important. Your importance depends upon theirs. (*Founder of World Jewish Congress, Nahum Goldmann – who maintained that he was unknown until he was publicly attacked by the redoubtable Rabbi Abba Hillel Silver.*)
Paranoid?	Remember that just because I am paranoid doesn't mean that I ain't got enemies. (*Henry Kissinger*)
Fatherly boast	I have never raised my hand to my son – except in self-defence. (*Lord Janner*)
Friends	The Prime Minister left tonight for a tour of all our friendly European countries. She will be back within a couple of hours.

196

Friendship	The Greeks say of a true friend: 'I have taken bread and salt with him.'
Genius	A Rabbi visited a kibbutz on the edge of the desert. He said: 'You kibbutzniks are so clever... You know how to settle where the trees are!'
Gossips	Q: What is the plural of 'gossip?' A: Women's Institute. (*Or if preferred 'Women's Branch' or as the case may be.*) [*This offensive and sexist definition has international variations, e.g. the Yiddish: What is the plural of 'Yenta?' – 'Hadassah' – for translation, try* Fiddler on the Roof – *and for 'Hadassah' read 'WIZO' or any other appropriate female organisation. GJ*]
Helpful	A driver stopped at a crossroads in a village. 'Excuse me,' he said to a passer-by, 'but does it matter which of these roads I take to get me to the next town?' 'Not to me, it don't' replied the villager.
Holes	First law on holes – when you're in one, stop digging! (*Denis Healey*)
Ideas	A friend once said to Einstein: 'When I have a good idea, I do not want to forget it. So I keep a notebook by my bed. What do you do?' Einstein replied: 'I do not understand your question. I have only had two or three good ideas in my life.'
Improvement?	A Yiddish edition of the complete works of Shakespeare appeared in New York. Its fly leaf contained the following remarkable inscription: 'Shakespeare – *ubergezetz und farbessert*' – literally: 'Shakespeare – translated and improved!' [*This is a useful illustration or riposte when dealing with those who wish to amend, update or otherwise allegedly improve upon some already excellent document, system, etc. GJ*]

Isolationism	A man once sat in a boat, boring a hole under his seat. 'Don't worry, shipmates,' he said to his fellow travellers. 'It's only under *my* seat, not yours...' (*Talmud*)
Knowledge	Everything I know about this subject would fit into a nutshell and still leave plenty of room for the nut. (*Lord Mancroft*)
Litigation	Litigants fight cases – lawyers win them. (*Janner's Law*)
Legislation	The effect of a statute is in directly inverse ratio to the amount of noise made during its passage. (*Janner's Law*)
Life?	Confucius says: 'I am asked why I buy rice and flowers? I reply: I buy rice to live and flowers so that I have something to live for.'
Men	Men who try too much to be macho do not amount to mucho. (*Zsa Zsa Gabor – quoted by Michael Foot, with reference to Dr Owen, October 1983*.)
News – and advertising	News is what somebody somewhere wants to suppress; all the rest is advertising. (*Lord Northcliffe*)
Opinions	A Russian Jew was asked whether he didn't have any mind of his own on political affairs. He replied: 'Yes, of course I do. I have my own opinions. But I don't agree with them.'
Optimism	An optimist says that the bottle is half full – a pessimist that it is half empty.
Orders	A Lufthansa pilot is reputed to have said: 'You *will* enjoy yourselves aboard this Lufthansa flight... Zat is an order!'
Photographs	The road to political oblivion is paved with good photographs. (*Janner's Law*)
Plagiarism	Copy from one book and that is 'plagiarism' or breach of copyright. Copy from two or more books and that is 'research'.

Power	Power is wonderful, absolute power is absolutely wonderful.
Public opinion	There was once a Russian doctor who bustled into the ward and said: 'I'm in a terrible hurry. Please give me the average temperature of all the patients...' (*Shimon Peres*) [*Useful when asked: 'What is the feeling in the UK about...? GJ*]
Quietude	Chinese proverb: May we live in uninteresting times.
Quotes	Resolution 242 is like most sacred texts – more often quoted than read. [*May be applied to most of its kind. GJ*]
Recession, depression – and recovery	Recession is when your neighbour is out of work; depression is when you are out of work; recovery is when the government is out of work...
Resignation	Never resign – unless a better job awaits. (*Janner's Law*)
Resolutions	The road to political ruin is paved with excellent resolutions. (*Janner's Law*) [*See also* Photographs].
Success	Mark Twain bemoaned that he had not seen the Niagara Falls, so they made up a special party to take him there. Afterwards his hosts said: 'What did you think of it?' Mark Twain paused: 'It's certainly a success,' he said.
Successors	Nothing succeeds like a successor.
Successful...	Be kind to people on your way up – you'll meet them again on your way down. (*US comedian, Jimmy Durante*)
Survival	The porcupine may be less attractive than the rabbit but it has a greater chance of survival and much less chance of being digested.
Systems	A system is only as good as those who attempt to deceive it. (*Janner's Law*)

Temptation	Do not blame the mouse – blame the hole in the wall. (*Talmud*)
Tolerance	Tolerance is the ability to put up with opinions which bother us little.
Intolerance	We *should* not endure intolerance; but we *must* not endure tolerance. (*Chaim Weizmann, first President of Israel*)
Secrets	The vanity of being known to be entrusted with a secret is generally one of the chief motives to disclose it. (*Samuel Johnson*)
	When a secret is revealed, that is the fault of the man who confided it. (*La Bruyère*)
	If you want to preserve your secret, wrap it up in frankness.
	Thou wilt not utter what thou doest not know, and so far will I trust you, gentle Kate. (*Shakespeare – Henry IV*)
	If you want another to keep your secret, keep it yourself. (*Seneca*)
Tradition	It is a long-established tradition ... as Lord Denning would say when he has a new idea...
Victory and defeat	Victory in war is the greatest of all tragedies – except defeat. (*Duke of Wellington*)
Wisdom	Just as the bee gathers honey from all flowers, so the wise man gathers knowledge from all men. (*Indian proverb*)

Offence

I don't just give offence, I take it. *(Churchill)*

Churchillian

Never has contempt been better expressed than that of Winston Churchill for Neville Chamberlain, thus: 'In the depths of that dusty soul there is nothing but abject surrender...'
'He looks at Foreign Affairs through the wrong end of a municipal drainpipe...'

Churchill described Prime Minister Attlee as: 'A sheep in sheep's clothing'; and said of Christian Socialist Chancellor of the Exchequer, Sir Stafford Cripps: 'There but for the grace of God goes God.'

Lady Astor was the first woman MP. She once said to Churchill: 'If you were my husband, I would flavour your coffee with poison.' He replied: 'Nancy, if I were your husband, I would drink it!'
On another occasion: 'Nancy,' said Winston, 'You are an ugly creature.'

'And you are drunk, Winston,' she retorted.

'At least *my* condition will have changed by the morning,' Churchill snapped back.

Withdraw

The late Will Paling, MP, once called Churchill 'a dirty dog'. The Tory benches erupted with cries of: 'Withdraw, withdraw...'

The old man rose to his feet. 'Not at all,' he said. 'I do not invite the Honourable Member to withdraw. On the contrary, I invite him to repeat what he has said outside this Chamber. And I will then show him what a dirty dog does to a paling!'

Top insult

Bernard Shaw sent Winston Churchill two tickets for the first night of *St Joan* – 'one for yourself – the other for a friend – if you have one.'

Churchill wrote back, returning the tickets

and regretting that he could not come to the first night. 'But I would like tickets for the second night,' he said, 'if there is one...'

No comment

Winston once tried unsuccessfully to get Lord Catto to make a statement on a particular issue. He got no results and complained: 'Alas – Lord Catto is lying doggo...'

Death wish

President Johnson attended the memorial service in Australia for a Prime Minister, recently drowned. He was asked by the press what he would do for peace. 'Anything,' he replied.

'Mr President,' came a voice from the back. 'Would you take a swim?'

Offensive person

A well known politician is reputed to have met a renowned and unpleasant lady on a dark night in a back street. The following morning he was charged with having an offensive person on his weapon.

Fence sitting

An American Senator described King Hussein as 'Forever Amber'. [*Could be used for anyone else who cannot make up his mind whether to stop or to go, on a particular issue or generally. GJ*]

Accountants and politicians

Aneurin Bevan coined a marvellous phrase for a heartless human being. Many wrongly believe that he applied it to the austere Sir Stafford Cripps. In fact it was used in rage when he was beaten by Hugh Gaitskell for the Treasurership of the Labour Party. Without naming his target, he said: 'The right kind of leader for the Labour Party is a *desiccated calculating machine* who must not in any way permit himself to be swayed by indignation ... at suffering, privation or injustice ... for that would be evidence of the lack of proper education and absence of self-control.'

'You, sir, are – as Bevan once said – a desiccated calculating machine!' is a splendid insult, especially when aimed at an accountant or a politician.

Enemies

Abba Eban said of a Cabinet Minister: 'It's not that ... has enemies. It's just that his friends cannot stand him!' [*This marvellous insult can, of course, be translated against any worthy opponent! GJ*]

Worst enemy

Herbert Morrison was once quoted as saying that he was his own worst enemy. 'Not while I'm alive, he ain't' Ernest Bevin retorted.

Compliment or insult?

One day, when Chancellor of the Exchequer, David Lloyd George, was making an important speech, a Conservative from the Opposition benches kept interrupting him. Eventually, Lloyd George exclaimed: 'I should think that the argument would be plain even to the colossal intellect of the Honourable Member.'

The Tory leapt to his feet. 'Is it in order, Mr Speaker,' he asked, 'for the Right Honourable Gentleman to refer to my colossal intellect?'

'Well,' replied Mr Speaker Lowther, very softly. 'I think it is not only in order, but is rather complimentary than otherwise!'

Disaster *v.* calamity

'If Gladstone fell into the Thames, that would be a misfortune; and if anybody pulled him out, that I suppose would be a calamity.' (*Disraeli on Gladstone*) [*This one is capable of innumerable variations, directed towards your current pet hate. Thus: 'If the Prime Minister/Leader of the Opposition/managing director of main competitors, were to fall out of an aircraft, that would be a misfortune – if his parachute were to open, that would be a calamity. GJ*]

Young parent

If you are faced with an inexperienced and youthful opponent, try the insult aimed by US Interior Secretary Harold Ickes at the then young Thomas Dewey, Republican candidate for President: 'Dewey has thrown his diaper into the ring.'

Lying

I do not accuse Mrs Thatcher of lying. She

merely has what psychologists call 'selective amnesia'. (*Denis Healey on Mrs Thatcher*)

Diplomacy   The opposite of 'secret diplomacy'? – 'megaphone diplomacy.' (*Denis Healey, describing insults being hurled across the world by Messrs Reagan, Thatcher and Andropov respectively.*)

Book review   An author wrote to the perpetrator of a fiercely offensive review: 'I am sitting in the smallest room in the house. Your review is before me. It will soon be behind me.'

Plagues   I was recently at a charity dinner, with my wife on my right, and a very persistent lobbyist on my left. During the first three courses, he regaled me with horror stories of the way that politicians of all parties had ruined his business and how no country could really survive its treatment by those of us elected to office. Finally, my wife said to him: 'But surely you do make *some* distinction between the policies of the two parties?'

'There's no difference between you,' he retorted. 'I say: A plague on all your houses.'

My wife smiled across at him. 'When the plague comes to our house,' she said, 'you *must* come and visit us!'

Memories   I always smile at Mr Smith's jokes. First at their elegant wit, and then again with nostalgia.

Mindless?   Mr Smith didn't say a word till he was ten. His mother didn't know whether he was dumb or just speaking his mind.

Repetition   . . . we were all glad to hear his speech again.

Speechmaking   Mrs . . . has proved the theory that the brain is a wonderful organ that never stops functioning from the moment of birth until one rises to speak in public.

Sleeptalking   Mr. . .'s speeches always do the audience some good; they either go away stimulated or wake up refreshed.

Non-contribution	He makes the same contribution to commerce (*or to the subject under discussion*) as Cyril Smith* does to hang-gliding... [*Or any other well known man of huge build. GJ*]
Libraries	Mr Smith's library was burned down. Both books were destroyed. And one of them he had not even finished colouring in. [*This one can be used for your favourite ignoramus. GJ*]
Genius	The chairman (*Foreign Minister, director or whomever-you-will*) was a man of few words which were quite adequate to express the full range of his ideas.
Unbiased assessment	No one thinks more highly of Mr Smith than I do – and I think that he's a pig!
One nation	Some Americans say that Yankees from the North are like haemorrhoids. If they come down and then go up again quickly, that's not too bad. But if they come down and stay down, that is a pain in the rear...
Manchester	He chose to live in Manchester, a wholly incomprehensible choice for any free human being to make. (*Mr Justice Melford Stevenson*) [*This remark may be transferred to any particular city of your hate. GJ*]
Manchester (or any other grimy city)	Manchester (*Pittsburg – or where-have-you*) is the place where the birds fly backwards so as not to get grit in their eyes.
Punishment	A man appeared before Mr Justice Melford Stevenson, charged with rape. The jury acquitted him. The Judge said: 'I see you come from Slough. It's a horrible place. You can go back there!'
Prizes	The first prize for the raffle was one week at Yarmouth-on-Sea. The second prize was two weeks at Yarmouth-on Sea. The third prize was a month at Yarmouth-on-Sea.
Thanks	At her husband's request, a wife gave him a plot

of land in the local cemetery as his birthday present. The following year, she refused to give him a birthday present at all.

'Why no present, darling?' he asked.

'Because you haven't used last year's yet,' she replied.

'And before leaving I would like to express my thanks to all those at Fire Station 37, Beryl on the switchboard, Chief Officer Hargreaves, Driver Jenkins. . . .'

Works, trade and **77** management

Branch opening

A friend asked a Mayfair prostitute: 'How's trade?'

'Marvellous,' she replied. 'If I had another pair of legs, I'd open a branch in Birmingham!'

Prostitutes

A prostitute is covered by the Factories Act because she is employed for the demolition of temporary erections.

Perks

Our staff reckon that they can only take the company's property off our premises at certain times...

Fringe benefits

On 'cabbage' (*the rag trade term for material offcuts*): We usually sell cabbage to our staff – if they don't pinch it first...'

Working hours

Alistair Cooke passed a country station and found the stationmaster tending his roses. 'How many hours a day do you work?' he enquired.

'Eight hours, sir. Five days a week.'

'Always eight hours? Always five days a week?' said Mr Cooke.

'Yes, always the same.'

'Why always the same?'

'Because if I worked less than eight hours, I wouldn't have enough money to buy roses. And if I worked more than eight hours, I would not have time to tend the roses...'

Short-time?

Employer: 'Did you work a full week last week?'

Employee: 'Yes – but I don't want any publicity...'

Occupational illnesses

Three well known diseases: *Plumbi pendulosis* — *swinging the lead; Haemophraemia* — bloody mindedness; and *Non digitus extractus* — failure to pull out the finger...

Tell-tale twitch   A man applied for a job as a television announcer. Unfortunately, he suffered from a very severe twitch of his right eye. His interviewer said: 'Wouldn't you be better off applying for a job with the radio?'

'No,' the man replied. 'I take one of my special pills and I'm all right for a couple of hours.'

'In that case,' said the interviewer, 'you'd better take one now and let me see how it works.'

The man fished in his pockets and pulled out a packet of contraceptives ... then another ... then a third ... then a whole pile of them, before finally producing a bottle of aspirin.

'I understand the aspirin,' said the interviewer. 'But why the contraceptives?'

The interviewee looked at him sceptically. 'Have you ever tried going into a chemist's shop and saying: "I'd like a (*wink*) bottle of (*wink*) aspirin, please"?'

Secretaries   Sign on noticeboard of large insurance company: 'Managers are asked to take advantage of their secretaries as early in the day as possible!'

Job description   Fred answered an advertisement, offering £1,500 for a man prepare to sleep with a gorilla. He asked whether he could have time to pay.

Unemployment   A miner applied for a job at a Rhondda pit. The manager told him to 'come back in the spring'.

'What do you think I am,' asked the man, 'a ruddy cuckoo?' (*Speaker George Thomas, now Viscount Tonypandy*)

Warning   The managing director of a great engineering company invited school classes to see round the works. One of the teachers was overheard at the end of the morning saying to his class: 'There you are, lads and girls. You have now seen where *you* may end up, if you don't do well in your O-levels!'

208

Passing the buck	An Ordinary Seaman was applying for promotion. He was asked to correct the following statement: 'It was me what done it.' He wrote: 'It was *not* me what done it.' [*Legend has it that he was immediately promoted to Rear Admiral! GJ*]
Industrial peace	Peace at work – a period of cheating, between strikes. [*Beam in on the industry or company currently in convulsion. GJ*]
Trade unions	A trade union is an island of anarchy in a sea of chaos. (*Aneurin Bevan*)
'Differentials' and 'anomalies'	If I earn more than you do, that is a 'differential'. If you earn more than I do, that is an 'anomaly'.
Management – and industrial disputes	The latest argument at a works renowned for its management problems got senior executives so upset that they began to stab each other in the front. [*Also useful to describe feelings in the Cabinet, Shadow Cabinet, boardroom – or where-you-will. GJ*]
Pay day?	A son asked his father for a loan until pay day. His father asked: 'When is pay day?' The son replied: 'I don't know. You tell me. You're the one who's working...'
Seagull management*	The European directors of a well known multinational described their head office people to me as 'seagulls'. 'They fly in ... make loud noises as they land ... and then fly off, fertilising all over you as they leave...' [**An advance on 'mushroom management'. GJ*]
Leadership	There are two types of leadership. One is where you go in front and lead from there. The other is: wait to see where people are going and then run around to the front and take over. (*Julius Berman, then Chairman of the Conference of American Jewish Organisations*)
Explanations	A personnel director was having great trouble in inducing an employee to sign up under a non-

contributory pension scheme – which was in fact far better for him than the current contributory pension scheme. But he refused to sign.

Eventually, the personnel manager sent the man to the managing director. 'Alex,' said the MD, 'you must sign. I know that you have been with us for 30 years without causing trouble, but that is no reason for not signing...'

Alex: 'I refuse.'

Managing director: 'Alex, you must sign – or I will give you the sack!'

Alex signed.

The next time the personnel manager saw Alex, he said: 'Why did you sign when the managing director asked you to – but you always refused me?'

Alex: 'Well, no one explained it to me properly before...'

Supervisors
Supervisory staff can do no right. They can only mitigate their wrong. (*Lord Goddard*)

Self-service
Two foremen were arguing over whether or not sex was a pleasure or a chore. The first, a married man with eight children, regarded it as a chore. The second, a bachelor, thought it was the greatest delight in life. To settle their argument, they called over young Fred, the apprentice. 'So you tell us, Fred,' they said. 'Is sex a chore or a pleasure?'

'It must be a pleasure,' said the boy.

'Why?'

'Because if it was a chore, you fellows would make me do it for you!'

Up yours
A worker removed the guard from a machine and lost two fingers on his right hand. He only noticed his loss when he said good night to the foreman!

Once a failure
A man was sacked for trying to kill his foreman. His shop steward begged the employers to give him a second chance.

Never resign

Frederick the Great intended to dismiss one of his Generals. The General wrote to him: 'After the battle, my head is yours. Meanwhile, I intend to use it to best effect on your behalf.'

Dismissal

The chairman of a large company called in his directors, one by one. Eventually, only the newest and most junior director was left outside the chairman's office. When his turn came, he found his colleagues sitting around a table.

Chairman: 'Bill, have you been having an affair with my secretary, Miss Jones?'

Bill: 'Certainly not.'

'Are you sure?'

'Absolutely. I've never laid a hand on her.'

'Are you absolutely certain?'

'Of course I am.'

'Very well Bill, then *you* sack her.'

References

'I am pleased to recommend him for any other job...'or 'I am pleased to provide him with a reference for any other job...' or 'He was fired with enthusiasm ...'

Discipline

A foreman was alleged to have assaulted a colleague, banging his head against a work bench. He alleged that the man had 'provoked him' – and the man was then dismissed.

The Transport and General Workers Union then brought everyone out on strike. Immediately, the management reinstated the man and sacked the foreman. The foreman's union then brought everyone out on strike. The management reinstated the foreman and cut the work bench in half.

Who dun it?

A woman complained to her personnel manager that she had been sexually assaulted. 'Who did it?' the manager asked. 'I don't know,' replied the girl. 'I'd never seen him before. But I think he must have been the foreman.'

'Why?'

'Because he was wearing a white coat and brown shoes – and I had to do all the work!'

**Erratic
leadership**

The following is a useful analogy, when explaining why the Prime Minister, president, managing director or other adversary is likely to perform some unpredictable and dangerous act:

Mr Brown is like the cross-eyed javelin thrower who does not break any records, but who certainly keeps his audience on its toes!

Auditors

An auditor is an accountant who comes onto the field after the battle is over and bayonets the wounded. *(Don Hanson [Arthur Andersen])*

Auditors – and actuaries

An auditor is like an actuary who has had his personality removed.

Accountancy

If someone asks me: 'What is two and two?', I answer: 'Are you buying or selling?' (*Lord Grade*)

Accountants

Three men apply for a job as an accountant. They are asked one question: 'What is two times two?' The first two fellows got it right. The third one replies: 'What figure did you have in mind, sir?'. He got the job.

Risks

A 'calculated risk' was defined by an airline pilot as one 'when the engineers on the ground make the calculations and the pilots take the risk'. [*Adapt for any situation where* others *make the calculation but the risk is yours. GJ*]

US petty cash slip

24th September – advert for typist	10 dollars
Violets for typist's desk	5.50 dollars
Week's salary for typist	120 dollars
Roses for typist	10 dollars
Candy for wife	75 cents
Lunch – typist and self	22.80 dollars
Typist's salary	190 dollars
Movies – wife and self	10 dollars
Theatre – typist and self	40 dollars
Candy for wife	75 cents
Lillian's salary	200 dollars
Theatre, dinner – Lillian and self	83 dollars
Doctor's bill – Lillian	780 dollars
Fur for wife (mink)	7,800 dollars
Advert for male typist	10 dollars

Flotation	An accountant and a client were swimming in the sea when the client was swept away. The accountant swam after him, dragged him towards the shore and when he was nearly in, said: 'Are you OK now? Can you float on your own?'
	The client replied: 'Even when I'm dying, he wants to talk business!'
The ripper	The mother of the Haifa Ripper said to her sister: 'It's a funny thing about my boy. He never brings home the same friend twice.'
	The sister said: 'How many people has he killed?'
	'How do I know?' replied the mother. 'My boy's a murderer, not an accountant.' *(Henry Knobil)*
Good company	Lawyer to judge, well known for his puritanical views and as a pillar of the Church: 'I appear for the plaintiffs – a God-fearing, limited liability company.'
Companies	Lord Thurloe once said: 'A corporation has no body to be burned and no soul to be damned...'
Unanimity	Two directors were doing a crossword. One asked: 'How do you spell "unanimously"?'
	The other: 'I am not surprised that you don't know. It's only a miracle that you can pronounce the word...'
Partners?	The owner of a hotel quietly watched as his barman put 50p in his own pocket, out of every £1 he took from a customer. When he saw the barman putting an entire £1 into his wallet, he pounced. 'What are you doing?' he asked. 'I thought we were partners!'
Civil servants	A civil servant – one who has a valid objection to any possible solution.
Success and failure	The head of the Civil Service, Sir Douglas Wass, pointed out to a distinguished and private dinner of top business executives and lawyers that *they*

could measure *their* success by winning or losing cases and by their balance sheets (respectively). 'We have no such base to judge ours,' he said. 'The success of a civil servant can only be judged by the absence of obvious failure!'

Police

A teacher in a local school required his class to write an essay on the police. Martin wrote: 'Them police are bastards.'

The teacher told the police of the comment. They invited Martin to the station and gave him the most marvellous day of his life. The next day the teacher set the boys another essay on the police. Martin wrote: 'Them police are *cunning* bastards!'

Spies

A Russian spy went to Wales and was told to see their contact in Abergavenny, who lived at 25 Cwmbran Terrace. The password: 'The space ship is in orbit.'

By mistake, he called at number 5 Cwmbran Terrace. A woman opened the door. 'Yes?' she enquired.

'The space ship is in orbit,' said the Russian.

'Oh,' said the lady, 'you've come to the wrong address. You will be wanting number 25. That's where Dai the Spy lives.'

Sailors

A sailor never wants to be where he is, but always longs to be where he is not. When a sailor stops complaining the time has come to start worrying... (*Prince Charles*)

Window cleaners

Raquel Welch once went on a brass-rubbing tour of the Gorbals. She was in bed one morning when she saw a window cleaner outside her room. She lifted back the covers and showed him one shoulder. He kept on working. She removed her nightdress and showed him her better points. He still kept on working. So she jumped onto the bed as God made her. The window cleaner opened the window, looked in, and said: 'Madam – have you never seen a window cleaner before?'

Public relations

Fact: In places, the fabled River Jordon is nothing more than a trickle.

Comment: 'This is what public relations can do for a river!' (*Henry Kissinger*)

Army legitimates

Four men were talking in a train. The first said: 'I am a brigadier; I am married; I have three sons; and they are all barristers.'

The next said: 'I am a brigadier; I am married; I have three sons and they are all soldiers.'

The third said: 'I am a brigadier; I am married; I have three sons; they are all chartered accountants.'

The fourth was silent. 'Well, aren't you going to teil us about yourself?' asked the first brigadier.

'Very well,' he replied. 'I am a sergeant major. I am not married. I have three sons. They are all brigadiers.'

Brains

Two army captains were grousing about the stupidity of their respective batmen. They decided to have a bet on which one was more stupid. Captain X called for his batman and said: 'Take this £5 note and buy me a colour TV set down in the village.' 'Yes, sir. Certainly, sir.' He saluted and went out into the mess room.

Captain Y then rang for his batman and said: 'Go to the orderly room immediately and see whether I am there.' 'Yes, sir. Certainly, sir.' The batman saluted and left.

The two batmen met in the corridor outside and compared notes.

'Fancy asking me to buy a colour TV set on an early closing day,' said the first. The second replied: 'Imagine making me walk half a mile when he could have used the telephone to see if he's in the orderly room!'

Class distinction

When I was serving in the British Army of the Rhine, I found a notice on our HQ board at Christmas. It read: 'Christmas parties will be held as follows: Officers and their ladies, 24 December; non-commissioned officers and their wives, 25 December; and other ranks and their womenfolk, 26 December.'

Press men

Newspapers are fiercely independent of pressure from their advertisers. Or are they?

Some years ago, I campaigned for legislation to ban the fraudulent 'guarantee' or 'warranty', which in reality removed more rights then it gave – especially when provided with a motor vehicle. I was commissioned to write a full-length feature for a London Sunday paper which carried the front page banner: 'THE fearless newspaper'.

My piece was pungent, accurate, documented and devastating. It was not published. Instead, I simply received my fee. I telephoned the Features Editor. He said: 'I'm sorry, but to publish your piece would have cost us a fortune. You effectively attacked every car manufacturer in the business.'

'So what?' I retorted. 'I thought you were "The fearless newspaper"!'

'That's all very well,' he retorted, "but you have to have a newspaper to be fearless in!"

Insurers

Insurance people present plans to keep you poor while you are alive so that you may die rich.

Insurance

The favourite uncle at a wedding dinner announced that he was going to give the bridegroom a life insurance policy. The bride burst into tears. When she was finally calmed, she blurted out: 'I don't like it ... I don't like it ... I don't want father to set light to Harry like he did to the warehouse ...!'

Whose worry?

A man owed $100,000. The night before the sum fell due for payment, he could not sleep. He tossed and he turned and he strode up and down. Eventually, he walked around to his creditor's house and knocked on the window. 'What is it?' asked the man.

217

'I'm very sorry,' replied the debtor, 'but I shan't be able to pay what I owe you tomorrow morning. I've been so worried about it that I couldn't get to sleep. Anyway, I've decided to wake you so that you can now stay awake worrying, while I get some sleep!'

Whose trade?

Morgan and Dai went on safari. Suddenly, a woolly creature dropped from a tree onto Morgan's back. 'What is it? What is it?' he cried out.

'How should I know?' Dai replied. 'Am I a furrier?'

Enterprise

Cohen owned a small tailor's shop and made a modest living. Then two firms of multiple-tailors opened on either side of him. 'What are you going to do now?' asked a friend.

'Don't worry,' said Cohen. 'Everything will be all right. I'll just change the name of my shop.'

'What good will that do you?'

'Plenty.'

'What will you call your shop?'

'I shall call it... *Main Entrance*!'

Value and worth

The famous painter, Rex Whistler, charged £500 for a portrait at a time when that meant big money. His client refused to pay, alleging gross overcharging for two days' work. Whistler sued.

In court, the client's lawyer challenged the artist: 'Is it right that you spent two days to complete this painting?'

'Yes,' Whistler replied.

'Then it follows, does it not, that you are seeking to charge £500 for two days' work?'

'Not at all,' the painter retorted. 'I charged £500 for a lifetime of experience which enabled me to paint the portrait in two days!' He won his case. [*Useful when dealing with the evaluation of time and service, in any circumstances. GJ*]

Jewish business

Three Jewish men met for dinner.

The first one said: 'Oi!'

The second one said: 'Oi yevay!'

The third said: 'If you boys are going to talk business, I'm off...'

Antiques

An American and his wife were in Portobello Road. 'It's not bad, Bessie,' he said. 'But they don't make antiques like they used to, do they?'

Wedding present

A father-in-law gave his son-in-law 5,000 shares in his business. 'There you are, lad,' he said. 'Anything else I can do for you?'

The son-in-law replied: 'Yes, Dad. Please would you buy me out?'

Commercial progression

A businessman gets on... then he gets honest... then he gets honoured...

Lobbying

As I was being wheeled on a trolley into the operating theatre at London's Royal Free Hospital, the anaesthetist came up to me, green clad and masked, syringe in hand. He leaned forward and said: 'Mr Janner, I understand that you are a Member of Parliament.'

'Yes,' I replied.

He paused, lifting his syringe: 'We anaesthetists,' he said, ominously, 'are very poorly remunerated!'

'Do please come and discuss the matter with me, when I have recovered consciousness,' I said.

Business talk

Movie Mogul Lou Wasserman once invited Sam Goldwyn to meet Clark Gable. 'But you mustn't talk business with him,' he said. 'Promise me – nothing about business and nothing about money.' Goldwyn agreed.

He duly arrived for the lunch with a brief case which he promptly opened, emptying onto the table $100,000 in 10 dollar notes. 'There you are,' he announced. 'This is what I am not allowed to talk to you about!' (*Michael Klinger*)

Excellence

The Head of Production of Metro Goldwyn Mayer once said to his redoubtable chief, Sam Goldwyn: 'We shall be making 30 films this year – 10 As, 10 Bs and 10 Cs.'

Goldwyn replied: 'I suggest that you make 30 As – the Bs and Cs will look after themselves!' (*Michael Klinger*)

Golfer – a top surprise

'I know you're not meant to take bets when you play against members,' said John Jones to the club professional, 'but I want to ask you a very special favour. As it's my silver wedding, I'd like to play one round with you for £100.'

'You know I can't do that,' said the professional. 'Anyway, I'd have to give you a very large handicap.'

'No,' said John, 'all I want by way of handicap is three gotchas.'

The professional, who did not want to let on that he did not know what 'gotcha' meant, said: 'OK. But keep it quiet.'

As they were about to tee off at the first hole, the professional felt a hand coming between his legs and grabbing him. 'Gotcha!' John shouted.

Discomforted, the professional prepared to tee off for the second time.

'Gotcha!' yelled John, as he grabbed his opponent.

'That's very nasty,' said the professional. 'But we've got 18 holes to go and you've only got one gotcha left!'

'That's right' said John. 'But how will you enjoy playing 18 holes, never knowing when the next gotcha's coming?' (*Bob Monkhouse*) [*Monkhouse used this joke to massive effect at an entertainment industry dinner – his speech won a standing ovation from his colleagues. Used with sensitivity, it may be told to illustrate any other situation in which you are proposing to keep your opponents, competitors, rivals or enemies in Damocletian suspense! GJ*]

Follow-up

Fred won a million pounds in a lottery. His wife said to him: 'What shall we do about all the begging letters?'

'Just keep sending them!' Fred replied.

How to become a millionaire

A bedraggled beggar wheedled a dollar out of Rockefeller, outside his Manhattan apartment block. After handing over the money, the millionaire enquired: 'Why don't you invest in some clean clothing, young man?'

'I appreciate the suggestion,' the beggar replied. 'But if you don't mind my asking, do I try to teach *you* your business?'

Time and emotion study

A wealthy and charitable friend tells how emissaries from a religious seminary called on him regularly, year by year. He always gave them a cheque for £100.

Then one year when the collector called, my friend said to himself: 'I don't really know these people. And there are many calls upon me. So I think I'll give them £50.' Which he did.

The man thanked him gravely and turned to leave. My friend said: 'Why didn't you try to get the other £50, like I usually give you?'

The man smiled. 'I've a taxi waiting outside,' he said. 'In the time I spend arguing with you and trying to induce you to give me the balance, I could probably make another couple of calls. And anyway, I'm grateful for the £50 I've got and I don't want to upset you.'

My friend gave him the balance – and told him to call again next year.

Fellow feeling

A burglar was caught in the garden of a millionaire's mansion, a transistor radio in his pocket.

'What do you want us to do with him?' asked the police.

'Let him go,' answered the millionaire. 'We all started small.'

The gift of language

Sign on shop: '30 languages spoken here.' Customer comes in and tries to make herself understood in French, but nobody can manage. Another customer says to the shopkeeper: 'I thought you spoke 30 languages here?'

Shopkeeper replies: 'That's the customers ...not us ...'

Luck

A man convinced Rockefeller that he should take a lottery ticket. It won a hundred thousand dollars.

'You have done me a great favour,' said Rockefeller to the man. 'I offer you twenty thousand dollars or four thousand dollars a year for life.'

'I'll take the twenty thousand dollars,' said the man, without hesitation.

'Are you sure?' asked the tycoon. 'You are a very young man ... Why have you made that decision?'

'Because with your damned luck, sir,' he replied, 'if I took the annuity, I would only live six months!'

Honour

'Next time a man says that his word is as good as his bond, take his bond!' (*Lord Home of the Hirsel – formerley Prime Minister, Alec Douglas Home)*

Energy

Britain is a lump of coal in a sea of oil on a bubble of gas. (*Clive Jenkins)*

Oil wealth

It's not clever just to have oil, you know. Sardines have oil and they are really stupid. They even get inside the tin and leave the key on the outside. *(Bob Monkhouse)*

Prophesies

It is very difficult to make a prophesy as to the future ... and in Israel, it is very difficult to be a prophet at all, because of the competition ...

Cash management	We have just created a new cash management programme. This means that we pay when we wish to ...
Debtors	If you owe £50, you are a *shnorrer* (a beggar, in Yiddish). If you owe £500, you are a businessman. If you owe £5 million, you are a millionaire. If you owe £500 billion, then you are Chancellor of the Exchequer *(or Minister of Finance)*.
Inflation	The Chancellor of the Exchequer is expecting to be immortalised by having his portrait, along with that of Her Majesty, on the first £1,000 notes.
Hyper inflation	The Chancellor of the Exchequer went into a shop and said: 'I don't think inflation is that bad. Look at those handkerchieves – £1 each. And shirts for £10. And trousers for £15.' His aide whispered quietly in his ear. 'I'm sorry, Minister. We're not in a man's shop. This is a laundry ...'
Magic	Asked how Israel copes with inflation at 400 per cent per annum, Eban replied: 'That's like the acrobat on the 100-ft wire who said: "My next trick is impossible!"'
A capital story	'Where is the capital of Saudi Arabia?' 'A third in Switzerland; a third in London; and the rest in Germany and the USA.' This story is matched by one I was told in Canada: 'What was the first Polish settlement in the Province of Ontario?' '30 cents in the dollar!'
Bankruptcy	'Nothing in your deposit box? Nothing in your wife's name? Nothing dug into the ground? – You're not bankrupt, brother, you're skint!'
Ultimate insolvency	Jack went bankrupt so often that he even put his tombstone into his wife's name.

Liquidation   Noah was the bravest man in history. He floated his company when the rest of the world was in liquidation.

Recession   A deep-sea diver feels tug on rope. Voice on intercom says: 'Come up quickly, the ship's sinking!' [*Suitable for comment on invitation to join political party currently in eclipse. GJ*]

'And this one, Miss Forbish, is the direct *line. . . .'*

Politicians and 80
philosophers

Objectivity   Those who are prominent in political life are only objectively described in their own memoirs. (*Abba Eban*)

Politicians   A politician is a person who approaches every problem with an open mouth. (*Adlai Stevenson*)

Principles   I am a man of principle – but one of my principles is expediency. (*Lloyd George*)

Compromise   Compromise is when you do today that which you swore yesterday that you would not do – and while all politicians compromise, none of them like to be photographed doing so...

Conservative   A lawyer was interviewed on his hundredth birthday. Journalist: 'I suppose that you have seen many changes in your time?'
     Lawyer: 'Yes – and I have been against all of them.'

Balanced concerns   'If I am not for myself, who will be for me? But if I am only for myself, what am I? And if not now, then when?' (*Rabbi Hillel*)

Middle of the road   The only part of the road worth driving on is the middle – each of the extremes is in the gutter. (*General Eisenhower*)

Experience   Experience tells us that politicians do not *always* mean the opposite of what they say.

Eggs and baskets   British aircraft manufacturers once suggested to Winston Churchill that he, the Cabinet and 40 other MPs should go up in the newly invented Comet jet aircraft, so as to give confidence to the public. But one of his ministers complained that if anything happened to the aircraft, it would be disastrous. The country would be plunged into over 60 by-elections at the same time.

Reluctantly, the old man agreed. 'It all goes to show,' he said, 'that it is potentially disastrous to put all your baskets into one egg...'

Opposition

To be in Opposition is no disgrace. In fact, it is an honour. But it is the only honour which politicians do not actively seek! (*Abba Eban*)

Governmental philosophy

If you do not know where you are going, you will probably end up somewhere else...

Publicity

He is the sort of politician who gets an erection every time he sees a microphone or TV camera. (*Israeli Cabinet Minister, Josef Burg, describing a colleague.*)

Media attraction

A microphone has the same effect on him as a lamp post has on a dog.

Sleep

MPs and Congressmen are people who talk in other people's sleep.

The oldest profession?

Some say that gardening is the oldest profession – because Adam was the first man on earth. But the Bible tells us that before the world was created, all was chaos and confusion. And you all know who created that... politicians!

Incipient modesty

Your first two weeks in Parliament, you wonder how you got there. Thereafter, you wonder how the others got there.

Substitute?

An MP died. Within a day, a young hopeful telephoned the national agent. 'I hope it's not too soon,' he said, 'but I'm wondering whether I might not take the place of the deceased...'

The national agent replied: 'If the undertaker has no objection, I certainly have none!'

Divisions

Two tourists were standing in the central lobby in the House of Commons, when the division bell rang. 'What's that?' one of them asked the other. 'I don't know,' she replied. 'I suppose one of them must have escaped...'

Person unknown

A Tory Whip telephoned one of his Members in the middle of the night, to tell him to come in to vote. A woman's voice answered the phone – but he heard a male voice in the background saying: 'Tell him I'm not here...'

'I'm afraid Mr ... is not here' said the voice.

Quick as a flash, the Whip replied: 'In that case, please tell the man who is in bed with you, whomever he may be, that he is required at the House of Commons to vote... at once!'

New councillor

Dai Jones is elected a Councillor for the first time. Delighted, he goes to the pub to celebrate.

'Your usual, Dai?' asks the barman.

'*Councillor* Dai, if you please,' Dai retorted.

When he went to collect his coat in the cloakroom, the attendant said: 'Good evening, Dai.'

He replied: '*Councillor* Dai, if you please.'

On the bus, the conductor said: 'Nice to see you, Dai.'

'*Councillor* Dai, if you please,' he replied.

And so it went on with everyone he met. And when he got home, he heard his wife's voice from upstairs: 'Is that you, Dai?'

'*Councillor* Dai, if you please,' he replied.

'Then you'd better hurry up,' his wife called out. 'Dai will be home at any moment!'

Surprise

St Peter provided a distinguished Pope with a bare cell, while giving a Congressman a fine, carpeted and thoroughly heavenly apartment. When challenged by the Pope, St Peter replied: 'We've had plenty of popes up here – but this is our first Congressman!'

Alas

There is nothing so 'ex' as an ex-MP.

Spot the wise man

Reagan, Mitterand and Thatcher met at a Conference. 'I need your help,' said Reagan. 'I have a problem. I have 18 guards. One of them is a KGB agent. And I cannot find out which one it is!'

I have a problem that, in its own way, is even worse,' said Mitterand. 'I have 18 mistresses. One of them is unfaithful to me. And my problem is

227

that I cannot tell which one.'

'My problem is worst of all,' said Mrs Thatcher. 'I have 18 people in my Cabinet. One of them is very clever. And I cannot find out which one it is!' [*This happy and – I hasten to add – apocryphal tale may, of course, be adapted to whichever Cabinet, committee or other national or organisational leadership you may desire to defame. GJ*]

Economy

A politician who claimed that it would be possible to get much the same results with half the expenditure illustrated his case with the tale of a Scottish riding school. They supplied each rider with only one spur on the principle that if you can get half the horse to go, there is a good chance that the other half will follow.

Differences of opinion

We specialise in harmonising contrariness. *(Sir Shridath [Sonny] Ramphal, Secretary General of the Commonwealth)*

Good relations

A son asked his father whether in the 25 years of his marriage he had never thought of divorcing his mother. 'Never,' said Dad.

'Never, ever?'

'No. I have never thought of divorcing her. Of course, there were many times when I wanted to murder her!' *(Union Leader, Jack Jones — explaining the relationship between the TUC and the Labour Party)*

Family tradition

Franklin D. Roosevelt was asked why he was a Democrat. He replied: 'Because my great grandfather and my grandfather and my father were Democrats before me.'

'What would happen if your great grandfather, your grandfather and your father had been horse thieves?' retorted the questioner.

'In that case,' President Roosevelt replied, 'I would have been a Republican.'

Mania

Soviet dissident, Leonid Plyush, told a group of MPs the sad story of his incarceration in Russian mental institutions. When asked what diagnosis he had received from the Soviet psychiatric experts he replied: 'Reformist mania with messianic tendencies.' His listeners agreed that he would have made an excellent MP.

Princely politics

It is very difficult to avoid making party political statements when you talk about almost anything. Sometimes, I fall into great elephant traps and no one notices. Other times, I trip into a very small trap – and all hell breaks loose ... *(Prince Charles)*

Open government	Sunlight is the most effective of all disinfectants ... (*US Supreme Court Justice Brandeis*)
Parliament	Our parliamentary system is not good – but it's the best we've got. *(Winston Churchill)*
	Parliamentary democracy is the worst form of government – until you look at all the others. *(Winston Churchill)*
Presidents and kings	What is the difference between a king and a president? A king is the son of his father.
Committees	If Moses had been a committee, the Israelites would still be in Egypt.
	A Parliamentary committee is a cul-de-sac into which ideas are lured, there to be quietly strangled ...
Committee inventions	A camel is a horse, invented by a committee.
Committee of one	Every committee must be made up of an odd number of people. Three members is too many.
Whipping	An MP complained that the 'whipping' had been so heavy that he could not even get out of the Commons to attend the christening of his son. His friend replied: 'You're lucky. You weren't there when your son was christened. I wasn't there when mine was conceived!'
Elections	A Scottish jury was informed by the judge: 'This is a simple case and no doubt it will not take you long to reach your verdict.'

After the jury had been out for three hours, the judge called them in. 'What's happened?' he enquired.

'We had no difficulty in reaching our verdict,' he was told. 'But the trouble is that we're still trying to elect a foreman ...'

The right of citizens in a democracy is to make the wrong decision. That right is one which the British people have massively exercised.

Democracy We cannot complain if a democracy exercises the rotatory principle and electors vote the wrong party into power . . . *(Abba Eban)*

Russian elections In the Soviet Union they have what are called 'Adam elections' – you have the same choice as he had.

Directions A Cabinet Minister got lost in a remote village. He lowered the window of his car and asked a passing villager: 'Where am I, please?'

The man replied: 'You are in your car, sir.'

'Thank you,' replied the Cabinet Minister. 'That reply is exactly like a Ministerial answer. It is brief; accurate; and it adds nothing whatever to the sum total of human knowledge!'

Withdraw, withdraw! MP Willie Hamilton was criticising Harold Wilson for wanting to go into the Common Market . . . then out of the market . . . then into the market again . . . He described such behaviour as: 'The politics of *coitus interruptus.*' The MP in front of him yelled: 'Withdraw . . . withdraw . . .'

Standard letters I sometimes use standard letters for those of my constituents' queries that are identical. For instance, I at one time received a huge postbag, carefully organised and orchestrated by the League Against Cruel Sports. Letters flooded in from all over the country, asking me to support the Bill against hare coursing.

My assistants prepared a large pile of standard letters saying: 'Thank you for your letter. I have carefully considered your views and I appreciate your writing to me.' To each I added a note: 'I agree with you – I will do what I can.'

Unfortunately, I also received on the same day a letter from a gentleman of eccentric views, complaining about a television broadcast in which I had said that a person's background must be taken into account when considering the cause of his criminal tendencies – and in

231

which I attacked the views of a judge who had declaimed to the contrary. The gentleman wrote: 'You are an idiot ... You have no understanding of people... You and your kind are leading this country into decadent disaster... You should be shot!'

The man must have been somewhat surprised to receive a standard reply, sent off by an unthinking aide. It concluded: 'I agree with you – I will do what I can.'

The truth

An opponent said: 'How do you know when ex-President Nixon is lying? When he spreads his hands out, he's telling the truth ... When he wags his finger, he's telling the truth ... When he shakes his fist, he's telling the truth ... But when he opens his mouth ...'

Emigration

A professor decided to emigrate. The Dean called him to his office: 'Why do you want to go?' he enquired. 'You have a very good job ... an excellent home ... splendid prospects ...'

'There are two reasons,' the Professor replied. 'The first is that when I come home in the evenings, I usually find my neighbour outside my door, dead drunk. He keeps swearing at me: "Just wait till we get rid of this Tory government and then we'll slit the throats of all you useless academics!" '

'But the Tory government is in for years yet' replied the Dean.

'Precisely,' said the Professor. 'That's my second reason.'

Tory advance

Conservative statesman: 'I see the *status quo* as the way forward.'

The choice before us

Vicar, blessing all parties before British election: 'We shall have three hymns today. In honour of the Conservatives: Now Thank We All Our God ... In honour of the Labour Party: Oh God Our Help In Ages Past ... And in honour of the Liberal-SDP Alliance: God Does Move In Mysterious Ways ...'

232

Why we lost   If you are travelling in a rocky ship and feel seasick, it is quite understandable that you would wish to throw the navigator overboard. *(Denis Healey)*

Advice to successor   When Harold Wilson handed over the premiership to James Callaghan, he is said to have left three envelopes in a drawer. They were to be opened in turn, in times of disaster.

Opening the first envelope, after the first disaster, Callaghan read: 'Blame your predecessor.'

After the second, he read: 'Sack your assistant.'

After the third: 'Prepare three envelopes...'

Successors   After Mrs Thatcher took over from Mr Callaghan, she is reported to have said to him privately: 'You certainly left us a lot of problems.' Jim replied: 'I didn't ask you to take them on, did I?'

Deterrent   Lord Birkett liked to tell the classic tale of the woman in the train who watched the man opposite her tearing up a newspaper and every now and again throwing tiny pieces out of the window.

'Why are you doing that, sir?' she enquired.

'To keep the elephants away,' he replied.

'But there are no elephants,' she protested.

'Yes,' he answered. 'It is indeed wonderfully effective.'

Hardly ever   The Captain of Gilbert and Sullivan's *HMS Pinafore* was asked whether he was ever sick at sea. He replied: 'Never.'

'What never?' chorused the sailors.

'No, never.'

'What, never?' the sailor insisted.

'Well ... *hardly ever*...' the Captain admitted.

[*Similarly: The Government – or the Opposition, or the company, or you – may* hardly ever *be mistaken, out of step, cheating... GJ*]

233

**Political
punishment**

W.S. Gilbert suggested that a judge should 'let the punishment fit the crime'. The following story may be adapted to suit whatever politicians you feel most inclined to insult at the time.

When Winston Churchill died and went to heaven, he was greeted by St Peter who directed him to his room: 'Straight down the corridor, eighth door on the left.' As he walked by, he saw Neville Chamberlain in a cubicle, embracing that great cabaret artist, Mae West.

When Winston arrived at his cubicle, he discovered his old sparring partner, Lady Astor – the first woman MP – lying on the bed. He stormed back to St Peter: 'It's disgraceful,' he thundered. 'After all that I've done for the world. It's bad enough putting me in a room with old Nancy Astor. But how can you do that while putting that dreadful Neville Chamberlain with the delicious Mae West?'

'Now, you mind your own business, Sir Winston,' Peter replied. 'How I punish Mae West is my affair!'

Foreigners and diplomats 82

Foreign Office

A tourist recently asked a policeman in Whitehall: 'Which side is the Foreign Office on?' He replied: 'It's supposed to be on our side – but I sometimes wonder ...'

Ex

When you are a distinguished ambassador, everyone wants you to make speeches and to be guest of honour. When you are an extinguished ambassador, you have to look both for a platform and for a livelihood...

**Ambassadors-
and journalists**

An ambassador is a man of virtue sent to live abroad for his country. A newswriter is a man without virtue who lies at home for himself. *(Sir Henry Wotton. The first quote, written in 1604, is well known. He added the second part later when a newswriter teased him about the lack of diplomacy inherent in his first definition.)*

**Peaceful
solution**

Our government is prepared to solve any industrial relations problem peacefully, if no other solution is available. [*Adapt to suit your circumstances – government, committee, organisation or as the case may be. GJ*]

**Silent
diplomacy**

Scientist Mark Azbel told of the need for silence by Jews and others oppressed by their rulers: 'A little bird freezes on a cold day and falls to the ground. A passing cow drops a cow pat on it. The bird, revived by the warmth, begins to chirp. A fox appears, hears the chirping, cleans the bird and eats it.'

Moral: 'Not everyone who covers you with manure is your enemy and not everyone who cleans you off is your friend.'

'More important: If you are deep in the shit, don't make a sound!'

Democracy?

Ivor Richard, former British Ambassador to the UN, was asked by an American friend why the United Nations is so undemocratic.

'Undemocratic?' he replied. 'Why do you say that?'

'Because we keep getting outvoted!'

Christmas Gifts – and diplomatic problems

A newly appointed British Ambassador to the USA arrived in Washington DC in mid-December. A newspaper man was chatting with him and asked: 'Ambassador, what would you like for Christmas?'

He replied: 'Well, a small box of American chocolates would do nicely.'

On Christmas Eve, the Embassy was shocked to hear the following broadcast: 'We asked various Ambassadors what they would like best for Christmas. The German Ambassador replied: "A generation of peace for all the world." The French Ambassador replied: "Love and fraternity between nations." The United Kingdom envoy replied: "A small box of American chocolates would do nicely." '

American and English

The American language differs from English in that it seeks the top of expression while English seeks its lowly values. *(Salvador de Madariaga)*

Never has one language done more to divide two nations. *(George Bernard Shaw)*

Solution

Whenever a government thinks that it has solved the Irish question, the Irish change the question.

Idealism

Yes, India is a country with great ideals – but it is peopled entirely by human beings. *(Prime Minister Mrs Indira Gandhi)* [*or the UK – or anywhere else! GJ*]

United Nations?

Former Secretary of State, Dean Acheson: When the United Nations is divided by 50/50, then the decision does not represent 'world conscience'. But add Yemen, Haiti and Portugal and it becomes world conscience. *(Dean Acheson, former Secretary of State)*

Equality?

Re: Israel and her Arab foes: 'They are many and we are one, but we represent 50 per cent of the conflict.' *(Yigal Allon)*

236

Majority power   If the Arab nations saw fit to declare that the earth is flat, they would get 82 votes at the United Nations – a majority would gladly state that fact to be true. What matters, though, is that they should not believe that the result is accurate. *(Abba Eban)*

Mind your language   Many years ago, a Canadian MP replied to a suggestion that their proceedings ought to be held from time to time in French by saying: 'If the English language was good enough for Matthew, Mark, Luke and John, it is good enough for us!'

Lost opportunities   The Jordanians never miss a chance to lose an opportunity. *(Abba Eban)* [*Adapt to suit circumstances/nation/government/situation.GJ*]

Promotion refused   The Arab General who conquered Egypt some 1,300 years ago expected the Caliph of Arabia to appoint him governor of the country. In fact, the Caliph only offered him the command of the troops in Egypt, while another man became governor.

The General refused this command, with the memorable phrase: 'Why should I hold the cow's horns whilst someone else milks her?' *(Anwar Sadat)*

Reflected glory   When I was in Antwerp, attending the massive rally which followed the explosion outside the synagogue in the diamond quarter, I walked in the procession alongside the Chief Rabbi of Belgium. He said to me: 'I am so grateful to you for coming. Our friends and ourselves got this set up very swiftly and yesterday morning we thought that no one would take part. We could not get the political leaders to come – nor even our own community. But when I told them that Lord Janner was coming...!' I was sorry to have to tell him that I was only the son of my father.

Shortly after, a man came up to me with a microphone and said, in French: 'I represent the only Jewish radio station in Europe. Please can I ask you some questions?'

I agreed: 'With pleasure.'

Switching on his machine, the man then said: 'I am now talking to that well known Jewish leader, Lord Janner.'

I replied: 'I'm afraid you are not. You are talking to his son.'

Turning not a hair, the interviewer said into the microphone: *'Chères auditeurs*, I am now speaking to *the son* of that well known Jewish leader, Lord Janner!'

Pure bred?

A polar bear has his little boy in tow. Son pulls at his tail. 'Dad,' he says, 'do we have any brown bear blood in us?'

'Certainly not, son,' replies the father. 'We're pure polar bear.'

A little later, tail tugged again: 'Dad. Have we any grizzly bear blood in our veins?'

'How many times do I have to tell you, son – we are absolutely pure polar bear.'

A little later: 'Dad, are you sure that we haven't any koala bear blood in our family?'

'Son, I've told you often enough, we are absolutely pure polar bear – with no other sort of blood in us at all. Only polar bear. But why do you ask?'

''Cos I'm flipping freezing!'

EEC virtues

What we need are all the attributes of our colleagues in the Common Market. We should have the sovereignty of Luxembourg ... the even temper of the Italians ... the flexibility of the Dutch ... the initiative of the Belgians ... the good nature of the Germans ... the reasonableness of the French ... But we do have in any event the sheer hard work and culinary art of the British ...

Is there life on Mars?

Yugoslavia is full of delegations. Like Rumanians, Yugoslavs remain terrified by the memory of Chamberlain's infamous description of Czechoslovakia: 'That small, distant country, of which we know so little...' So they welcome guests and their country is almost overrun by delegations, from East and West.

Three scientists were recently discussing whether or not there is life on Mars. The American said: 'We think, on the whole, that there probably is some form of primitive life on the planet...' The Russian said: 'We are far more sceptical. On the whole, we think that there is probably no form of life, however primitive, on the red plant.' The Yugoslav said: '*We* are absolutely *certain* that there is no life on Mars – otherwise we would long ago have had delegations from there.'

Precedence

When the late Aga Khan was due to be guest at a luncheon in the House of Lords, the host wrote to the Garter King of Arms on the question of precedence. After a long wait, he received the following reply: 'The Aga Khan is believed to be a direct descendent of God. English Dukes take precedence...'

Brainwashing

Chief Rabbi Rosen of Roumania tells of his first visit to America. On landing, he was surrounded by press men who asked him some very abrupt and even rude questions. For instance: 'Rabbi, are you not brainwashed in your country?'

He replied: 'Yes, I suppose we are. But then so are you, in a different way. The difference between us and you, though, is that *we* do not believe what *we* read in the newspapers and you do.'

One of the problems of their suspended disbelief is that even when Roumanian newspapers or radio are telling the truth while other people's are lying, Roumanians are so suspicious that they still prefer to believe other people's lies.

Ten Commandments

If Moses had had to descend from Mount Sinai and submit his Ten Commandments to the scrutiny of Israel's parliamentary committees, I doubt whether they would ever have become law. *(Abba Eban)*

Peace
A peace treaty is more impressive when it has two signatures on it. *(Abba Eban)*

Negotiating with Russians
'They can't accept a big concession. They have got to extort it from you.' *(Henry Kissinger)*

Socialist
Why is the Soviet Union like an aeroplane in flight? Because it's cold; it makes you feel slightly sick; and you cannot get out of it.

Russia
A juggernaut that doesn't jug. *(Adlai Stephenson)*

Ignorance
About the policies and motives of the Soviet Union, there is no knowledge – only varying degrees of ignorance. *(President Truman)*

Sharing
A Soviet citizen who wished to join the Communist Party was interviewed by an official, who asked: 'If you were given two houses, what would you do?'

He replied: 'Give one to the Party, comrade, and keep one for myself.'

'Now suppose that you are given two cars. What would you do?'

'Give one to the Party and keep one for myself.'

'Now suppose that you were given two shirts.'

'Oh, I'd keep both of them for myself.'

'Why would you give one of your houses and one of your cars to the Party and not one of your shirts?'

'You don't understand. I've already got two shirts.'

Siberian parrot
A Russian dissident trained his parrot to say: 'Down with Brezhnev... Down with Marx... Down with Lenin ...'

One day, the KGB called on the dissident. In panic, he shoved the parrot into his refrigerator.

The KGB men searched the house and

eventually opened the refrigerator. The parrot emerged, shivering.

After an expectant pause, the parrot talked: 'I love Brezhnev ... I love Marx ... I love Lenin...'

'Little bastard,' snarled his master. 'After 5 minutes in Siberia, you join the Party...'

Communist society

An East European was asked the following question by his 18-year-old son: 'Do you think that we already have 100 per cent Communism here, or is it going to get worse?'

State secret

Some years ago, a Moscow man was arrested for rushing naked through the streets, yelling: 'Kruschev is a fool!'

The Judge sentenced him to 25 months' imprisonment. 'You get 6 months for indecent behaviour,' he said, 'and 19 months for betraying State secrets.'

Love of Russia

An old man was studying Hebrew on a park bench in Moscow. A KGB man came up to him and said: 'What are you reading?'

'I'm studying Hebrew.'

'What's the use of that to you?'

'It's the language of Israel.'

'Old man – you will never get there...'

'Never mind, then. It's the language of Paradise.'

'But what happens if you go to the other place?'

'That will present no problem. I already speak Russian.'

Long distance

When Kosygin died, he entered hell. He begged the devil to be allowed to keep in communication with friends on earth. 'Certainly,' Satan replied. 'But you will need plenty of change for the telephone.'

'What do calls cost from here?'

'To the United States, 50 roubles; to South America, 40 roubles; to the United Kingdom, 50 roubles; to India, 55 roubles...' and so on, in a long list, ending with: 'and to the USSR, one rouble...'

'Why is it so cheap to the USSR?'

'Because,' replied Satan, 'it's only a local call...'

Patriotism

Kogan in Kiev applies for a visa for Israel. A few nights later, he hears loud banging on his door. He pulls the blankets over his head. The banging continues. Eventually, he calls out: 'Who is it?'

'The postman.'

'Go away, please.'

The banging restarts. Eventually Kogan opens the door and five KGB men rush in, knocking him to the ground.

'Which is the best country in the world?', one of them asks, sitting on his head.

'The Soviet Union.'

'And where do children get the best education?' demands another, twisting his leg.

'The Soviet Union.'

A third twists his arm behind his back. 'Where is the best food, the best culture, the best of everything?'

'The Soviet Union.'

'In that case,' enquires the man in charge, 'why do you want to leave for Israel?'

'Because in Israel,' said Kogan, 'the postman does not come at 2 o'clock in the morning.'

Moscow morale

A man phoned his friend in Moscow: 'How are you, Ivan?' he asked.

'Fantastic ... marvellous ... unbelievable ... fabulous...'

'OK,' said his friend. 'I see you've got someone with you. I'll phone back later...'

Emigration

Brezhnev once asked Kosygin: 'How many Jews are there in the Soviet Union?'

'About 3 million,' Kosygin replied.

'Then tell me: if we opened the doors and allowed as many Jews to leave as wanted to go, how many would emigrate?'

242

After a moment's thought, Kosygin replied: 'I'd say about 15 million!'

Vive la difference!

Malcolm Rifkind, Minister of State at the Foreign Office, tells of his discussion with his Soviet opposite number on a visit to Moscow. He complained about the Soviets' failure to allow Jews to emigrate from their country. The Russian replied: 'The matter of emigration from the Soviet Union is a controversial one. But how would you like me to raise with you the question of immigration into the United Kingdom, which is also a controversial matter?'

Rifkind replied: 'I would be happy to discuss that with you. But there is a difference, you know. People are trying to get *into* my country...'

Russian tragedy

Moshe Goldstein, a long-serving activist in the Communist Party, applied for a visa to emigrate to Israel. He was called before the Commissar who said to him: 'Goldstein, I don't understand. You have always been a loyal member of the Party. And a proud Soviet citizen. Why do you suddenly want to go to Israel?'

Goldstein replied: 'Comrade Commisar, you do not understand. I am a Jew.'

Commissar: 'So what? Are you not in a position of authority within the Party? Have you not a good living, a nice flat, a fine *dacha*, a car? You are not discriminated against in any way. So why should you want to leave?'

Goldstein: 'But Comrade Commisar, what if things change and unrest grows in the villages and the towns and they start hanging Jews and chess players?'

Commissar: 'I don't understand. Why should they want to start hanging chess players?'

Détente

A Soviet dignitary boasted to an American acquaintance that they had found a new way to make a lion share a cage with a lamb. 'If you don't believe me,' he said, 'then when you come to the USSR we will show you...'

True enough, on his next visit the American was taken to Moscow Zoo and there in a cage was a lion lying in one corner and a lamb in another.

'That's wonderful' said the American. 'You must have a very remarkable lion and a very wonderful lamb...'

'The lion is a good one,' replied the Russian. 'But we have a new lamb every morning.'

One all

For years, I had written to Ambassador Smirnowski, Head of the Russian mission to the UK. My complaints about their treatment of Jews, dissidents, Baptists and other minority groups were all ignored. Then, one day, he came to the Commons for tea, as guest of the Anglo-Soviet Parliamentary Group – of which I was and remain a member in good standing. The Chairman introduced us. I said: 'Your Excellency. I am very pleased to meet you. I did not believe that you really existed.'

'Why not?' he asked.

'How could I accept the existence of a person who fails to answer so many letters?'

Ambassador: 'Well, I am very pleased to meet you too. I did not believe that a man who wrote so many contentious letters could be so pleasant...'

Match drawn...

Dissidents

My wife and I were invited by the Prime Minister to an official luncheon for Egyptian President Mubarak.

Introducing me to the guest of honour, Mrs Thatcher said: 'Now, Greville Janner is one of my favourite dissidents. In the Soviet Union, of course, they lock up their dissidents. Here we invite them to lunch!'

Faith, religion and ethics – **83**
and some Jewish
favourites

Faith

An Italian priest was walking along a cliff top when he slipped and fell – but was caught by a slender sapling, growing out of the cliff. He looked down 300 ft at the sea and up at heaven and cried out: 'Is there anyone up there – help!' And a mighty voice cried out: 'I am here. Fear not. Let go of the tree and I will keep you safe.'

The priest looked down 300 ft at the raging sea and the rocks. Then he cried out: 'Is there anyone else up there – help, help!'

Greater faith

A nun was driving her little Fiat along the road when it ran out of petrol. She left the car and walked 10 miles to the nearest filling station. Regretfully, they said that they had no jerry can and no other container of any sort. 'Surely you have something which I could put the petrol into?' she pleaded. Thoughtfully the attendant said: 'Well, I can only offer you an old chamber pot...'

Gratefully, the nun accepted. The pot was filled with petrol; she walked back to the car. And as she was pouring it into the petrol tank, a passing motorist leaned out of the window, saying: 'Well, sister, I wish I had your faith!'

Fowl language

A man was standing on the steps of the cathedral, shooing away the pigeons. 'Bugger off... bugger off...' he said.

A priest emerged and listened to this performance. 'My man,' he said, 'you really shouldn't talk to pigeons like that. Not on the steps of this House of God. You should say: "Shoo... shoo... shoo..."'

'Look,' he said. 'I'll demonstrate. Shoo...

shoo... shoo....' he said to the pigeons. They all flew away.

'There,' said the priest to the visitor. 'I told you all you had to say was: "Shoo... shoo... shoo..." and they'd all bugger off, just the same!'

God?

Suffragette: 'Put your trust in God. *She* will provide.'

Epistle

An epistle is the wife of an apostle...

End of the World

Prominent physicists predicted that a flood would signal the end of the world in three days.

A television station called on leading religious personalities to advise on how people should act.

The Pope urged his flock to recant for their sins; the Buddhist monk instructed his people to seek inner peace by searching for their inner selves; the Rabbi told his followers: 'OK. We've got three days to learn how to swim.'

Spoilsport

The advantage of having a Scottish granny is that though she doesn't prevent you from falling into sin, she does prevent you from enjoying it...

Optimism

An optimist thinks that all is for the best in the best of all possible worlds. But they say in the Vatican that a pessimist is one who thinks that he is right.

Miracles

A very wicked client, charged with fraud, told me this story, in a cell at the Old Bailey: Martin O'Riley was crossing a road when he was knocked down by a car. He was about to get up and walk away when he observed that it was a Rolls Royce, so he lay down again.

The chauffeur emerged from the front of the Rolls and a lady, dripping with jewels, from the rear. Between them, they helped him onto the back seat and took him off to the London Clinic where he was kept for treatment for some three months at her expense.

Thereafter, O'Riley was transferred to the

Imperial Hotel, Torquay, where he convalesced for six months – again at the woman's expense. By that time, he felt well enough to start suing.

The case came to court some two years later and O'Riley sat throughout in a wheelchair. He won his case and received a massive award of damages. As he was being wheeled out of court, counsel for the defendants came up to him and said: 'Mr O'Riley, you fooled the court. I believe that you have even fooled your own counsel. But you have not deceived me. The moment you step out of your wheelchair, you are for the high jump!'

'Oh, that's ridiculous,' said O'Riley. 'I have thought of all that. I am booked on the next plane to Lourdes. And there we shall see the most amazing miracle in the history of mankind!'

Outside support

I am afraid that I cannot be called a pillar of your church. But I would like to be described as a buttress – supporting you from the outside! [*Ideal for speeches in other people's churches. GJ*]

Civilisation

Mahatma Gandhi was asked: 'What do you think of Western civilisation?'

He replied: 'I think it would be a very good idea.'

Double crossing

I once travelled from Amman in Jordan to Damascus in Syria and back again in a day. I was somewhat surprised to find a large sign at the frontier: 'Double crossing only permitted for diplomats and for certain priests.' (*Rt Rev. Robert Runcie, Archbishop of Canterbury*)

True

A man writes to God: 'I am desperately in need of £100. Please, God, help me!' He addresses the letter to heaven – and posts it.

In a special, kindly, post office department, the letter is opened. The clerks decide to have a whip-round. They collect £80 and post it back, 'with love from God'.

The following day a letter arrived at the post

247

office: 'Thank you, dear God, for answering my letter. But I think I ought to tell you that those wretched people in the post office stole £20!'

Whose religion?

Father Brown (Roman Catholic) and the Reverend Green (Anglican) were arguing furiously over a theological matter.

The priest held up his hand: 'Come, let us not quarrel,' he said. 'You and I are both doing God's work – you in your way and I in His!'

Us

We are proud of the inhabitants of our island. There are the Scots who take themselves seriously – as well as anything else they can lay their hands on; the Welsh, who pray on their knees and on each other; the Irish, who will die for what they believe in, even if they do not know what that is; and the English, who proclaim that they are self-made men, thereby absolving the Lord from a heavy burden.

Ethics

A son asks father at dinner: 'What are ethics?'

'Leave me alone to eat,' father replies.

'But I must know. I have to write an essay tonight, which I must hand in tomorrow. Ethics is the title.'

'I see. Well, suppose I am closing the shop at night and I find a £10 note on the floor. I check the till and make sure that we are not £10 light. Then, what do I do? I tell my partner, that's what. And I split it with him. That's ethics.'

Jewish jokes

A Jewish joke is a joke which Jewish people have heard and non-Jewish people would not understand.

Recognition

It was Balaam who said: 'How goodly are thy tents O Jacob, thy dwelling places O Israel' – and he was not Jewish. (*Parasha Balak in* Exodus)

Solutions

As a Jew you should understand that it is better to have a problem with no final solution than a final solution with no problem! (*Professor Chouraqui*)

Apartheid

During the Second World War, the United States fleet paid a courtesy call in Durban. A society lady who was running a big dance one night asked the American authorities to send half a dozen of his boys along, but to ensure that they included no Jews.

Six big black men duly arrived.

'I'm terribly sorry,' said the hostess, 'but I'm afraid that there must be some mistake.'

'No, ma'am,' replied the leader of the party. 'Major Rabinowitz never makes mistakes!'

Co-habitation

In an article in *The Spectator* (24 April 1982), publisher Anthony Blond told the following anecdote: 'The door of my house in Chester Row sports a Mezuzah (a little silver badge of Jewishness). At a *Spectator* party, my wife remarked to Enoch Powell that she often saw him walking past the house. "Ah," remarked the observant statesman, "you must live near the Jew."

"No," she replied, "*with* the Jew." '

Jewish wedding

The Jewish bridegroom traditionally treads on glass, breaking it into thousands of pieces. Why? 'To celebrate the last occasion when he will be able to put his foot down...'

Persistence

A woman was lying on a beach in Miami. She turned to a man lying alongside her and asked: 'Excuse me, are you Jewish?'

He replied: 'No, I'm not.'

A few minutes later, the woman turned again to the man and said: 'Are you sure you're not Jewish?'

He replied: 'I'm certain.'

Five minutes later, the woman again addressed the man: 'Excuse me, are you absolutely certain that you're not Jewish?'

He replied, angrily: 'All right. So I'm Jewish.'

The woman paused: 'Now isn't that funny,' she said. 'You don't look Jewish!'

Barmitzvah baskets

A well known Rabbi was addressing a Jewish boy on his Barmitzvah (his confirmation, at the age of 13). He said: 'You have a special responsibility, Brian. You are an only child. Your parents have, as it were, put all their eggs into one basket – and you are that basket!'

Half Jews

How come that when someone is half Jewish, we so seldom get the top half? (*Chaim Weizmann*)

Anti-anti-Semitic

A Jewish man was sitting in the corner of a compartment, while two other travellers sat chatting. One said to the other: 'Where are you going?'

'To Brighton.'

'Oh, that used to be a nice place. But it isn't any more. It's full of Jews.'

'Where are you going, then?' asked his friend.

'To Bournemouth.'

'Bournemouth! You talk of Brighton but you should see what's happening to Bournemouth, with all those Jewish hotels...'

The Jew lowered his newspaper and looked at them over the top. 'You know where you two boys should go,' he said. 'You should go to hell. There are no Jews there!'

Many of my best friends...

When King Khaled of Saudi Arabia first greeted US Secretary of State, Henry Kissinger, he launched into his renowned attack on the Jews and Israel ... and how they had taken over the world's banks and financial institutions, its communications and its newspapers, its television and its radio. 'They have even infiltrated into positions of high power in the Foreign Ministries of the world,' declaimed His Majesty.

Then, realising what he had said, the King added: 'But you, sir, we welcome warmly – not as a Jew, but as a great human being...'

Secretary Kissinger replied quietly: 'Your Majesty, many of my best friends are human beings...'

**The best
deal – Jewish
style**

A Warsaw butcher's shop was due to open at 7
a.m. A long queue had formed by 5.30.

On the nail of 7, the proprietor emerged from
the shop. 'Sorry,' he said. 'Not serving Jews
today. All Jews go home please.'

Four ill-clad old Jews silently left the queue
and drifted into the dawn.

A few minutes later, the proprietor came out
again. 'Sorry,' he said. 'We can only serve Party
members today. The rest of you should go
home.' Half the queue evaporated.

Five minutes later he was back. 'Sorry,' he
said. 'We can only serve officials and
functionaries of the Party today. The rest of you
must leave.' Only a handful remained outside the
shop. The proprietor looked at them: 'Sorry,' he
said. 'Today is Tuesday. No meat until
Thursday.'

One of the last survivors looked at his
neighbour. 'There you are,' he said. 'Those
bloody Jews always get the best deal!' (*Told by
Rabbi Hugo Gryn, after a visit to Warsaw in
1981*)

**Repeat
business**

A tailor made a suit for an Anglican parson. He
refused to accept any charge. The parson sent
him a lovely bible.

Two weeks later, the same tailor made a suit
for a Roman Catholic priest. Again, he refused
to charge. The priest sent him a magnificent
prayer book.

The tailor was later visited by a Rabbi and
made a suit for him. He made no charge. The
Rabbi sent him another Rabbi.

**The curse of the
Plotnik
diamond**

Dealer shows woman a magnificent diamond.
'This, madam, is the Plotnik diamond. Is it not
beautiful? It is one of the largest in the world and
is very valuable. But there is a curse which goes
with the Plotnik diamond...'

Customer: 'What curse is that?'

Dealer: 'Mr Plotnik!'

Who likes fish? In 1958 the Roumanian Minister of the Interior announced that permission would be given for people to go to Israel. Instead of sending off those who had long since applied to join relatives, they invited applications. Thousands of Jews queued up to apply.

Chief Rabbi Rosen went to see the Minister, who said: 'What do you want, then? Is this not what you have always been asking for?'

The Rabbi told him the story of another Rabbi who issued an invitation to people in the village to join him for a fish dinner. When they arrived, he gave them nothing to eat.

'What's this, Rabbi?' they protested. 'We thought you were going to give us dinner.'

'Oh, no,' replied the Rabbi, 'I just wanted to know which of you liked fish.'

'Well, Minister – I think that you are just trying to find out which of us like fish...' said Chief Rabbi Rosen.

He was right. It was not until much later that the flow of emigration began. They simply wanted to know how many Jews would leave if given permission.

Oedipus A Jewish couple sent their son to a psychiatrist. He returned and his mother enquired what had happened. '*Nu*?' she said.

'He says I've got an oedipus complex.'

'Oedipus shmoedipus,' his mother retorted. 'You just go on loving your mommy!'

Blessing 'God bless the Tsar – and keep him far away from us!' (*Fiddler on the Roof*)

Perspective Ezra Kolet, leader of India's tiny Jewish community – about 7,000 souls out of a population of some 780 million: 'You may take it from me, Ladies and Gentlemen. Numbers are not important!'

Holy deduction How do you know that Jesus was Jewish? Well, he went into his father's business; lived at home until he was 33; and his mother thought he was God!

Permanent job   Teddy Kollek, Mayor of Jerusalem, kept seeing a man sitting on the roof of his house, looking up at the sky with binoculars. One day, he called out to him: 'What are you doing up there?'

'Looking out for the Messiah' came the reply.

'Why are you doing that?'

'I am being paid for it.'

'How much?'

'Not much. Just a few pence a day...'

'That's pretty poor pay...'

'I know. But at least the job is permanent!'

'When I give my speech tonight, I want everyone to pay attention. . . .'

Free love?

'Do you believe in free love?'
'Have I ever sent you an invoice?'

Love and money

'If I lost all my money, darling, would you still love me?'
'Of course I would darling. But I'd miss you...'

Uncertain future?

A sex questionnaire to college students included: 'Are you a virgin?'
One girl replied: 'Not yet.'

Premarital

Two businessmen talking: 'I never slept with my wife before I was married. Did you?'
'I don't know John. What was her maiden name?'

Welsh virgins

The day after his wedding, Dai returns home.
'What's happened?' asked his mother.
'I found out that Bridget is a virgin,' he said. 'So I left her.'
'Quite right,' said his mother. 'If she's not good enough for the rest of the boys in the village, why should she be good enough for you?'

A woman of worth

After the marriage service, the bridegroom thanked the Rabbi and said to him: 'What do I owe you?'
'Give me as much as you think that the bride is worth,' the Rabbi replied.
The groom handed him a crumpled fiver.
The Rabbi looked at the bride – and gave the groom £4 change.

Marriages

A parson had two ties – a black one for funerals and a white one for weddings. One day, he arrived at a wedding wearing a black tie.
'Why are you wearing a black tie, Parson?' he was asked. 'That's the wrong one...'
'Have you seen the bride?' he replied.

In love

A well known peer married at a comparatively advanced age. His wife is an attractive Mediterranean lady. When the noble lord fell ill, his wife replied to a telephone enquiry as follows: 'He is much better, but he is still under heavy seduction.'

Real ale

A barren woman attended her doctor's surgery for artificial insemination. 'What will happen?' she asked.

'I just get a bottle from the fridge and spray you with a syringe,' he replied.

He went out to the refrigerator but found the bottle was empty and the syringe missing. He walked back into the room, wearing no trousers.

'What's happening now?' asked the woman.

I'm afraid we've run out of bottled,' he said. 'You'll have to make do with draught!'

A wife in the business

I went into the beer business. My wife said: 'I'll drive the people to drink and you can sell it to them.'

Tribute by host to wife

I would like to thank my wife for working so hard and so extensively for the success of this function. She deserves all the credit for this lovely affair – I hope that she will get it from the hotel...

Always right

Wife: 'I have my faults. But being wrong isn't one of them.'

Corny

Bridget approached Gwyneth, the village gossip, and said: 'Gwyneth, you have been going around saying that my husband has a corn on his John Thomas!'

Gwyneth replied: 'Certainly not. I didn't say that. I just said that it *felt* as if he had a corn on his John Thomas!'

Stupidity

Smith came home and found his wife in bed with another man. 'What the hell do you two think you are doing?' he asked.

The wife turned to the other man. 'There you are,' she replied. 'I told you he was stupid!'

Naked truth

Man comes home and finds his wife lying naked on the bed. 'Why aren't you wearing anything?' he asks.

'I keep telling you,' she replies, 'I haven't anything to wear...'

He marches over to the cupboard, throws upen the door and then says: 'Hello Persian lamb ... Hello ocelot ... Hello mink ... Oh, hello Sam ...! Hello Persian lamb ... Hello coney ...'

Raffles

A girl came home one night with a fur coat. Her husband said: 'Where did you get that from?'

'I won it in a raffle,' she replied.

The next night, she arrived home wearing a diamond ring. 'And where did that come from?' her husband enquired.

'I won it in a raffle' she said.

The next night, the girl arrived in a Rolls Royce Silver Cloud. 'All right, darling,' said her husband. 'I know... you won it in a raffle...' She nodded.

The girl said: 'Darling be a pet and run my bath for me.'

Shortly after, she came upstairs and found that the bath had only an inch of water in it. 'What's the matter, darling?' she asked. 'Why don't you run me a decent bath?'

'Oh, sorry, darling... but I didn't want your raffle ticket to get wet...'

Wrongdoing

Mabel, aged 18, arrived home at four in the morning – wearing a mink coat.

'Did I do wrong?' she asked her mother.

Mother replied: 'I don't know whether you did right or wrong dear – but you certainly did well!'

Abortion

Some years ago, Gwyneth got into a certain condition and came up to London for an abortion. She was told that the best doctors were all in the Harley Street area and she came across a house with a sign – Dr Ralph Vaughan Williams. She rang the bell; a woman came to the door and when she said she wanted Dr Ralph Vaughan Williams, was told: 'I'm afraid that Dr Vaughan Williams is busy at present.'

'But I have come all the way from the Rhondda to see him!'

'Well, come in for a moment and I will see if he can spare a few minutes for you.'

The woman returned shortly. 'I'm pleased to tell you Dr Vaughan Williams will see you,' she said, 'but you'll have to be patient. He is busy re-orchestrating *The Men of Harlech*.'

'And about ruddy time too!' Gwyneth replied.

Love

My wife liked to talk to me while she was making love. She used to phone me from a motel room... Got me so used to it that she would use me to time a boiled egg. It was always soft-boiled... *(Bob Monkhouse)*

Wives

Behind every successful man stands an amazed woman.

Three speech

A woman sued for divorce, claiming that her husband had only spoken to her three times in the course of their marriage. She applied for custody of the three children.

The fodderless child

Our daily diet grows odder and odder.
It's a wise child who knows his fodder.
(Reproduced by kind permission of Ogden Nash)

Fertility

A turtle lives 'twixt plated decks
Which carefully conceal its sex.
To me, how clever is the turtle
In such a fix to be so fertile! *(Ogden Nash)*

Garlic

The Italians invented birth control – they call it 'garlic'.

Necessity

Gwyneth was on night shift. She arrived home to find her husband, Morgan, in bed with her best friend. She looked down at her sadly and said: 'Bridget – I have to – but you!'

Birth control

When people talk to me about the need to keep

258

down the number of children, I remind them that I was the fifth! *(Clarence Darrow)*

Mothers
A parent's place is in the wrong...

Pen pals
For many years, Charlie in London and Bill in New York were pen pals. They had never met.

One day, Charlie received a letter from Bill, saying that he intended to come to London. 'Please cable back if it's convenient,' Bill wrote.

The following exchange of cables ensued:

Charlie: 'Delighted to welcome you. Will meet you at station.'

Bill: 'Thanks – am black. Charlie.'

Charlie: 'Don't care if black. Come. Will meet you at station.'

Bill: 'Am Catholic.'

Charlie: 'Don't care if black Catholic. Come. Will meet you at station.'

Bill: 'Am hunchback.'

Charlie: 'Don't care if black Catholic hunchback. Come. Will meet you at station.'

Bill: 'Have only one eye in centre of forehead.'

Charlie: 'Don't care if you are black Catholic, hunchback with only one eye in middle of forehead. Will meet you at station. How do I recognise you?'

Don't wait
Two men were due to fight a duel. One telephoned the other: 'Charlie, don't wait for me... If I'm not there within 5 minutes, please start without me!'

Romance
Fall in love with yourself and you are in for a lifetime of romance. *(Oscar Wilde)*

Self-love
He is a self-made man, and he worships his creator. *(Disraeli on John Bright)*

Deviation

Psychiatrist: I have good news and bad news for you. The bad news is that you are a homosexual. The good news is that I love you!

Aspirations

Dai informs his wife that he is buying a new suit. 'It's very modern,' he said. 'It includes a 14-inch zip.'

'Dai,' she answers, 'you remind me of that company director across the road. He has a double garage and rides out every morning on his bicycle.'

Identification

A man was lying naked on a beach, sunbathing, when he saw three beautiful girls coming towards him. He grabbed at the only clothing within reach – his hat – and put it over his face.

The three girls stopped and looked down at him. The first said: 'Well, it's not my husband.' The second said: ' You're quite right. It is not your husband.' The third one said: 'He's a stranger – he doesn't live in the village...'

The bird

A farmer came to town and bought a live chicken. Waiting for his train home, he decided to go to the movies. The woman at the cash desk said: 'I'm sorry, young man, but we don't allow animals in here.'

The farmer went round the corner and stuffed the chicken into his trousers. He returned to the cinema, paid for his ticket, and sat down in the stalls. Eventually, two women came and sat beside him.

It was very hot and the chicken became itchy. So he opened up the front of his trousers and the chicken extended its neck.

One woman said to the other: 'Mary, do you see what I see?'

'Certainly I see what you see. If you've seen one, you've seen them all!'

'I'm not sure,' said Mary. 'This is the first one I've seen that eats crisps!'

260

Evolution   In law each of us must look after his 'neighbour' – or, as it is sometimes put, each of us is his brother's keeper. Which reminds me of the monkey in the zoo discussing the principles of evolution and asking: 'Am I my keeper's brother?' [*There is also the tale of the herring, who was separated from his best friend, the whale. He responded to enquiries about his friend's whereabouts with the world's worst pun: 'How should I know? Am I my blubber's kipper?' GJ*]

'Perhaps learned counsel would like to re-phrase that
question. . . ?'

The rule of law

This country is planted thick with laws from coast to coast. If you cut them down – and you're just the man to do it – do you really think you could stand upright in the wind that would blow then? (*Robert Bolt – from* A Man for All Seasons)

International law

Famous professor, Hersch Lauterpacht, used to say: 'International law is not much good. It creates laws which the wicked do not obey and the righteous do not need.'

Single-handed

A man asked to be recommended to a one-armed lawyer. When asked why, he replied: 'I'm sick of being told: ''On the one hand this — and on the other hand that''.'

Lawyers

It is untrue that lawyers do nothing. They just get together and decide that nothing can be done.

St Peter and Satan had an argument. Satan suggested that they should each consult a lawyer.

'I'm not surprised that you made that suggestion,' said St Peter. 'Lawyers, after all, are so much more accessible to you...'

Alleged motto of the Law Society: The man who is his own lawyer has a fool for a client.

Respected professionals

A foreigner was being shown around Westminster Abbey. His guide pointed to a splendid monument: 'There lies a great and honest man and a most distinguished lawyer,' he said.

'That's interesting,' the foreigner replied. 'I never knew that in England you buried two men in the same grave!'

Oh, hell!

A businessman arrived at the pearly gates and was cross-examined by St Peter. He demanded his basic civil right – to be represented by a lawyer.

'Sorry,' said St Peter. 'We haven't any up here.'

Socialist lawyers

The expression 'socialist lawyer' is a contradiction in terms – like 'military intelligence'. (*Michael Foot*)

Bright boy

A car dealer's son was trying to sell his own vehicle – but failing. His father told him to turn back the clock to 6,000 miles. The following week, father asked his son whether he had sold the car. 'Certainly not.'

'Why not then?'

'Well, it's only got 6,000 miles on the clock so I decided to keep it...'

Contracts

It was a curious contract. The first clause forbids you to read any of the others.

Costs

Two partners fell out and sued each other. Their lawyers tried to settle the disputes, but failed. Eventually, the case reached court.

Outside the courtroom, Morgan said to his counsel: 'Look, Dai and I used to be very good friends. We were in happy partnership for years. Perhaps we can have a chat and see if we can settle our differences on our own?'

The lawyer replied: 'Why not? But I must warn you. The amount in dispute between you is now less than the legal costs. So even if you settle your dispute, you've got to decide who is going to pay the costs.'

Morgan went to Dai and the two of them disappeared. Half an hour later they returned, beaming.

'Have you settled the case?'

'We have,' replied the partners in unison.

'Well, who's going to pay the costs then?'

'Oh, that was easy,' said Dai. 'We've solved the problem. He'll not pay his and I'll not pay mine!' (*Judge Bernard Gillis*)

Wrongdoing

When visiting Egypt, one of our guides explained his *modus operandi*. 'If you have to do wrong,' he said, 'you must know the right way to do it.'

Bribery

When we know that one of our customers will not accept the whisky that we send him for Christmas, we send even more the following year – because then we know that it will be sent back and we can drink it ourselves...

Ears

The famous American lawyer, Clarence Darrow, told the story about how easy it is for a lawyer to ask one question too many.

A man was accused of biting off another man's ear. His lawyer cross-examined the witness: 'Did you see my client biting off the victim's ear?'

'No sir.'

Instead of stopping there, he went on in triumph: 'So how can you testify that my client bit off the victim's ear?'

'Because I saw him spit it out!'

Conducting a case

If the facts are on your side, hammer on the facts... if the law is on your side, hammer on the law... if neither is on your side, hammer on the table...

Leave law to the lawyers

There were too many cart drivers in a Russian village, so the municipality decided to issue licences. But each prospective applicant had to pass an examination.

Ivan came for his examination and was asked: 'Suppose that your cart stuck in deep mud, what would you do?'

'I'd lash my whip over my horse's head and I'd cry out: "giddy up".'

'And if that didn't work?'

'Then I'd get out of the cart and down in the mud and I'd put my shoulder to the back of the cart and I'd push with all my might and at the same time lash my whip above the horse's head and shout "giddy up".'

'And if that was no good?'

'Then I'd get the passengers out of my cart and they'd have to come down in the mud and push along with me and I'd lash my whip above the horse's head and shout "giddy up".'

'I'm sorry,' said the examiner, 'but you've failed.'

'Why?'

'Because a good cart driver never enters the mud.'

And that explains why you should let your lawyers get on with their job ... and why you should not enter into matters that come within the expertise of others.

Modesty

So I asked myself the question ... We lawyers frequently ask ourselves questions because in that way we know that we will get prompt and intelligent answers... (*Lord Denning*)

Chancery

The court of a well known Chancery judge, now retired (and nameless) became known at the Bar as the 'din of inequity'.

Justice?

When I was a puisne judge – sitting on my own, in my own court – I could be sure that justice would be done in that court. But now I sit in the Court of Appeal with two brother judges, the odds against justice being done in my court are two to one!' (*Lord Denning*)

Interviewed on his 81st birthday, Lord Denning was asked whether it was not correct that he bent the law, in order to do justice. He replied: 'Certainly not. I just develop it...'

Whisky and water

Former Lord Chief Justice, Lord Goddard, was asked what was the difference between whisky and water. He replied: 'If you make the former in private, that is a felony; if you make the latter in public, that is a misdemeanour.' [*Happily, the distinction between felonies and misdemeanours has now been abolished. GJ*]

Dissenting voices	Master of the Rolls, Sir John Donaldson, tells of an occasion when he sat in the Court of Appeal with his great predecessor, Lord Denning. At the end of a case, Denning turned to him and said: 'Well, John, I think we must allow this appeal, don't you?'
	Donaldson replied: 'No. It must be dismissed.'
	Denning turned to the third judge: 'What do you say?' he asked.
	'I'm sorry, Tom,' he replied, 'but I agree with John. The appeal must be dismissed.'
	'In that case,' said Lord Denning, 'the two of you will just have to deliver dissenting judgments!'
Equality of opportunity	Courts of this country are like the Waldorf Hotel – open to all! [*High Court judge, explaining the inaccessibility of justice. GJ*]
Perjury	Counsel, cross-examining a man who alleges his arm and shoulder were hurt in an accident: 'Show me how high you can raise your arm, please...' The witness raises his arm a few inches, clearly with great effort and difficulty.
	'Now show me how high you could raise it, *before* the accident...'
	The arm goes high into the air. [*This tale is, of course, best told with the appropriate demonstration. GJ*]
Chinese praise	Chinese man in the witness box in a stamp theft case was praised by the judge. He replied: 'Philately will get you everywhere...'
The truth	There are three stories in any law suit: the plaintiff's, the defendant's, and the truth.
Juries	Welsh juries are against crime – but they are not too dogmatic about it. (*Lord Elwyn Jones*)
Ducking the question	Lawyer to witness: 'Did you get the letter?'
	Witness (contemplating whether he should answer yes or no – and after a long pause): 'Not necessarily.'

Evidence

Lawyer defending client on charge of causing grievous bodily harm: 'It is our case, my Lord, that there is no evidence that any such affray took place. If it did, we shall prove that my client was not there. If he was there, there is no evidence that he took part in the affray. And in any case, the other man hit him first.'

Unwise counsel

Counsel: 'I hope that you are following me...'
Judge: 'Yes – but where are you going?'

Trials

At the 1981 Sheep Dog Trials, how many were found guilty?

Misconception

As Mr Justice James Cassells was swearing in a jury, one of the jurymen asked to be excused.
'What is your reason?' asked the Judge.
'My wife is about to conceive,' he replied.
'I don't think that is what you mean,' replied the Judge. 'I think that what you mean is that your wife is about to be confined. But whether you are right or I am right, I agree that you ought to be there...' (*Lord Elwyn Jones*)

Appeal

A businessman had to leave court before the end of the long, hard-fought trial. He left word for a telegram to be sent to him, to inform him of the result.
At the end of the case, the lawyer sent a telegram as arranged: 'Justice has been done,' it read.
The client immediately sent a reply: 'Appeal at once.'

Punishment for the crime

A man was convicted of a peculiarly unpleasant offence with a dog. The magistrate ranted at him: 'I cannot think of any punishment worthy of this horrible crime...'.
A voice from the rear of the court cried out: 'Give him the cat!'

Trouble

The court was packed when Fred appeared to plead guilty to a peculiarly unpleasant offence with a swan. Journalists and the public jostled for position. The magistrate asked him: 'Have you anything to say to the court before we pronounce sentence upon you?'

'Yes, sir,' said Fred. 'If I'd have known that it would cause all this trouble, I'd have married the flipping bird!'

Brevity

Judge to accused: 'Have you anything to say before I pass sentence?'

Accused: 'Yes, guv – for gawd's sake keep it short!'

Forgiving

An old Cockney usher used to take visitors to the Lord Chief Justice's Court when Lord Goddard presided: 'Lord Goddard,' he would say, 'is famous as a forgiving judge. Very forgiving. For giving five years... ten years... life...'

Language problems

Policeman giving evidence of arrest: 'So I cautioned the man and asked him if he could explain his presence, in the early hours of the morning, carrying what appeared to be a house-breaking implement. He made a lengthy reply in a language which I subsequently discovered to be Greek. I told him that I was not satisfied with his explanation and I duly arrested him.'

Cross-examination

The policeman gives evidence of having observed disgusting behaviour by a courting couple in a car. They deny it, maintaining that had he been in a position to observe, they would have heard him coming.

Counsel: 'Was it not a gravel path? What size shoes do you take? Was it not in the silence of the night? I put it to you that had you been near to that car, they would have heard the tramp of your feet...'

Constable: 'No sir.'

Counsel: 'You say that they would not have heard the tramp of your feet? Why do you say that?'

Constable: 'I was riding my bicycle.' [*This sort of horror explains why young lawyers are*

No charge
PC: 'You are under arrest, sir. I am taking you to the police station where you will have to stay the night.'
'And what's the charge, officer?'
'No charge, sir. All part of the service.'

Gaol
Any 8-year-old child will tell you that a place from which you are forbidden to leave is a 'prison'. (*Tom Stoppard*)

Balls
A prisoner went round the cells, selling tickets for the Warder's Ball. One of his mates complained: 'I don't want to buy a ticket for any screw's dance!' The seller replied: 'It's not a dance. It's a raffle!'

Bribery
Lord Goddard once remarked: 'Bribery is like a sausage – difficult to describe, but very easy to smell!'

Corrupt?
It's not corrupt if you can eat it, drink it or sleep with it.

Commission
A well known company found difficulty in putting its 'commission' (*slush, payola, or what-have-you*) through its books. But as it has a hunting lodge in Scotland, it listed the items as 'hunting expenses'.

A visiting customer from Nigeria was provided with a suite at Claridges and a girl in it. Unfortunately, he contracted a certain illness for which he had to be treated at the London Clinic. The cost of that treatment went into the books as: 'Repairs to gun...'

Corruption
Be specially careful not to bribe tax or factory inspectors or other public officials. 'Do not feed the hand that bites you...'

Gifts
Sir Joshua Hassan, Chief Minister of Gibraltar, making a presentation of small Wedgwood box

270

to British Foreign Secretary: 'This comes well within the parameters of what a Minister is permitted to accept!' [*In other words – it did not cost much, but what a charming way to put it! GJ*]

Choice of language

A man could not get a good job because prospective employers kept finding out that his father had died in the electric chair. Eventually, he learned to reply to questions about his father thus: 'My father was at one of the great educational institutions in this country. He occupied the Chair of Applied Electricity.'

Written evidence

A man appeared in a lawyer's office: 'I have come to you because God has told me you are the best lawyer in the country.'

The lawyer replied: 'If that happens again, please get it in writing.'

Rubbish

To get rid of rubbish nowadays, all you have to do is to wrap it in silver paper, put it on the back seat of your car, and some silly sod will steal it. (*Bob Monkhouse*)

Tact

A company official was in the witness box, giving his opinion. 'Do you consider yourself an expert?' asked the cross-examining lawyer.

'Well, no,' said the man modestly. 'But I am something of a judge.'

'What is the difference between an expert and a judge?' asked the lawyer.

'An expert sometimes makes mistakes,' replied the official. 'A judge – never!'

Judge's functions

Lord Asquith was discussing the functions of the various branches of the judiciary. He said: 'It is the function of the judge in the Queen's Bench Division to be quick, courteous and wrong. But it must not be supposed that it is the function of the Court of Appeal to be slow, crapulous and wrong – for that would be to usurp the function of the House of Lords.'

Conviction

A famous hanging judge, Mr Justice Avory, was discussing with Mr Justice Travers Humphreys the unhappy way in which the courts were being conducted by their junior colleagues.

Avory: 'Any of these young members of the Queen's Bench Division can secure the conviction of a guilty man. But it takes an old hand like you or me to make sure that the innocent do not escape!'

Leading counsel

Litigant arrives at court to find that whilst he is represented by junior counsel only, his opponent has both a junior and a leader. He tugs the gown of his advocate: 'How are you going to manage?' he said. 'The other side have a QC and a junior...'

'I'm as good as any two of them,' replied the junior.

A few minutes later, the client again tugged the barrister's gown. 'I'm worried,' he said. 'I've noticed that when the QC is talking, the barrister behind him is thinking. But when you are talking, no one is thinking!'

Petty theft

Judge – commenting on defence that accused 'only stole a very small sum': 'You either are dishonest or you are not – like a woman – who cannot be just a tiny bit pregnant!'

Guilt

A man appeared in a Magistrates Court. Magistrate: 'Did you steal these goods?'

'Yes.'

'Did you take them home?'

'Yes.'

'Did you then sell the goods?'

'Yes.'

'Do you want to say anything to me?'

'Yes. I want a lawyer.'

'What is the point in getting a lawyer when you are so obviously guilty on your own admission?'

'Well, I would just like to discover what he'd find to say for me!'

Speed

An American criminal complained that in New York you are liable to get mugged between the time that you rob the bank and the time that you reach the getaway car.

Terrorism

The Mafia Godfather arrived at the Pearly Gates.

St Peter: 'I'm not sure that we will have you in here. I'll have to ask The Boss.'

'I haven't come to be invited in,' said the Godfather. 'I have come to give you three minutes to get out.'

'*The first part will drive everyone to drink – the second part doubles the tax on liquor. . . .*'

Food for thought

Political life has many drawbacks, one of which is *not* malnutrition. *(Abba Eban)*

Shortage

What is 200 yards long and eats cabbage? A queue outside a food shop in Warsaw.

Patience – and head waiters

Description on head waiter's tombstone: God finally caught his eye.

We serve all . . .

A man came into Grubbs with an alligator on a leash. He said: 'Do you serve lawyers here?'

Mr Grubb replied: 'Of course we do.'

'In that case,' said the man, 'I'll have two salt-beef sandwiches for me and a lawyer for my alligator...' [*For lawyers – use doctors, Methodists, Mongolians, – or whatever other audience you are addressing. GJ*]

Never satisfied

The host asked his house-guest: 'Will you have coffee after dinner?'

'No thank you. Just brandy.'

'Will you have cocoa before you retire?'

'No thank you. Just tea.'

'Will you have tea for breakfast?'

'No thank you – coffee.'

'Would you like boiled eggs or scrambled eggs?'

'One of each please.'

After breakfast, the host asked his guest: 'How were your eggs?'

'Not good.'

'Why?'

'You boiled the wrong one!'

Staff training

Two waiters pass behind diner's chair. One says to the other: 'Look – she's eaten it!'

Fifty-fifty

A well known hotel in London's West End became a favourite haunt of Arab guests. So it started serving a new delicacy: camel and chicken stew.

A dissatisfied diner called after the head waiter. 'This is meant to be camel and chicken stew,' he said. 'But I can't taste any chicken.'

'Oh, I can assure you, sir,' the waiter replied, 'it's fifty-fifty – one camel, one chicken!'

Drink fast

Like a Scottish (*or Greek or Israeli or what-you-will*) wedding reception – plenty for everyone, but you have to be quick...

Prescriptions

A down-and-out tries to beg a pound from a passer-by.

'What is it then? Drugs?'

'Don't indulge.'

'So I suppose you smoke yourself silly?'

'As a matter of fact, I never smoke at all.'

'Then there is only one answer. Gambling...'

'Certainly not. That's a mug's game...'

'Then never mind the quid. You come into the car with me and let me take you home to meet my wife. I would like her to see what happens to a man who doesn't drink, take drugs, smoke or gamble!'

Conferences

Some politicians and many business people suffer from a disease called conference syncopation – making irregular movements from bar to bar...

Glass houses

Two guests at a cocktail party. One says to the other: 'Look, old man I shouldn't drive if I were you. Your face is getting all blurry.'

Drink and drive?

A Scottish hotel applied for a drinks licence. This was refused because 'the roads in the vicinity of the hotel are unsuitable for drunken driving'.

Blood thicker than whisky...

A Scottish friend of mine always carried a hip flask of whisky. One day he fell and felt damp around his hip. 'My God,' he said, 'I hope it's only blood!'

Ugh!   After a party, Fred was found wandering on the rooftops. The drinks were on the house.

Wonder drink   Mankind has always been amazed at the miracle of water. And in many languages, that wonderment has been built into its name. English – what-er; French – *Eau*!; Hebrew – *ma-yim, (mah* meaning what); German – *wass-er;* Spanish and Italian – *agua (Ah! – gua).* *(Chief Rabbi Sir Immanuel Jakobovits)*

Mirage   'Drink makes you really look beautiful, Brenda.'
   'But I haven't been drinking, Charlie.'
   'I know. But I have!'

No room at the inn?   Smith is refused a room at a famous hotel. 'I'm sorry, sir, we are full up,' said the head receptionist.
   'If Prince Philip were to come here,' said Smith, 'you'd find a room for him, wouldn't you?'
   'I suppose we would,' said the receptionist.
   'Well, I've got news for you,' Smith retorted. 'He isn't coming. So I'll have his room.'

Record   The following message was allegedly put out by a certain Eastern airline: 'Ladies and Gentlemen, we are now flying at an altitude of 27,000 feet. If you look over to your right – that is, the starboard side – you will see that we are above the Indian Ocean. If you look carefully, you will note a tiny, yellow speck. That is a life raft. In it there are four people. They are your crew. This message is recorded...'

Early bird   Cyril decided to beat the latest underground strike by hitch-hiking to work – he got up at 5.30 so as to beat the traffic.

Hopeless   Two strangers occupied the upper and lower bunks in a sleeper compartment of a long-distance train. They wished each other good night and the man on the lower bunk was just about to drift away when he heard a voice from above him: 'Oy! Am I thirsty! Am I thirsty! Am I thirsty!'

Again: 'Oy! Am I thirsty! Am I thirsty! Am I thirsty! Am I thirsty!'

Exasperated, the man below clambered out of his bunk; fetched a glass of water from the side and handed it up to his travelling companion who thanked him most profusely. 'God bless you! And good night!' he said.

Five minutes later, just as he was about to sleep, the man in the bunk below heard a voice from above him moaning out: 'Oy! Was I thirsty! Was I thirsty! Was I thirsty!'

Procrastination

A visitor to Ireland asked a professor: 'What is the Gaelic for *mañana*?'

The professor replied: 'I regret that we do not have any word in the Irish language that conveys quite that same sense of urgency!'

Timeless

A vicar remarked to his parishioner: 'I don't mind you looking at your watch during my sermon. But when you put it up to your ear and shake it...'

Brevity

We no longer know how to be brief. For instance: the Lord's Prayer consists of 56 words; the Ten Commandments 297 words; the United States Declaration of Independence 300 words; and the EEC Convention on the Importation of Caramel – 26,911 words.

I am sorry that I have had to write such a long letter. I did not have the time to write a short one. (*Horace Walpole*)

God gave man two ears and one mouth so that he may listen twice as much as he speaks! (*King Faisal*)

Former Israeli Prime Minister, Levi Eshkol, once chaired a meeting. A speaker, who was likely to be boring, asked him: 'How long shall I speak? There's so much to say. I don't know where to begin...'

Eshkol replied: 'Then I suggest that you start at the end...'

Apologies

Counsel apologises for the length of his speech.

Judge: 'Don't worry – you have shortened the winter for us...'

Apologies for lateness

Better the President late than the late President. [*Favourite apology of the late Lord Fisher of Camden, my predecesor as President of the Board of Deputies of British Jews. GJ*]

Time and tide

They believe in casting their bread on the waters – but only when the tide is coming in. (James Callaghan)

Take your time

An El Al plane was landing in New York. The pilot announced: 'Ladies and Gentlemen, we hope that you enjoyed this flight on El Al and that we shall have the pleasure of your company on future flights.' Then, forgetting that his loudspeaker was still switched on, he added: 'Now all I need is a nice cup of coffee and a woman!'

A pert air hostess rushed up the gangway towards the cockpit. An old Mama put her hand gently on her passing arm: 'Don't hurry, darling,' she said. 'Give him time to have his coffee!'

Confidence

Cricketer Learie Constantine told how he was once walking down the steps of a pavilion on his way to bat when he heard the following telephone conversation: 'You want to speak to Learie Constantine? Oh, I'm sorry, he's just going in to bat. Would you like to hold on?'

Repetition

Leonid Brezhnev was accustomed to making 3-hour speeches. One day, he said to his aide: 'I am not quite as young as I was. I think that I would prefer in future to make only 1-hour speeches. Kindly prepare future speeches on the basis of 1 hour only.'

The next time that Mr Brezhnev made a public speech, he read out his script – and it lasted 3 hours. Afterwards, he said to his aide: 'I don't understand. I gave you instructions that my speeches in future were to be drafted to last 1 hour and not 3. Why did you draft this one for 3 hours?'

'Comrade Leonid,' said the aide, 'this one was drafted as you asked – for 1 hour only. But I gave you three copies!'

Time

Captain of aircraft, about to land at Belfast Airport: 'The time locally is 16.00 hours. Kindly put your watches back two centuries...'

In conclusion   'Has he finished?

   'Yes, he finished a long time ago, but he is still going on.'

'Last thing I remember, everyone was drinking my
health. . . .'

Communication

The operator at a London hospital received a call asking for the sister in charge of a particular ward. When the sister was put through, the caller enquired: 'How is Mrs Goldberg?'

'Doing very well,' sister replied.

'Is her stomach condition improving, then?'

'Yes. The doctor is very pleased with it.'

'Is her blood pressure better?'

'Yes, much better.'

'And how about Mrs Goldberg's chest. Is the infection clearing well?'

'Very well. But tell me, who is enquiring?'

'This is Mrs Goldberg. Nobody tells *me* nothing, *dollink*!'

Ambition

The Minister of Health visited a hospital and was introduced to three international rugby players, lying in adjoining beds. He asked the first man: 'What's the matter with you?'

'I have piles, sir,' replied the man.

'And what are they doing for you?'

'They give me a brush and some ointment and I apply it to myself.'

'And what's your ambition now?'

'To get back to the rugger field to play for England, sir, as soon as possible.'

'Well done, my boy. I wish you luck.' And he turned to the second man.

'What's the matter with you, then?'

'I'm afraid that I've got venereal disease.'

'Oh dear. And what treatment are they giving you?'

'They give me a brush and some ointment and I apply it to myself'

'And what's your ambition?'

'To get back to the rugger field to play for England again, as soon as possible,' he said.

'Well done, my boy,' nodded the Minister and turned to the third bed.

'And what's your trouble?'

'I have laryngitis,' the man whispered.

'What are they doing for you?'

'They give me a brush and some ointment and I apply it to myself.'

'And what is your ambition?'

'To get the brush before the two other fellows...'

Majority for good health

In 1982, my car suffered a blow-out on the M1 and we were all saved by the presence of a crash barrier – and the driver and myself wearing seat belts. At Question Time the following week, I paid tribute to that crash barrier – and asked the Minister of Transport to ensure that any road works which meant that traffic had to flow in both directions on the same side of the road should be kept as rare and as brief as possible.

She started her reply by saying 'how glad the whole House would be to hear of the Honourable Member's fortunate escape – and at his presence in good health here today.'

This evoked cheers from my side and laughter and cries of 'resign' from that of the Minister. Which reminded me of the classic story of...

The lone Conservative Councillor in a Welsh Labour stronghold fell ill. He was visited in hospital by the mayor, who said:

'My dear Dai, I am here not only in my personal capacity, but especially as Mayor of our town, deputed to bring to you a resolution which I will now read: "We the City Council of Ebbw Vale do wish Councillor Dai Jones a most speedy recovery to robust good health." I am pleased to tell you, Dai, that this resolution was passed – by 13 votes to 12, with 6 abstentions!'

Rare?

Patients in a psychiatric hospital were undergoing group therapy. One asked: 'Why are we all here?' Another immediately replied: 'Because we're not all there...'

Mad?

A psychotic builds castles in the air; psychopaths live in them; psychiatrists collect the rent.

Inferiority

A man told his psychiatrist that he was suffering from a severe inferiority complex. The psychiatrist said: 'I am sorry' sir, but I cannot help you.'

'Why not?'

'I'm afraid that you just *are* inferior!'

Listen!

Man visits a psychiatrist's office and says: 'My trouble is no one listens to me.' The psychiatrist says: 'Next...'

Lost voice

A singer who had lost his voice knocked on the door of his doctor's surgery. A nurse appeared. The man whispered: 'Is Dr Jones in?' The nurse whispered in reply: 'No – come in quickly.'

The doctor arrived after about 15 minutes, wrote out a prescription and recommended 'plenty of ice cream'.

The singer duly lodged the prescription with the chemist and went off to the ice cream parlour. He whispered: 'What flavours of ice cream do you have?'

The ice cream man replied, whispering: 'Strawberry and vanilla.'

Singer: 'Do you have laryngitis too?'

The ice cream man whispered: 'No – just strawberry and vanilla.'

Limits on DIY

John needed a pacemaker but could not get one swiftly under the National Health Service. So he went privately to a distinguished consultant. 'I can do the job for you with pleasure,' said the surgeon. 'But I'm afraid it will cost you £5,000. These gadgets are very expensive.'

'I have a friend who is brilliant with electronics and gadgets,' said John. 'If I provide my own pacemaker with his help, will you do the implant for me?'

The surgeon agreed. John produced the pacemaker and the surgeon planted it in his chest and wired him up.

Three months later, John returned for a check-up. 'Any problems?' The surgeon asked.

John replied: 'Only one. Whenever I get an erection, the garage door opens!'

Just right

Sign over pharmacy: 'We dispense with accuracy.'

Fair

Dentist to patient: 'Now, we're not going to hurt each other, are we?'

Medical prophecy

An American doctor gave his patient six months to live – and sent him a bill for $500. By the end of the six months, the bill was still not paid. The doctor than gave his patient another six months...

Nurses

Occupational nurses are a race apart. I once asked one what you do when you have a patient brought in with a bleeding leg. She replied: 'You bind up the bleeding wound; you elevate the bleeding leg; and you call in the bleeding doctor.'

Accidents at work

There is no such things as an Act of God when you are dealing with accidents in industry. The fact is that God has a down on inefficient managers... (*Bill Simpson, then Chairman of the Health and Safety Commission*)

Emergencies

An employee was lying on the operating table in the factory's sick bay, clenching his teeth, while a doctor sewed up a large wound on his scalp. A pair of pliers had fallen from a scaffold and split open his head. I asked him: 'Haven't you got a hard hat?'

'Yes' he said.

'Where is it, then?'

He replied: 'It's in my locker.'

'Why do you keep it in your locker?'

'It's there for emergencies,' he answered.

Contribution

Mary goes to the doctor with a pain in her stomach. She returns home and asks her husband. 'Don't you want to know what the doctor said?'

'All right, then, tell me.'

'I must have sexual intercourse at least 20 times a month.'

'Ah, I see. Then put me down for four.'

Deafness Doctor to personnel manager at very noisy steel works. 'I don't know why you don't just hire deaf people in the first place and then you wouldn't have to worry...'

Too late When I asked a steel worker why he was not wearing his ear muffs, he replied: 'I'm already deaf!'

Asbestosis A man inhaled so much asbestos that it took three weeks to cremate him.

Compensation Apprentice: 'What is a cubic foot?'

Foreman: 'I don't know – but I will make sure that you get full compensation.' [*Or could be a reply by a shop steward. GJ*]

Theatres A woman who had been sitting towards the back of the stalls left her seat during the interval. When she returned, she found a man lying across the seat. She asked him to move. He just groaned. Eventually, she called the manager. 'Come on, come on, my man... please move along,' he said. The man opened his eyes and said nothing. 'If you don't move, I'll have to call the police,' said the manager.

Eventually, the policeman arrived with his notebook. 'Very well, where do you come from?' asked the officer.

'From the balcony,' the man groaned.

Fall from grace Fred fell 80 ft from a scaffold. By good fortune, he managed to clutch hold of a rope about 20 ft from the ground. After a few moments, he let it go and fell on his head.

His friend picked him up and said: 'Fred – why did you let go of that rope?'

He replied: 'I was afraid it was going to break.'

Self-recognition   An employee had his ear cut off at work. He was told to go to the local hospital and have it stitched back on. When he arrived, he had left the ear behind.

'Where is the ear?' they asked. 'Why didn't you bring it with you?'

'I couldn't tell whether it was mine,' he replied. 'It had no pencil behind it!'

Illness uncured   A man suffering from constipation went to his doctor who provided him with a suppository, telling him to leave it in his back passage overnight and that if it did not do the trick, to come back in a couple of days.

Two days later, the patient returned. 'It was useless,' he said.

'Did you do as I recommended?' asked the doctor.

'Well,' said the patient, 'we haven't got a back passage in our house. So I put it on top of the refrigerator. For all the good it did me, I might just as well have shoved it up my rear end!'

Open certificate   Morgan was an overworked businessman. He suffered a severe heart attack and his doctor told him that he had to keep 'very quiet' until further notice – no stress, no excitement, no exertion.

'But what about bed with Gwyneth?' he asked. 'Bed is for sleeping purposes only,' said the doctor.

Some months later, when Morgan was feeling much better, he said to Gwyneth: 'Well, it's Friday night and I am quite recovered now.'

'I'm not taking any chances,' said Gwyneth. 'You'll have to get a doctor's certificate before I am prepared to resume our previous arrangements.'

So Morgan went back to the doctor, who examined him and proclaimed himself fully satisfied. 'You may return to work on a part-time basis,' he said. 'You are doing very well.'

'Then how about bed, with Gwyneth?'

'That should be all right. Everything in moderation, of course.'

'Gwyneth won't allow even moderation without a certificate from you.'

'Then I shall provide one,' said the doctor, and sat down at this desk, took out his pen and began to write.

Morgan came quietly up behind him. 'If it would not be a nuisance,' he said, 'would you be kind enough to head your certificate: "To whom it may concern"?'

Operations

Two eunuchs met. One asked the other in a high-pitched voice: 'Did I tell you about my operation?' [*If you have had an operation, this may conveniently be adapted to: 'As one eunuch said to the other – have I told you about my operation?' GJ*]

Mother-in-law

'I hear that your mother-in-law is in hospital!'

'That's right.'

'How long has she been there?'

'In three weeks, please God, it will be a month!'

'It'll be a much better speech if you don't read from your notes. . . .'

Age

The young look forward; the old look back and the middle-aged look around.

The ages of man

You are young if it is as easy to go upstairs as it is to go down; you are middle-aged if it is easier to go down than up; and you are old if it is just as difficult to go in either direction.

Tired

Two men were visiting a brothel on the top floor of a 20-storey block. The lift broke down and they started to climb. One said to the other: 'Wouldn't it be awful if we got to the top and found that the girls weren't there.'

After 10 floors, the other replied: 'Wouldn't it be awful if we got to the top and the girls *were* there!'

Distinction

To appear really distinguished, you need grey hair, a wide girth and piles. The grey hair gives you an appearance of wisdom; the girth an appearance of prosperity; and the piles a look of anxiety that can easily be mistaken for true concern.

Alternatives

A distinguished US Senator was asked how he felt on his 80th birthday. 'Very well, thank you,' he replied, 'considering the alternative...'

Very nearly

A friend asked an 80-year-old man who had just married a young girl: 'How are you managing?'

'Marvellous,' he replied. 'We do it nearly every night. Nearly on Monday... nearly on Tuesday... nearly on Wednesday...!'

Don't delay

A streaker ran across Westminster Bridge and passed three elderly ladies. Two of them immediately had a stroke. The third one did not reach out her hand in time.

Pensioner's marriage

Two pensioners married. On their honeymoon night, the husband reached for his wife's hand – and held it tenderly. On the next night, he did the same. On the third night, he reached out for her hand but it was not there.

'What's the matter, Mary?' he asked.

'I am sorry, dear,' she replied. 'I am too tired tonight…'

What for?

Two old men were sitting on a bench in a boulevard. One said: 'Do you remember how we used to run up and down here when we were young, chasing girls?'

The other replied: 'I remember running up and down – but I've forgotten what it was for.'

Wrinkles

Two old ladies in an old people's home decide to go streaking. A retired sailor is sitting with his wife watching them. She says: 'Look at those two. What are they wearing?'

'I don't know – but whatever it is, it needs pressing!' [*This may be adapted for a named hotel, club or other institution. GJ*]

Happy ending

Goldstein, aged 75, married a 30-year-old. He boasted to a friend how they had done it six times every night during their honeymoon.

Friend: You can die from this!

Goldstein: So she dies, she dies!

Enjoy!

Sound, sound the clarion, fill the fife,
To all the sensual world proclaim
One crowded hour of glorious life
Is worth an age without a name. *(Thomas Mordaunt [1730 – 1809])* [*Both these last two quotations are especially useful in eulogies – the second one, for those who died young. GJ*]

Time – and life – and death

Days are scrolls; write on them that which you want to be remembered. *(Spanish-Jewish Sage, Bachya)*

Tact

Jones the Bread, Morgan the Tailor and Evan the Bookie went to the races. Unfortunately, a horse leapt over the rails and smashed into poor Jones, knocking him down and killing him. Morgan and Evan considered the problem: 'Who should tell Mrs Jones?'

Morgan said: 'I'm only a tailor. I have no tact. Evan, you tell her. You're a bookie, so you know how to explain losses...'

So Evan went to the village and knocked on the door of the Jones's terraced home. A lady came to the door.

'Excuse me, madam,' said Evan. 'I'm sorry to disturb you. But are you Widow Jones?'

'There's no Widow Jones here,' she replied.

'Do you want to make a bet?' asked Evan.

Not now!

Paddy was dying. The priest came to administer the last rites. 'My son,' he said, 'do you renounce the devil now and for ever more?'

The unfortunate man looked up, his eyes pleading. 'Oh, Father,' he replied, 'this is really no time to be making enemies, anywhere!' [*This tale is great for use when asked a question which could lead to instant unpopularity among the audience – as where you are a visitor to the USA and are asked to criticise America's foreign policy, or a guest in the UK and invited to comment on that of Britain. GJ*]

Wrapping it up

David was away on business. He telephoned his wife. 'Any news?' he asked.

'Yes. The cat has died.'

'How terrible. But fancy you telling me like that. Why didn't you wrap it up... Like saying: "The cat's not well..." or "The cat is up a tree..."?

The next time he was away David phoned his wife. 'Any news?'

Wife: 'Yes. I'm afraid mother-in-law's not well. In fact, she's up a tree...'

Will

An old man was dying. His children and his grandchildren were gathered round his bed, waiting patiently. Every few minutes, the old gentleman pointed down to the floor with two fingers of his right hand. Eventually, the eldest son said: 'He is trying to tell us that's where he's put the money...'

So they started pulling up the floorboards all over the house – but they found nothing.

That evening, the father rallied and started to chat. Eventually, the son said to him: 'Tell me, father, what were you pointing two fingers at the floor for?'

'Oh that,' replied the father. 'I was just too weak to point them upwards.'

Wills

A man climbed to the top floor of a block of apartments, to the home of a well known call-girl. As she opened the door, he had a heart attack and dropped down dead. His executors asked their lawyers this question: 'Are we bound to carry out the testator's last wish?'

Eternal distrust

During the Congress of Vienna, Metternich was informed that the Russian ambassador had died. 'I wonder what was his motive!' he exclaimed.

Right dead

Here lies the body of William Jay
Who died defending his right of way
He was right – dead right – as he walked along
But he's just as dead as if he'd been wrong.
(Epitaph on pedestrian's tombstone)

The angel of death

A girl died in the arms of her elderly lover. He was charged with manslaughter. He explained his sad situation to the judge thus: 'My arms were around her; her arms were around me. Her legs were around me and mine around her. My lips were on her lips and her lips on my lips. Her breasts were on my chest and my chest on her breasts. My lord, I do not know how the angel of death managed to get in!'

Floral tribute

Everyone is condemned to the sadness of attending funerals – I treasure one true anecdote which has added a moment of consolation to many a cremation service.

An elegant lady cousin had to attend both a funeral and a wedding on the same summer's afternoon. So she donned a smart, navy blue suit, but put her attractive new, floral hat into a paper bag. As it was covered with gay and realistic, artificial flowers, it was hardly suitable headgear for a cremation.

In the entrance of the crematorium, a solemn black-clad man – obviously a cloakroom attendant – held out his hand for her parcel and she gave it to him. Then she sat quietly at the back.

Moments later, the coffin was wheeled noiselessly into the funeral hall. It was crowned with a magnificent floral tribute – her hat!

My cousin sat transfixed during the service, which reached its silent climax as the doors at the far end of the hall slid apart and the coffin rolled gently away, still bedecked with her hat.

The service over, she joined the mourners around the back where all the wreaths had been laid against the chapel wall, accompanied by a simple sign: 'In memory of the Departed'. She stood silently – wondering whether she dared remove her floral tribute from the rest. Watching the sad faces of the family of the deceased, she decided that her hat must be sacrificed. She went to the wedding hatless. When she returned that evening, her hat was gone.

Brotherly love

During the lingering final illness of my wife's beloved uncle, Emeritus Chief Rabbi Sir Israel Brodie, I often sat by his bedside while he told me marvellous and generally whimsical tales from the *Talmud*. My favourite explains the nature of brotherly love: I have used it often and always with impact at functions of and for charities, fraternal organisations and the like . . .

A father died and left his fields in equal parts to his two sons, one of whom was a bachelor and the other married with many children.

One moonless night, after the harvest had been

brought in and stacked, the bachelor brother crept into his field and carried half a dozen sheaves from his pile, took them across the boundary line and quietly placed them on his brother's heap. The next morning, he was amazed to find that the two piles were still the same size.

The following night, the brother repeated the process. Still the piles were no different.

The next night, the bachelor tried again. This time, as he was carrying the bundles across his field, he met his married brother, coming in the other direction and himself laden with sheaves. 'What are you doing?' he asked. 'Please let me give you some of my wheat. I do not need it. I am single and have no family to keep. You have a wife and children – many mouths to feed.'

'Not so, brother,' came the response. 'You must save for your old age. You will have no wife or children to look after you. You must keep the corn for yourself.'

So the two brothers stood together and looked up to heaven and called on the *Holy-One-Blessed-Be-He*. 'Tell us,' they called out, 'which one of us is correct?'

A voice descended from above. 'You are both right,' it said. 'And so great is your love that upon these fields will I build my Temple.' And tradition has it that He did.

Death

Cicero: Life is a great play. The final act is a tragedy.

De Gaulle: Life is a magnificant voyage, ending in a shipwreck.

Hell

Stalin died and went below. Shortly thereafter, St Peter answered a knock on the door. He found the devil outside, seeking political asylum.

Life after...

'The House of Lords? Life after death, my boy...' *(Ex-Cabinet Minister – now a Peer)*

Index